W9-AGB-611

solutions@syngress.com

With more than 1,500,000 copies of our MCSE, MCSD, CompTIA, and Cisco study guides in print, we continue to look for ways we can better serve the information needs of our readers. One way we do that is by listening.

Readers like yourself have been telling us they want an Internet-based service that would extend and enhance the value of our books. Based on reader feedback and our own strategic plan, we have created a Web site that we hope will exceed your expectations.

Solutions@syngress.com is an interactive treasure trove of useful information focusing on our book topics and related technologies. The site offers the following features:

- One-year warranty against content obsolescence due to vendor product upgrades. You can access online updates for any affected chapters.

- "Ask the Author" customer query forms that enable you to post questions to our authors and editors.

- Exclusive monthly mailings in which our experts provide answers to reader queries and clear explanations of complex material.

- Regularly updated links to sites specially selected by our editors for readers desiring additional reliable information on key topics.

Best of all, the book you're now holding is your key to this amazing site. Just go to **www.syngress.com/solutions**, and keep this book handy when you register to verify your purchase.

Thank you for giving us the opportunity to serve your needs. And be sure to let us know if there's anything else we can do to help you get the maximum value from your investment. We're listening.

www.syngress.com/solutions

SYNGRESS®

SYNGRESS®

HACK PROOFING YOUR IDENTITY

IN THE INFORMATION AGE

Protect Your Family on the Internet!

Teri Bidwell

Michael Cross Technical Editor

Ryan Russell Technical Reviewer

Syngress Publishing, Inc., the author(s), and any person or firm involved in the writing, editing, or production (collectively "Makers") of this book ("the Work") do not guarantee or warrant the results to be obtained from the Work.

There is no guarantee of any kind, expressed or implied, regarding the Work or its contents. The Work is sold AS IS and WITHOUT WARRANTY. You may have other legal rights, which vary from state to state.

In no event will Makers be liable to you for damages, including any loss of profits, lost savings, or other incidental or consequential damages arising out from the Work or its contents. Because some states do not allow the exclusion or limitation of liability for consequential or incidental damages, the above limitation may not apply to you.

You should always use reasonable care, including backup and other appropriate precautions, when working with computers, networks, data, and files.

Syngress Media®, Syngress®, "Career Advancement Through Skill Enhancement®," and "Ask the Author UPDATE®," are registered trademarks of Syngress Publishing, Inc. "Mission Critical™," "Hack Proofing®," and "The Only Way to Stop a Hacker is to Think Like One™" are trademarks of Syngress Publishing, Inc. Brands and product names mentioned in this book are trademarks or service marks of their respective companies.

KEY	SERIAL NUMBER
001	GT6YUJ8KFC
002	2PBP9MJ5MR
003	83N5M44ER4
004	VZW233N54N
005	NFG4R77TG4
006	NV88HTR46T
007	XC5CMU6NVH
008	KTCD54MPE4
009	SGD34Y5GFN
010	T945AQ2YT5

PUBLISHED BY
Syngress Publishing, Inc.
800 Hingham Street
Rockland, MA 02370

Hack Proofing Your Identity in the Information Age

Copyright © 2002 by Syngress Publishing, Inc. All rights reserved. Printed in the United States of America. Except as permitted under the Copyright Act of 1976, no part of this publication may be reproduced or distributed in any form or by any means, or stored in a database or retrieval system, without the prior written permission of the publisher, with the exception that the program listings may be entered, stored, and executed in a computer system, but they may not be reproduced for publication.

Printed in the United States of America

1 2 3 4 5 6 7 8 9 0

ISBN: 1-931836-51-5

Technical Editor: Michael Cross
Technical Reviewer: Ryan Russell
Acquisitions Editor: Catherine B. Nolan
Developmental Editor: Kate Glennon
Cover Designer: Michael Kavish
Page Layout and Art by: Shannon Tozier
Copy Editor: Mary Millhollon
Indexer: Claire Splan

Distributed by Publishers Group West in the United States and Jaguar Book Group in Canada.

Acknowledgments

We would like to acknowledge the following people for their kindness and support in making this book possible.

Ralph Troupe, Rhonda St. John, Emlyn Rhodes, and the team at Callisma for their invaluable insight into the challenges of designing, deploying and supporting world-class enterprise networks.

Karen Cross, Lance Tilford, Meaghan Cunningham, Kim Wylie, Harry Kirchner, Kevin Votel, Kent Anderson, Frida Yara, Jon Mayes, John Mesjak, Peg O'Donnell, Sandra Patterson, Betty Redmond, Roy Remer, Ron Shapiro, Patricia Kelly, Andrea Tetrick, Jennifer Pascal, Doug Reil, David Dahl, Janis Carpenter, and Susan Fryer of Publishers Group West for sharing their incredible marketing experience and expertise.

Jacquie Shanahan, AnnHelen Lindeholm, David Burton, Febea Marinetti, and Rosie Moss of Elsevier Science for making certain that our vision remains worldwide in scope.

Annabel Dent and Paul Barry of Elsevier Science/Harcourt Australia for all their help.

David Buckland, Wendi Wong, Marie Chieng, Lucy Chong, Leslie Lim, Audrey Gan, and Joseph Chan of Transquest Publishers for the enthusiasm with which they receive our books. And welcome back to Daniel Loh—glad to have you back Daniel!

Kwon Sung June at Acorn Publishing for his support.

Ethan Atkin at Cranbury International for his help in expanding the Syngress program.

Jackie Gross, Gayle Voycey, Alexia Penny, Anik Robitaille, Craig Siddall, Darlene Morrow, Iolanda Miller, Jane Mackay, and Marie Skelly at Jackie Gross & Associates for all their help and enthusiasm representing our product in Canada.

Lois Fraser, Connie McMenemy, Shannon Russell, and the rest of the great folks at Jaguar Book Group for their help with distribution of Syngress books in Canada.

Author

Teri Bidwell (GCIA) is an independent security consultant, a GIAC Certified Intrusion Analyst, and a member of The SANS Institute GGIA Advisory Board. Additionally, Teri has over 10 years experience designing and building secure computer infrastructures for companies of all sizes. She has taught multiple courses and written articles on various topics related to computer security and analysis of computer intrusions. Teri is also a contributing author to the Syngress publication *Hack Proofing Your E-Commerce Site* (ISBN: 1-928994-27-X). As an independent security consultant, Teri assists companies and individuals evaluate and reduce their risk for computer network intrusion; her specialties include creating security policies, establishing secure administrative procedures, and installing both firewalls and intrusion detection systems.

Technical Editor and Contributor

Michael Cross (MCSE, MCP+I, CNA, Network+) is an Internet Specialist and Programmer with the Niagara Regional Police Service and has also served as their Network Administrator. Michael performs computer forensic examinations of computers involved in criminal investigations, and has consulted and assisted in cases dealing with computer-related/Internet crimes. He is responsible for designing and maintaining their Web site at www.nrps.com, and two versions of their Intranet (one used by workstations, and another accessed through patrol vehicles). He programs applications used by various units of the police service, has been responsible for network security and administration, and continues to assist in this regard. Michael is part of an Information Technology team that provides support to a user base of over 800 civilian and uniform users. His theory is that when the users carry guns, you tend to be more motivated in solving their problems.

Prior to working for the Niagara Regional Police Service, Michael worked as an instructor for private colleges and technical schools in London, Ontario, Canada. It was during this period that he was recruited as a writer for Syngress Publishing, and became a regular member of their writing team. Michael also owns KnightWare, a company that provides Web page design and other services. He resides in St. Catharines, Ontario Canada, with his lovely wife, Jennifer.

Technical Reviewer

Ryan Russell is the best-selling author of *Hack Proofing Your Network: Internet Tradecraft* (Syngress Publishing, ISBN: 1-928994-15-6), and *Hack Proofing Your Network, Second Edition* (Syngress Publishing, ISBN: 1-928994-70-9). He is an Incident Analyst at SecurityFocus, has served as an expert witness on security topics, and has done internal security investigation for a major software vendors. Ryan has been working in the IT field for over 13 years, the last seven of which have been spent primarily in information security. He has been an active participant in various security mailing lists, such as BugTraq, for years, and is frequently sought after as a speaker at security conferences. Ryan has contributed to four other Syngress Publishing titles on the topic of networking, and four on the topic of security. He holds a Bachelor's of Science degree in Computer Science.

Contents

Online Theft

Tthink of your computer's hard drive as an online "wallet" that can contain the following:

- Computer login accounts

- Screen names

- Electronic commerce account numbers

- E-mail addresses

- Computer and domain names

- Computer IP addresses

- Passwords, passwords, and more passwords

**Viewing Hidden
Programs**

Hidden programs are pro-
grams that run on your
system without your being
aware of them. Some of
these programs are called
spyware, which is soft-
ware that secretly gathers
personal and organiza-
tional information from
your computer, monitors
your Internet activity,
and/or obtains other information about you. You
can see if hidden pro-
grams are running on
your system using Task
Manager on systems
running Windows
XP/NT/2000.

Chapter 3 Keeping Your E-mail Private   103

E-mail Privacy Is Not Just About SPAM

Check privacy policies of Web sites to determine what they do with any information they acquire from you.

If you receive SPAM, check the message to see if they provide a method to be removed from their mailing list. Look into software or services provided by your Internet Service Provider to have e-mail flagged and/or deleted before reaching your inbox.

Disable cookies to prevent information from being sent to Web sites.

Chapter 4 Self Defense on the Web   151

Employer-Provided Internet Access

According to the FBI, the vast majority of corporate information theft occurs by employees taking advantage of access to information they probably shouldn't have. Companies have every right to protect their own informational assets by monitoring how those assets are being used.

SafeKids Kid's Pledge

1. I will not give out personal information, such as my address, telephone number, parents' work address/telephone number, or the name and location of my school without my parents' permission.

2. I will tell my parents right away if I come across any information that makes me feel uncomfortable.

3. I will never agree to get together with someone I "meet" online without first checking with my parents.

4. I will never send a person my picture or anything else without first checking with my parents.

5. I will not respond to any messages that are mean or in any way make me feel uncomfortable.

6. I will talk with my parents so that we can set up rules for going online.

7. I will not give out my Internet password to anyone (even my best friends) other than my parents.

8. I will be a good online citizen and not do anything that hurts other people or is against the law.

Answers to Your Frequently Asked Questions

Q: I keep getting these embarrassing pop-up ads on my computer for things like viagra and pornographic sites, but I've never visited anything like that on the Web! Does this mean someone else is using my computer?

A: No. What it means is that you've visited some fairly innocuous Web site that has set a cookie or installed some spyware on your computer that is displaying those ads. If that's the case, you should follow the instructions in Chapter 4 for deleting cookies and temporary files from your computer, and blocking ad-ware. You might have installed some software that contains spyware within it. It's easy to do if you download software from the Internet frequently. If this is the case, the pop-up ads won't go away until you remove the spyware from your computer.

NOTE

Most browsers have an option that allows you to enter your personal information profile. A form typically asks for the kind of information you'd put on a business card. The browser can then insert the information into Web forms, e-mails, or news postings without having to retype it. This feature makes life easier, certainly, but it also stores private information you might not want to be viewable by everyone. There is a small risk that the information might be shared with the wrong service, your computer could be stolen, or the information could otherwise be obtained without your knowledge.

Foreword

Even though I've spent several years studying how criminals break into computer systems, I thought I was just being paranoid the first time I saw one of those signature capture devices at the local electronics store. You know the kind I'm talking about, where the clerk slides the receipt from your credit card onto a flat pad, and you sign your name onto it using a pen that writes on the slip in ink but also records an imprint of your signature electronically. Needless to say my curiosity got the better of me. I asked the clerk, "What happens to my signature after I sign the slip?" I figured that my signature was sent to the financial network that approved the charge on my credit card, in order for it to be compared against my original credit application, similar to the way banks use the signature cards they keep on file.

The clerk replied, "All of the signatures are stored on the store's server, in the backroom. We (the store) hold on to all of the electronic signatures just in case the credit card company ever needs to verify that you signed a receipt." This was definitely not the response I expected.

I then asked the clerk "Well, is the server in the back room locked up?" Again, I received an unexpected answer.

"No, it's in the office out back that the executive staff for the store use."

"Is access to the computer restricted?" I continued.

"Well, there's only one person who knows how to work on that system, so nobody else usually touches it," he replied.

"Is the data on the computer ever backed up?"

"You know, that's a really good question." Again, not the answer I was looking for.

Truthfully, I'd have been happier to be told that my signature was sent to a big credit card company. At least they'd have a dedicated computer security staff to protect all of that data. But here was this man telling me that my private information was easily accessible to various people.

After digging into the technology behind the devices used by the store, I learned that my signature was encrypted before being sent to the computer in the back room; thereby significantly reducing it's value to any thief. Thank goodness. However, the entire incident made me wonder: How much technology out there is making mistakes with people's private information by storing it insecurely, using weak encryption, and ultimately putting it into the hands of untrained operators for whom security is not the primary focus?

If you're like most people, your day includes writing checks or using a debit card at stores, using credit cards at the gas station, or using an ATM terminal to get cash. If you're among the growing numbers of Internet users, you've probably also bought a thing or two online, and might even do your banking or trade stocks online as well. Each time you enter into any of these transactions, you must share private information about yourself with the outside world. Most people don't give it a second thought. But do you know how your private information will be used? Is your private information safe from theft?

You may not care about the answers to these questions until you find out one day that someone else has stolen this private information and used your identification to commit your name to a legally binding agreement such as a credit card charge, a loan application, a driver's license, or a variety of other agreements. What do you do? How do you repair the damage? How can you prevent it from happening again?

Hack Proofing Your Identity is designed to answer these questions, and teach you the methodology of how to find answers to questions this book will inevitably be unable to address. Unfortunately, it is impossible to anticipate all the possible ways in which someone might steal your identity given the current rapid evolution rate of new technology. Instead, we hope this book will teach you how to think about your personal information in a new way; how to recognize when you are unnecessarily putting yourself or your family at risk for identity theft, and how to recognize opportunities to reduce that risk by making small changes in the way you manage your personal privacy, both online and offline.

Like other books in the Syngress "Hack Proofing" series, this book includes more than just a bullet list of things you should do—it also provides explanations and shows you examples that illustrate the reasons *why* you should do them.

Chapter 1, *What is Identity Theft?*, starts us off with a definition of identity theft, what it is, how it happens, and shows how identity theft is more prevalent than you think.

Chapter 2, *Protecting Your Hard Drive*, guides us through the various steps of protecting our hard drives through the use of strong passwords, updated anti-virus software, and proper handling of temporary files. There's a lot more hiding on your hard drive than you may be aware of, and identity thieves are everywhere and know what to look for.

Chapter 3, *Keeping Your E-mail Private*, shows us how e-mail opens up your computer to the outside world. Discussions of viruses, malicious code, SPAM, and e-mail fraud are included, as well as tips for protecting your personal information and preventing any potential computer damaging security breaches.

Chapters 4 and 5, *Self Defense on the Web* and *Connecting to the Internet Safely*, will look at what a network is, how your network and the Internet can be used in identity theft, and how to avoid common mistakes that make it easy for a thief to do his work. As you examine the risks of various types of network and Internet connections, we will demonstrate a few surprisingly simple ways to access other computers. These demonstrations are intended only for educational purposes—to show you the kinds of information other computers on your network can see.

Chapter 6 takes on the sensitive topic of *Are Your Kids Putting You At Risk?* Unfortunately, children can be at risk on the Internet if they are not properly educated about the dangers of sharing personal information (both their own and that of their parents). On the flipside, children could be breaking the law without even knowing it, depending on their interests or proficiency with computers, by downloading copyrighted material, accessing the Internet with a connection provided by their parent's employer, and so on. This chapter stresses the importance of proper education, and offers some suggestions for monitoring your child's activities online.

Chapter 7 offers suggestions and possible answers to the question, *What to Do If You Become A Victim?* This chapter offers helpful tips on contacting law enforcement, filing reports, contacting credit bureaus, and rebuilding your finances after becoming a victim of identity theft.

Finally, Chapter 8, *Configuring Your Browser and Firewall*, offers some practical step-by-step instructions for setting up your Internet browser and personal firewalls to further protect your computer from intruders or identity thieves

Unlike other books in the Syngress series, this book is not directed exclusively at a high-tech audience. We assume you have at least one computer in your home that's connected to the Internet, perhaps another one at work, and regularly use e-mail and surf the Web. If you are an IT professional, you may already know most of the technical information in this book; however, you might not have applied this knowledge to the protection of your own private information. This book will help technical and non-technical people alike understand how to better protect private, personal information and avoid becoming a victim of identity theft.

—Teri Bidwell, GCIA

Chapter 1

Identity Theft: Are You At Risk?

Solutions in this chapter:

- Defining Identity Theft
- Understanding What Electronic Information Is Private
- Striving for Theft Prevention
- Keeping Private Information Private

☑ Summary

☑ Solutions Fast Track

☑ Frequently Asked Questions

Introduction

The use of a seal, card, or other identification while making a purchase or signing a contract is a custom almost as old as history. As merchants and their customers have begun using the Internet in recent years to conduct business online, they have been challenged to find digital forms of identification that mimic traditional, trusted forms, such as hand-written signatures and photo IDs. Because traditional forms of identification don't work well on the Internet, no universal form of ID has been found to be suitable for companies wanting to conduct business online.

Web site owners, merchants using computers to track purchases, and electronic service providers have each been forced to reach their own, unique solutions for identifying customers using only computers. Many merchants using electronic commerce rely on passwords. Some have embraced electronic identification known as *digital certificates*. Most attach an account name or number, e-mail address, physical address, telephone number, and other identifying information to their customers as well.

Each company with whom you do business electronically increases the number of identifiers associated with you. These digital forms of identification (like passwords) require safeguarding just like any traditional form (like a license). However, because they are not tangible (you can't see or touch them), your traditional notions of how to lock up your belongings do not apply. Not only does that put you at risk, but, just as thieves often prey upon people struggling to understand what's happening around them, cyber criminals can more easily take advantage of people for whom locking up their *digital* information is a new concept.

Today, you are asked to sign credit charge slips using signature-capturing devices designed to copy your signature for storing electronically. You can type your credit card numbers into a Web form and a product will magically appear at your door several days later. An unprecedented number of homes are exposing private information, stored on their computers, to the Internet 7 days a week, 24 hours a day. These are all completely new challenges to our traditional notions of personal identification, and these challenges bring with them new responsibilities for protecting personal information.

Businesses and consumers are beginning to look at personal identification in a way never before required. No longer is it sufficient to keep your wallet on your bed stand where it's safe each night. You need to understand how to protect your identity in its digital form as well.

In this chapter, we investigate the forms of identification that make up your identity in an Internet-enabled world. We begin by focusing on physically securing the sources of information that identify you as an individual, using tangible security methods. We finish the chapter by introducing some of the ways you can protect your personal information using the less tangible features of your computers and the Internet. Those methods are covered in depth in this book's remaining chapters.

Defining Identity Theft

Identity theft is a crime involving someone impersonating a victim for the purpose of financial gain or other personal gain. The victim could be an individual or a business, and the perpetrator could be one person or several individuals acting as part of a theft or fraud ring. Often, the theft of a person's or business's identity is used to commit other crimes as well, such as credit card fraud, submitting loan applications in another person's name, and so on.

Impersonating someone for personal gain has been a problem for centuries, but it has become more prevalent as easily accessible information about people has become more prevalent. Whereas common targets for identity theft used to be the very rich or famous, today ordinary citizens are much more likely to be victims. Here are a few statistics that have been accumulated in recent years by various U.S. government agencies:

- Identity theft is a crime that happens to ordinary people, just like you and me; the average age of victims is 41.

- The U.S. Secret Service estimated the cost of identity theft at $745 million in 1997. Since that time, identity theft has become more prevalent, with total costs estimated in the billions to victims, financial institutions, and taxpayers.

- The number of new cases of identity theft is on the rise. This relatively new trend is the result of the Internet's influence on easy information access.

- Identity theft affects people with good credit or high income more often than it affects those with a poor credit history or low income.

- Identity theft was reported to the Federal Trade Commission (FTC) in 69,370 complaints from November 1999 through June 2001 (www.consumer.gov/idtheft/charts/01-06c.pdf).

- Identity theft was reported to the FTC at a rate of about 3,000 calls per week, up from 2,000 the year before, according to FTC Chairman Robert Muris in April 2002 (www.technews.com).

- Identity theft costs victims an average of 175+ hours and $1,000 in out-of-pocket expenses to clear their names, according to The Identity Theft Resource Center (www.idtheftcenter.org/html/facts_and_statistics.htm).

For the sake of clarity, here are a few examples of actions that constitute identity theft:

- Having your wallet stolen is not identity theft. However, if your wallet is stolen and, subsequently, the thief uses your driver's license and credit card to make a purchase, the crime becomes identity theft.

- Losing your ATM card does not constitute identity theft. However, identity theft occurs if you lose your ATM card and someone finds it and then obtains your PIN (personal identification number) to withdraw money from your bank account or uses your ATM card in some other way for financial gain.

- Having your cell phone stolen is not identity theft unless the thief makes calls using your phone or uses the data stored on your phone in some way in an effort to impersonate you.

Take a Risk Factor Test

Take this test to determine your risk factors. If more than half of the following statements are true, you are at high risk for identity theft. Keep these risk factors in mind when reading the solutions presented in the rest of this book:

- You receive at least one loan solicitation or preapproved credit offer each week.

- You usually toss preapproved credit or loan solicitations in the trash without shredding.

- You usually toss old banking or credit documents in the trash without shredding.

- Mail is delivered to you in an unlocked mailbox.

- You send mail by placing it in an unlocked mailbox.

- You carry your Social Security or Social Insurance card in your wallet.

- Your Social Security Number is printed on the health insurance card in your wallet.

- Your Social Security Number is printed on your driver's license.

- Your Social Security or driver's license number is printed on your personal checks.

- You make purchases online using a credit card.

- You seldom check whether a site is "secure" before using a credit card to make an online purchase or before disclosing private data, such as your Social Security Number, to a Web site.

- You seldom read Web site privacy policies before disclosing private information.

- Your online account with your bank, health insurer, or stockbroker uses your Social Security Number as your account number.

- Your bank doesn't require a password before allowing you to make a withdrawal in person.

- The password for your online bank account is written down in an unlocked location.

- Your ATM PIN is written down in your wallet or on the ATM card.

- You sometimes share your name, address, e-mail address, and/or phone number with Web sites.

- You don't use privacy software to remove identifying information from your computer.

- You seldom take advantage of programs designed to opt-out of information sharing.

- You haven't seen your credit report in the past year.

- Your Internet-connected computer stores private or financial information and is not protected from the Internet by both a firewall and antivirus software.

Why Do They Do It?

Identity thieves might want to impersonate someone else for a couple of reasons. In one form of the crime, an opportunistic thief obtains several pieces of information about a victim and uses the information to obtain goods or services for free, for a short period of time. For instance, the thief opens a credit card account using your Social Security Number, name, and address, and then the thief makes several purchases. By the time you receive the unfamiliar billing statement, the thief has stopped using the new stolen account, to avoid being caught. This type of thief typically obtains one or two credit cards, a Social Security Number, or a driver's license, i.e., to use in committing the crime.

Another form of identity theft involves someone with the goal of long-term impersonation. For instance, someone opens a bank account in your name and then has the statements sent to his own location instead of yours. Another example of this type of crime involves someone obtaining employment or government benefits by using a stolen Social Security Number. New accounts are opened using the thief's address, and the accounts are used for a long period of time. In extreme cases, a thief might maintain the alternate identity for months or years, in an effort to hide their own identity. If you're a victim of this type of crime, you might not discover it until the next time you view your credit report, are denied a loan due to bad credit, or observe inaccurate employment data on your Social Security records. Consider the following victim's statement provided to the FTC on July 13, 1999 (taken from the U.S. Federal Trade Commission's consumer protection Web site at www.ftc.gov):

> "Someone is using my name and Social Security Number to open credit card accounts. All the accounts are in collections. I had no idea this was happening until I applied for a mortgage. Because these "bad" accounts showed up on my credit report, I didn't get the mortgage."

How Do They Get Away with It?

Most people go about their busy day making purchases using credit cards, writing checks, and using their ATM cards at automated teller machines, without giving it second thought. Each time you enter into one of these financial transactions, however, you share private information about yourself with others. Of course, you can't just stop sharing private information entirely, without being denied the services you need to use. You must find a middle ground in which you are cognizant of the information you routinely share while protecting as much private information as possible from being shared unnecessarily.

Before you can understand how to protect your private information, you need to examine the ways in which your private information can be obtained and stolen, possibly without you even realizing it. Bear in mind, each one of the items discussed in this section is something that could and does happen but is certainly not guaranteed to happen to you. As you read, think about whether the situations might apply to you, given your routines and habits. Later, we'll examine ways in which you can make changes to routines and habits in order to prevent the kinds of thefts described here.

Dumpster Diving

Dumpster diving is when someone goes through someone else's trash in order to obtain useful information or items. Your trash contains a lot of valuable information about you unless you take steps to prevent that from happening. For instance, you might discard bank records, loan forms, or old bills that have valuable data on them. When you obtain new checks, you might discard your old ones. A dumpster diver might retrieve those old checks, thereby allowing her to begin using your bank account right away.

If you have a credit card, you probably also receive preapproved credit offers in the mail. Credit companies buy mailing lists from credit bureaus and other sources, and send these offers to people who are known to use credit cards. Most people just toss them in the trash as junk mail, without even opening them. However, an enterprising thief might rummage through your trash, retrieve these preapproved offers, and send them in. Most preapproved offers have a convenient change of address section, which the thief fills in with her own address, then signs your name to the application form. Some preapproved offers or even existing credit card statements come with checks inside, ready for your use in consolidating bills. If you toss the checks in the trash, a thief can retrieve them from your garbage, sign one, and use it to make a large purchase in your name.

Dumpster diving isn't a federal crime, unless you do something else in the process that is illegal. It's also not addressed very well by state laws at the present time, other than by the laws against trespassing on another person's property. For instance, if your trash bin has a sign on it that says "No Trespassing," you could feasibly argue that someone taking an item from it is stealing; however, it would be difficult to demonstrate that the discarded item had sufficient value to be considered "stolen property." That argument is made even more difficult by the 1988 Supreme Court ruling in *California vs. Greenwood* that rummaging through someone's trash does not, in fact, violate their right to privacy. There *are* certainly actions you can take to minimize your exposure to dumpster diving, which are discussed later in the section titled "Striving for Prevention."

What You Can't See Can Hurt You

The Computer's Recycle Bin

People who might be savvy enough to shred their paper trash might not be thinking about the trashcan on their computers. Your computer's recycle bin might contain files with private information in them that you've deleted over time. If someone gains access to your computer while you're away from it, those files might provide useful information.

For instance, let's say you make an online purchase using a credit card, and the Web site provides you with a confirmation form showing what you purchased along with the credit card number and shipping address. You keep the confirmation page on your hard drive until you receive the merchandise. After you receive the merchandise, you delete the confirmation form because it's no longer needed. The form remains in your recycle bin until you empty it. Even then, the file isn't irretrievable. It can be restored using special undelete software, which is discussed in greater detail in Chapter 2.

Shoulder Surfing

Shoulder surfing is what people do when they watch over your shoulder to see what you're typing on a keyboard. For example, when you step up to an ATM machine and enter your PIN, the person behind you might watch your fingers to see what numbers you enter. If you are sitting at an Internet café, the person sitting next to you might be watching as you type a Web or e-mail password. You have no way of knowing whether the person watching is able to use your PIN or password, but don't assume they cannot.

Experienced shoulder surfers are extremely good at memorizing numbers quickly, as you type them, and can remember very long passwords, credit card numbers, and so forth. In an extreme form of shoulder surfing, the thief might carry a small camera designed to record your keystrokes for later playback.

Social Engineering

Social engineering, also called *pretexting*, is a term used for a variety of scams and con games involving tricking a victim into voluntarily giving up private information that's useful. Pretexting is an attempt to elicit a specific response to a social situation the perpetrator has engineered; for example, someone gives you false information for the purpose of obtaining otherwise forbidden information from you. You might receive the false information via postal mail, e-mail, computer chat program, Web site, telephone, or in person. An example of this is the Nigeria 419 e-mail scam described in Chapter 3. The Nigeria 419 scam is designed to trick you into disclosing your bank account number. In any case, you are asked to give up information that you would not normally give to just anyone. Most of the time, the victim has no idea he or she has disclosed information under false pretenses, unless it results in a crime that can later be traced back to having disclosed information to the person doing the social engineering.

As an example of social engineering, an identity thief might pose as a potential landlord or employer in order to obtain a copy of a victim's credit report. Or, let's say you needed to find someone's address and couldn't find it using one of the online "People Search" type programs. You might phone up the gas company and pose as a relative. The phone conversation might go something like this, in which the gas company clerk is tricked into disclosing the address you're looking for:

> You: Hello, I'm Joe User's daughter. We just moved my dad to a senior community, and I need to make sure he changed his gas service over to his new address. Bless his heart—he doesn't remember things the way he used to! Can you tell me the address that's showing on his account?
>
> Gas Company clerk: I show his address is 555 Shady Lane. Is that the retirement home?
>
> You: Yes it is; thank you very much. Bye.

Social engineering is by far the most effective, least costly, and hardest to prevent method of obtaining private information. Technology can't be used to block it, and people targeted have to be on their toes in order to even notice it when it's happening. What's more, it's not illegal unless someone uses the obtained information to commit a crime.

Unfortunately, most people have an even harder time noticing social engineering when it's happening using a computer. Some of the most successful social engineering scams today are sent to victims via e-mail. When you can't see a person's facial expression or hear his or her voice, inferring their intent when they ask you for information can be difficult. You need to be even more vigilant online than in person against social engineering, due to the numerous places a thief can hide on the Internet.

Digging Deeper...

The U.S. Graham-Leach-Bliley (GLB) Act

The 1999 Graham-Leach-Bliley (GLB) Act (www.ftc.gov/privacy/glbact/glboutline.htm) set privacy requirements for U.S. financial institutions to prevent social engineering from being used to obtain financial data. However, it doesn't cover forms of business that are not financial institutions, and it doesn't cover financial institutions outside the United States. The GLB Act makes it illegal for someone to impersonate you to your bank in order to obtain private information your bank might possess. It also makes it illegal for financial institutions to share your financial data, such as credit card numbers, with telemarketers.

The GLB Act defines personal, identifying information as any information you provide to a financial institution in order to obtain their service or product. It goes on to define nonpersonal, publicly available information as any information available in public federal, state, or local government records, or any information that a financial institution believes is lawful to make public. It goes on to say that a financial institution can't just assume information is public. It must take into account whether the consumer has requested that the information not be disclosed and whether the type of information is generally made available to the public. As a result of the GLB Act, financial institutions must now disclose privacy statements that describe how your private information is used. They must allow you to opt-out of information sharing as well.

You can read more about consumer privacy provisions of the GLB Act at www.ftc.gov/privacy/glbact/index.html.

Physical Theft

If you leave your purse or wallet in a place where it can be stolen, it probably will be. A wallet full of credit cards with a driver's license and possibly a PIN written down on a piece of paper is like hitting the mother lode for an identity thief. Likewise, leaving a copy of your tax return lying on the counter near the printer at work invites the same kind of theft as if you had left your social security card lying there.

Unfortunately, most people forget that physical theft of identifying information involves more than just credit cards, driver's licenses, and ATM cards. Wallets also sometimes contain:

- Social Security cards
- Access key cards for work
- Health insurance cards
- Student or employee ID cards
- Video rental membership cards
- Other membership cards (health clubs, shopping clubs, and so on)
- Receipts with credit card numbers on them
- Checks or deposit slips with bank account numbers
- Identifying information about family members

Theft of private data isn't limited to the paper and plastic in your wallet, either. Personal digital assistants (PDAs) and cell phones can contain valuable personal information, especially if you use your PDA or cell phone to make online purchases. If your cell phone is Web-enabled, it might contain cookies or files that contain private data, such as name, address, phone number, or credit card numbers. These devices need to be protected from physical theft just as you would protect your wallet. Private data is also available on credit card and bank statements, tax returns, and other documents stored in the home, where visitors might have access to them.

Unfortunately, you might not necessarily have control over stolen electronic data. In March 2002, the New York Times reported a story about a former employee of the Prudential Insurance Company who was arrested and charged with stealing the identities of colleagues from a company database containing 60,000 names. The case is one of the largest potential identity theft cases ever, according to Federal prosecutors in Brooklyn. While Donald Matthew McNeese of Callahan, Florida, worked in the tax department at Prudential, he stole the database of personnel records. He then sold some of the names over the Internet as part of a credit card scam. McNeese also posted information about some former colleagues on the Internet for free, for anyone to use. According to the complaint, one person had $2,000 charged to his credit card as a result. Unfortunately, no one knows how many others might have private information in circulation.

Online Theft

When thinking about theft of credit cards and other forms of identification, most people think about their wallet or purse, because that's where they physically carry their identification cards. But because your private information is also stored on your computer, you should think of your computer's hard drive as an online "wallet" that can contain the following:

- Computer login accounts
- Screen names
- Electronic commerce account numbers
- E-mail addresses
- Computer and domain names
- Computer IP addresses
- Passwords, passwords, and still more passwords

These items identify you indirectly by identifying your computer. For instance, your computer's IP address is an identifier, assigned by your Internet Service Provider (ISP), and is unique to your computer. The login account name also assigned by your ISP is unique to you. Nobody else has the same e-mail address as you. If one or several of these pieces of information can be matched up with an appropriate password, phone number, or your home's street address, together they might provide sufficient evidence of your identity to fool a service provider into believing an imposter is actually you. For this reason, you need to secure the items in your "online wallet" to the same extent you would secure the items in your physical wallet.

Back in the 1970s, a common form of credit card fraud involved a thief dumpster diving for the carbon copy layer of a charge slip, on which the credit card number could easily be read. The thief subsequently used the credit card number to make a purchase from a mail order house or other merchant that didn't require a signature or other form of identification in order to make a purchase. In today's online world, a thief might use a variety of computerized means to steal your credit card information.

Online information theft takes two main forms. The first is a direct attack on servers that store a lot of data about people. Examples of this are computers providing Internet-based shopping services or computers used by government agencies to provide services to a large number of people. A thief with sufficient computer intrusion knowledge might target a shopping Web site (by attacking the server) in an attempt to steal a list of customer credit card numbers, phone numbers, or addresses.

Instead of stealing the information, the attacker might have as much to gain by *changing* the information found on the server. A hacker recently told me a story about his teenage friend a few years ago. The teenager and his friends who frequented an electronic message board were learning how to break into computers. They had targeted the Department of Motor Vehicles (DMV). The teen was angry with his mother for some perceived mistreatment, so he added a couple of charges of Driving Under the Influence (DUI) to her DMV record. The mother's license was revoked, and she was forced to protest the DUIs. In the process of investigating the mother's claim, the DMV uncovered the boy's activities.

Another way online thefts occur is from attacks directly on the source of the data being sent to servers, such as data on computer disks stored in the home. While your computer is connected to the Internet, a thief might connect to your computer's disk remotely to retrieve the same type of data. He might engage in scanning techniques to determine the services you are running on your computer as clues to the type of software (and therefore the type of data) present on your computer. If you do business with a Web site that sends purchase confirmations to you via e-mail, a thief with the ability to read your e-mail might be able to obtain your credit card number from the confirmation; hence, the attacker might attempt to steal your e-mail password by intercepting it directly from the network as it traverses from your computer to an Internet e-mail server.

The attacker might also attempt to steal your online private information through indirect means. For example, she might trick you into inadvertently installing software that appears to have a useful purpose but actually is a malicious program, known as a *Trojan Horse*, which sends private information about you to the thief. (Programs that appear to have a benevolent purpose but actually contain hidden malicious code are commonly called Trojans, after the famous horse of Troy.) A thief might send you a Trojan password-recording program disguised as a humorous image or Web link in an e-mail, with the intent to retrieve the stored passwords from your computer at a later time. Or, she might trick you into entering passwords or other private information into what appears to be a legitimate Web server but is actually a Trojan Web server designed to record any data you provide to it. You'll learn how you can protect yourself from these kinds of attacks throughout the book and specific information about antivirus protections in Chapter 2.

Privacy Erosion

Along with the proliferation of affordable computers has come a proliferation of opportunities to use computer technology to spy on others. Sometimes, spying might be warranted, as in the case of a parent who uses Web-monitoring software to protect a child from online pornography. In other cases, spying clearly isn't warranted, as in the case of a Trojan that records passwords. Mostly, privacy erosion happens in the gray area—where legal boundaries haven't yet been clearly drawn between the need to protect citizens from crime versus their own privacy rights, employers' privacy rights, merchant rights, software manufacturers' rights, and Web site owners' rights.

One aspect of privacy erosion involves an employer's right to monitor its employees as they conduct business online using the Internet, versus an employee's right to privacy while at work. Another involves advertisers using various electronic methods to track the surfing habits of customers, in an attempt to tailor advertising to be better suited to the needs of customers, versus the customer's desire to surf anonymously. Both of these practices can be considered good business or spying, depending on which side of the issue you're standing.

In this same category, you can find some relatively new search engines on the Internet designed to help you find that long lost someone or locate background information about missing persons, potential tenants, employees, roommates, and so forth. It's possible to use any number of Web sites—such as Yahoo! People Search (http://people.yahoo.com) or US SEARCH.com (www.ussearch.com)—to easily and quickly locate public records, criminal records, and court records, for instance.

These services typically only report information on the Internet that can be obtained through other means, however, and are regulated by the 1999 GLB Act as to what kinds of information can not be disclosed. Social Security Numbers, for instance, are not provided as part of those searches. Information not regulated by the GLB Act can be disclosed, however, and remains useful for obtaining details about particular individuals. Some less scrupulous Web sites will even disclose a Social Security Number if it is found in public records.

The proliferation of public information sites on the Internet in recent years has presented an incredibly convenient opportunity for thieves to anonymously gather large amounts of personal information about potential victims. Prior to the creation of these Internet-based services, obtaining public information, such as marriage, health, or court records, was much more difficult. A thief would need physical access to a specific phone book or a credit bureau, for instance, or would need to know how to navigate government procedures to obtain public records. He might have needed to disclose his own name in order to obtain public records from a government agency.

Obtaining certain classes of information, such as financial or credit data, requires a requestor to demonstrate a specific business need or right before being given access to restricted data. This is still true, but the Internet makes it easier for that same restricted data to end up in the hands of those who don't have the rights to it if it becomes subsequently published on a Web site or stolen from an online server.

Many public information searches on the Web allow you to choose not to have your private information disclosed by them, a process known as *opting out* of their service. Some sites don't provide this option. We present some specifics about which ones allow you to opt-out, and how to do that, later in this chapter in the section "Keeping Private Information Private."

Limited Enforcement Resources

A February 2002 article in the *Denver Post* (http://nl3.newsbank.com, article ID 1093052) reveals the extent to which municipal police departments sometimes lack the funding and expertise to pursue Web criminals. Police know about chat room predators and the selling of Social Security Numbers on the Internet but are sometimes hindered by budgetary, legal, and logistical complexities; following the electronic trail to the perpetrator can often end in expired service provider logs, false addresses, or a quagmire of multijurisdictional search warrants, subpoenas, and other paperwork. Municipal law enforcement agencies might face budgetary constraints that hinder purchasing the computing equipment or training officers in essential skills necessary for tracking criminals' online activities. That doesn't mean computer crimes aren't being solved, but it does mean the Internet poses new challenges for law enforcement. Solving these problems is a complex issue but is happening; some of the solutions are at a national level, some are at the local level, and others involve partnerships between law enforcement and the private sector. If you'd like to know more about this topic, consider reading Syngress Publishing's *Scene of the Cybercrime: Computer Forensics Handbook* (ISBN 1-931836-65-5), which deals exclusively with the challenges facing the collaboration between law enforcement and IT communities.

Recognizing Identity Theft When It Happens

According to the Federal Trade Commission, 69,370 victims of identity theft were reported in the period from November 1999 through June 2001. Figure 1.1

shows the types of theft involved in those complaints. By and large, credit card fraud was reported most often, followed by unauthorized telephone or utility service. In this section, we examine each type of crime associated with identity theft, focusing on how you can recognize when each type of information theft or financial fraud has occurred.

Figure 1.1 Identity Thefts by Type

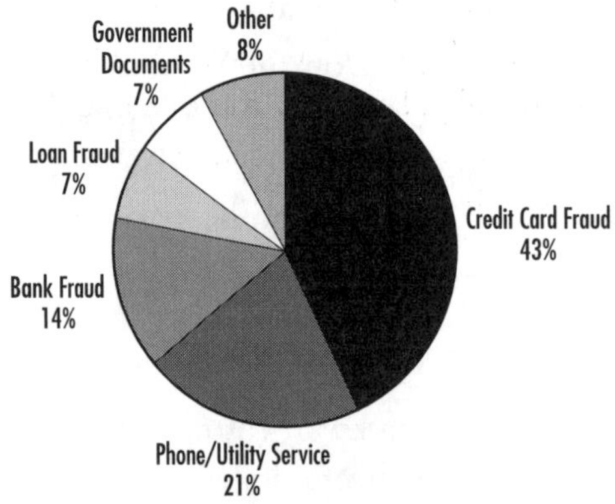

Unauthorized Credit Cards

Receiving a statement for a credit card you don't recognize is a tip-off that someone else has obtained a credit card in your name. Being familiar with the statements you should receive each month and the dates they normally arrive will help you notice when something unexpected arrives in your mailbox. Keeping a list of statements you should receive and verifying each month that you do receive them will also help you notice if someone has changed the address on one of your credit cards without your permission.

If an identity thief obtains the number of one of your existing credit cards and uses it to make a purchase, you'll notice unauthorized charges on the next month's billing statement. Always keep copies of purchases you make and compare them to the monthly statement as a way to flag unauthorized charges.

Unauthorized Phone or Other Utility Services

Your telephone service can be stolen even if the phone is never out of your possession. For instance, thieves who can *clone* cellular phones might discover how to configure their own cellular phone to use someone else's service. You will notice long distance or other charges you didn't make on your monthly bill, if this happens. Carefully reviewing phone statements each month will help you detect this type of theft more quickly.

Figure 1.2 is a very simplistic diagram showing how cell phone cloning works for one type of service. A cell phone is programmed with an electronic serial number (ESN) when you buy it. The phone identifies itself to the cellular service of your choice by sending its ESN and a mobile identification number (MIN). You can think of a MIN like a telephone number. A thief can use a scanner to pick up an ESN and MIN during transmission; they can then program the numbers into a different cell phone. Calls placed on the cloned phone are then indistinguishable from calls placed on the original phone, at least from a billing standpoint. Switching to a different cellular account or service and a different cell phone effectively changes your ESN and MIN. Newer types of cellular services claim to be able to prevent cloning, but they are not perfect. All are vulnerable to some extent.

Figure 1.2 Cellular Phone Cloning

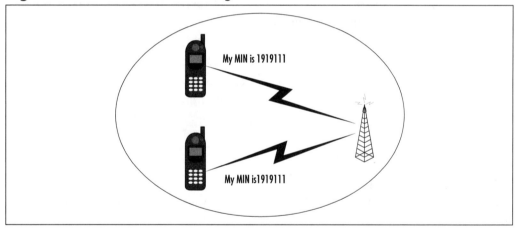

Bank Fraud

Bank fraud involves someone making unauthorized withdrawals from a bank account, either in person, by check, by electronic fund transfer, or by ATM card. One of the more common types of bank fraud involves a thief obtaining your bank information by stealing your bank statement from your unlocked mailbox and then, while pretending to be you, she changes the account's address. After the address is changed, she can order an ATM card and use your account for quite awhile, because it might take one or two months for you to notice that your bank statement has stopped arriving.

Bank fraud can also involve someone opening an entirely new account in your name. If a bank isn't careful to check a photo ID, an imposter might need only your Social Security Number and an address to set up a new account. Of course, there's also the possibility that a determined thief can create a falsified photo ID with his photo, your name, and address. If your mailing address is used to set up the new account, you might discover the account when you receive a bank statement in the mail. Or, you can find out about a new bank account by viewing your credit bureau report.

Fraudulent Loans

If someone obtains a loan in your name, that's loan fraud. The loan might be to make a purchase of a business or personal asset, automobile, real estate, and so forth. Typically, the thief will use the loan proceeds to make a purchase but make no payments. Or, he might just run off with the money. The delinquent payments are reported on your credit report, which might prevent you from obtaining a legitimate loan due to bad credit. You might not discover what's occurred until the loan has been sent for collection.

Like credit card accounts, if a thief uses your address, you'll receive payment information in the mail that you won't recognize, provided you are familiar with the statements you should be receiving. If he uses his own address, you might not notice the unauthorized loan until you are denied credit or review your credit report.

Government Documents

Someone might attempt to obtain a job using your Social Security Number to avoid disclosing the person's real identity. It's not difficult to envision this scenario for an illegal immigrant, for example, but other situations also apply. If this happens, you might notice the thief's earnings on your Social Security Statement. You might notice that your Social Security or military identification card has gone missing, or the thief might have obtained your Social Security Number from the Internet or by other means. Someone might steal or forge your driver's license or other government-issued identification in order to obtain services in your name, or someone might file a fraudulent tax return in your name.

Other Forms of Identity Theft

Other types of identity theft reported include obtaining medical services, leases, securities, investments, and other illegal activities committed in the name of the victim.

Understanding What Electronic Information Is Private

Common sense tells us that the contents of your wallet make up your identity. Certainly that is also true for the contents of your filing cabinet, including bank statements, credit card statements, tax returns, insurance policies, loan applications, mortgages, court records, and other documents that contain personal, private information, such as Social Security Number, driver's license number, tax ID number, name, address, phone number, employer, financial status, or any of the same information for a relative or business partner. Many people tend to think of "private" information as only concerning their finances.

Unfortunately, the privacy protection for your identifying information offered by the GLB Act (described in the sidebar in the "Social Engineering" section) doesn't cover nonfinancial institutions, such as your health club, medical services provider, cable TV provider, or Internet Service Provider (ISP). What does this mean for you? It means there is a large category of information that is not defined by Federal law as either public or private. Certain types of information are not classified as private yet can be used to obtain private information that is classified.

For example, you likely provided the same kind of private information to your favorite video rental store as your bank when you initially set up accounts at both places. As a result, either institution is as interesting as the other to an identity thief trying to obtain, say, a credit card number or Social Security Number. If I can obtain your name, address, and video rental card, I can impersonate you to the video rental store and pretend to change the credit card number on your account, thereby learning the credit card number. While your video rental card number is not classified by the GLB as private data, it can be used to obtain your credit card number, which is.

Such unregulated, or undefined, private information might not be subject to legal protections against sharing, so you need to provide your own protections for it. Whereas today, in 2002, you can expect privacy policies from financial institutions to inform you about how your private data will be used, you can't expect to be informed by nonfinancial institutions. Some common electronic sources of unregulated private information include the following:

- Account information for merchants that store private data about you

- Account information you store online

- Account information you use to connect to the Internet

- Cell phone numbers or contact lists stored in a cell phone

- Online messaging to parties whose identities are not fully known

- Online purchase confirmations sent via e-mail or stored on your hard drive

- Unencrypted files stored on your computer or personal digital assistant

- Unencrypted information sent over the Internet

- Web site cookies

- Web sites or services asking for and storing more data about you than is needed

The very act of participating on the Internet requires several forms of identification in order to receive the service. First of all, in order to even connect to the Internet, you have an account name and password with your ISP, which provides an IP address for your computer and possibly an e-mail address. You might have an AOL screen name. You might also have a chat room screen name by which others know you. If you have a Web-enabled cell phone or PDA, it too has a serial number that identifies the phone itself.

As an example of how this type of information can be used, let's consider an identity thief with computer intrusion skills. She could use your ISP account and password to impersonate you while making online purchases or conducting other business online. There is a possibility that she could use social engineering in combination with your information to obtain your credit card number from your ISP, by reciting your account name and password as evidence of her alleged identity. You need to protect your ISP account login and password as carefully as you would your credit card number itself.

If you have a personal digital assistant on which you store sensitive information—such as passwords for online trading accounts, online banking accounts, or ISP accounts—that information can be used by an identity thief to obtain unauthorized access to the online accounts, which in turn might disclose private financial data to the thief. Your PDA thus needs to be protected as carefully as the information it contains. The same goes for the data in a cellular phone with Web capability for reading e-mail or storing other private information.

When you interact with Web sites, they might store small text files on your computer that contain private information, such as name, address, telephone number, or other data. These files are called *cookies* and are not defined as private information by the GLB Act. Yet, they can be used to obtain private information that is defined by the GLB Act, if they contain, say, a credit card number or other information that leads to an unprotected credit card number.

Although not explicitly defined as private, nonprivate data can sometimes be used to obtain the financial data an identity thief is looking for. By taking steps included in this book to protect these sources of information, you can better protect yourself against identity theft. In Chapter 2, we take a look at how to protect passwords and files that are stored on your hard drive. In Chapter 4, we discuss methods of protecting your private data as you surf the Web.

If someone were to prominently hold a video camera near you while you used your online banking service and recorded your finger movements as you typed your online banking password, you would probably consider the resulting video image to be private information about you, because it could so easily be used to access private information as defined by the GLB Act. Your typing can also be viewed or captured as the resulting data traverses the Internet, unless it is protected.

One of the primary difficulties associated with the Internet is that you can never be certain that your typing isn't recorded as you share private information with your ISP, Web sites, e-mail servers, or other online services. Is this a huge problem? No; otherwise, the FTC would be getting more than 3,000 calls a week reporting identity theft. However, being aware of your surroundings and observing the ways in which your private data can be recorded provides opportunities for you to make changes in the way you manage your data, thereby increasing your overall protection from identity theft. In Chapter 5, we talk more about protecting your home computer using network protections, such as firewalls and correct permissions on shared files.

What You Can't See Can Hurt You

Biometrics: The Ultimate Identification

A biometric is an electronic representation of a unique part of your body, one that looks different than anyone else's. For example, your fingerprint is unique to you and becomes a biometric when you imprint it on paper or allow an electronic device to turn it into an encoded file. The patterns on your retina are also unique to you, and they can be scanned using a laser to produce an electronic representation and stored in a file on a computer disk. Cameras can also be used to identify you based on your entire facial image.

Continued

Many institutions have turned to biometrics as the ultimate identification, because there can be no duplication among individuals. You might think that your biometric identifies you beyond refutation. However, confidence in biometric identification requires confidence in the ways in which that identification is protected from theft, in the same manner as any other form of identification.

Like any other computerized file, a biometric representation must be stored on a computer disk or an identification card, or transferred over a network to another computer in order to be useful in allowing you to be identified. It must be compared against a database someplace, where the original biometric image is stored. During the time it's stored on disk, in transit across a network, or available to a database program on a server, it's vulnerable to the same types of theft that plague any other type of information. A file containing a biometric image can be intercepted and copied, interpreted, decoded, deciphered, replayed, or disseminated in much the same way as any password, unless it is properly protected with encryption, secure networks, secure computers, and privacy policies.

Striving for Theft Prevention

Is it possible to completely protect yourself from identity theft? Unfortunately, the answer is no. If a thief is determined, he or she will figure out a way to obtain your information. But you don't have to make it easy. You can take steps to reduce the amount of private information that's "out there." You can track it down and ask for it to be removed, and you can avoid handing out private data in the first place. Specifically, you can help prevent theft in the following ways:

Know how your private information will be used. As mentioned earlier in this chapter, the GLB Act requires financial institutions to provide you with a privacy statement indicating the types of information they request and how personally identifying information will be protected. Even though nonfinancial institutions might not be required to provide a privacy statement, many do. Take time to read through the statement and understand what it means. If a company you do business with doesn't publish a privacy statement, they might still have an unpublished privacy policy. Ask to view a copy of it. Chapter 4 describes the provisions of a good privacy policy.

Know your credit standing. Being turned down for credit is often the first indication that you've become a victim. By that time, much of the damage to the victim's finances and reputation has been done. Catching an identity thief early, before she's had much time to run up large purchases, is the best way to keep the damage to a minimum. Order a copy of your credit report often, and review what it says about you at least once a year. Compare it to your own records of credit card accounts, bank accounts, and so forth, and correct any information on the report that is inaccurate. See Chapter 7 for more information about contacting credit bureaus to make corrections to your credit bureau report.

Keep accurate records. If you should find yourself a victim of identity theft, you'll need to provide police with accurate information about credit cards and bank accounts. You'll also need to know what financial information is correct, in order to identify unauthorized accounts. This will be easier if you do the following:

- Make a list of the credit card account numbers you have and keep track of their balances.

- Pay attention to billing cycles. If you miss a bank, loan, or credit card statement, track it down and find out why you didn't receive it as expected. Ensure the return address wasn't changed without your permission.

- Make a list of the contents of your wallet. Make a list of the account numbers and passwords you use online but keep it locked in a safe or encrypted if stored on a computer disk.

Guard your mail. The following physical-world precautions are useful in protecting against online theft:

- Prevent someone from stealing mail out of your mailbox by getting a lock for it or using a P.O. box.

- Drop mail into a post office mail receptacle instead of using your home mailbox to send mail.

- Use a shredder to dispose of junk mail or any documents containing private information.

- Protect your name and address from being published whenever possible. Online people search services usually only require a name and address to perform a search. The information they provide might include Social Security Number and other sensitive information useful to an identity thief.

Protect credit cards. Remember, credit card account numbers and any information that can be used to obtain a credit card number from a merchant is just as vulnerable as the credit card itself. To protect your credit card numbers:

- Keep the number of credit cards you carry in your wallet or purse to a minimum. Only carry one credit card, if possible. Keep the others in a safe at home.

- Clear your wallet or purse of receipts that display private information.

- Put passwords on credit card accounts. Don't tell anyone your passwords or credit card PINs. Close accounts that aren't needed.

- Take steps to protect credit card numbers when using them to make online purchases, such as making sure Secure Sockets Layer (SSL) is being used before entering credit card numbers. Chapter 4 talks more about safety on the Web.

- Never disclose credit card numbers over the telephone or via e-mail. If you can't avoid disclosing a credit card number via e-mail, use the encryption methods presented in Chapter 3.

- Always cut up and discard credit cards for closed accounts.

Protect bank accounts. Just like credit card numbers, your bank account name and number are just as vulnerable to theft and misuse as checks and ATM cards themselves. To protect your bank accounts:

- Ask your bank to use a password to make financial transactions. If your bank doesn't offer this service, consider moving your accounts to another bank. Don't tell anyone your password. Protect the password as you would your ATM card itself.

- Carry your checkbook only when needed.

- Don't use checking account routing numbers when making purchases on the Web. If you use a credit card, you are allowed by law to request a charge back if the merchandise is not satisfactory, but you don't have this protection when paying by check. If a credit card is stolen, your limit of liability is typically $50, but this limit doesn't apply to unauthorized withdrawals from a checking account.

- Don't write down bank passwords or PINs. Don't use passwords that are simple to guess, such as maiden names or pet names. Chapter 2 offers more advice about choosing secure passwords.

- Never discard unused checks or bank statements in the trash without shredding.

Protect government and other identification. Most forms of military ID display your Social Security Number, and many employer badges do too. Don't forget that protecting your Social Security Number also means protecting anything on which it is printed. Ways in which you can protect your Social Security Number include:

- Don't carry your social security card in your purse or wallet. Keep it safely locked up at home.

- Carry passports or other forms of government ID only when needed.

- Don't have your Social Security Number printed on personal checks.

Lock up financial records in the home or office. You have no way of knowing if your household help, roommate, or a relative will end up being an identity thief. To protect your financial records at home and in your office:

- Don't leave financial records lying around at home or the office where coworkers, hired help, roommates, or relatives can view private information.

- Don't share your computer with others.

- Don't share financial, banking, or stock trading Web accounts or passwords with others.

Be aware of your surroundings. As you share private information in public places, be cognizant of your surroundings. To keep yourself aware:

- Know if someone is standing behind you, and check to see if they're watching you type.

- Be alert for anyone sorting through your trash bin.

- I advise people no to use Web kiosks or public Internet terminals for financial transactions.

- Be alert for people attempting to trick you into disclosing information you don't need to disclose.

- Educate yourself about common scams committed via telephone, mail, e-mail, and in person. Learn to recognize when you're being tricked into disclosing information you shouldn't disclose.

Keeping Private Information Private

The primary goal in the security steps discussed in the preceding section is to reduce the amount of information that's "out there" about you. Every time you keep your address out of a database, that's one fewer place an identity thief can obtain it. In this section, we'll look at some actions you can perform on an ongoing basis to keep your private information private.

Protecting Your Social Security Number

Contrary to popular belief, very few laws restrict private companies and individuals from requesting your Social Security Number. Although Social Security Numbers were never intended for the purpose of identification, they have become de facto national ID numbers as more and more companies have decided to use them to identify customers. Many organizations prefer to use your SSN as an account number, if for no other reason than it's unique for each individual. For this reason, if an identity thief can obtain your SSN, opening false bank accounts, acquiring credit card accounts, or obtaining false loans is a simple matter.

When possible, you should resist giving out your SSN. The existence of Social Security fraud can't be denied, with over 92,847 allegations in fiscal year 2000, according to a report from the Social Security Administration (www.ssa.gov/oig/Testimony05222001.htm).

People whose SSN is less readily obtainable might be passed over by an identity thief in favor of victims for whom obtaining an SSN is easier. By keeping to a minimum the number of institutions storing your SSN, you reduce the number of opportunities for it to be made available to others without your knowledge.

Figure 1.3 demonstrates an extreme case for resisting disclosure each time an SSN is asked for. This is a real Web page I found on the Internet. There is nothing on this page to convince you that you should trust what will be done with your information after you type it in and hit the Submit button. There is no indication of the name of the organization asking for it. There is no indication of why you should type in your SSN, or what you would gain if you did. Worse, there is no information on the Web page disclosing the site owner's intent for using your SSN after you type it in. For all you know, the page owner might intend to put it on a list to be sold on the Internet.

Figure 1.3 Example of Improper SSN Use on a Web Page

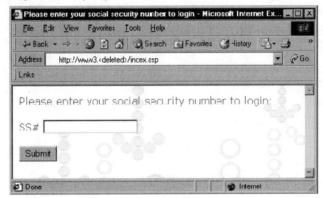

By law, governmental agencies requesting your Social Security Number must provide you with a statement indicating the following four pieces of information:

- Whether disclosure of the information is mandatory or voluntary

- How the information will be used

- Other potential routine uses of the information

- The consequence should you not provide the information

The law requires disclosing your SSN to the IRS, for example, but does not require you to disclose it to your bank. You give your SSN to your bank voluntarily. Does that mean you have a choice in deciding to whom you want to disclose your SSN? Yes; it does. You can ask if the requesting party would allow you to set up your account using different, arbitrary numbers.

The ultimate step you can take to protect your Social Security Number is to pursue legal action against the bank or to support legislation regulating the use of Social Security Numbers as identifiers for software and Web applications. However, the company, organization, or individual requesting your SSN might not be able to accommodate your request. In most cases, you might have no choice but to either disclose your SSN or be denied the goods or services you want to obtain.

NOTE

Companies and individuals do not have to provide a statement of use when they request your Social Security Number, so you should strive to answer the government's statement of use questions for yourself, before deciding if disclosing your SSN is actually necessary. When you're asked to provide your Social Security Number, ask the merchant, Web site, or individual:

- Can I use some other arbitrary number instead of my Social Security Number?
- Am I required by law to provide you my Social Security Number?
- For what purpose is my Social Security Number being requested?
- What will happen if I refuse to provide you with my Social Security Number?

There are many perfectly legitimate reasons why a company or online Web site might ask for your SSN. In some cases, your SSN is requested so that a credit check can be performed prior to selling you goods or services. A Web site requiring your SSN might be using your number as an account number or password to authorize you for using an online application.

However, neither of these actually *requires* a SSN in practice. Credit checks can be performed using other identifiers. Web sites can use an arbitrary account number or password. Ask if the merchant or Web site will accept an alternate identifier.

For example, let's say you're ready to join the ranks of online banking customers, but you discover that your bank requires that your online account number be your Social Security Number. Convincing the bank to stop its practice of using SSN for online transactions might prove to be rather difficult, because an expensive retooling of the bank's Web application would likely be required. Using an arbitrary account number might also make it more difficult for the bank to report your interest earnings. The bank might not be willing to use special accounting procedures just to accommodate your individual request.

If you choose to disclose your SSN to an online banking service, you can take steps to ensure that your data is protected while in transit from your computer to the bank. You can read and understand the Web site's privacy policy. You can also take steps to ensure that you are really dealing with a legitimate Web site. We'll discuss these topics in detail in Chapter 4.

In the end, it's up to you to decide if doing business with a given company is worth the risk of handing out your SSN. But don't assume that individuals, companies, or Web sites will automatically tell you when you have a decision to make about disclosing it. You need to take the initiative and ask questions before automatically handing it over.

Taking Advantage of Marketing Opt-Out Programs

Another action you can take to keep your private information private is to pursue every opportunity to tell direct marketers, financial institutions, and companies with whom you do business that you don't want them to share your private information with third parties. Telling a company that you don't want them to disclose private data to others is known as *opting out* of information sharing.

Digging Deeper...

Opt-Out Scams

The GLB Act requires financial institutions to provide you with information about opting out of information sharing. Many other types of companies also provide opt-out procedures you can follow to eliminate or reduce the amount of private data circulating "out there." Some might send you opt-out information by postal mail or e-mail. You should take advantage of these opportunities wherever possible but be sure to verify that the phone number or address provided for opting out is actually correct for the given service, before you respond to the e-mail or make the phone call. It could be a scam intended to trick you into making a long-distance phone call or some other action that benefits the person responsible for the scam.

At the current time, there's no one single place you can call to opt-out of direct marketing mailing lists, telephone lists, or other sources of circulating information about you. About half the states in the United States have their own opt-out list programs. The Direct Marketing Association has created one too, plus individual businesses may or may not provide an opt-out program for information they collect about their customers. Some online search engines provide this, which we examine next.

Using Search Engine Opt-Out Services

Several search engines exist on the Internet that allow people to find people on the Internet. These search engines might report your name, address, telephone number, and/or e-mail address to anyone, unless you opt-out of their services. The following people-search engines allow you to specify your information as unlisted and typically include their opt-out instructions in their online privacy policies:

- AnyWho (http://anywho.com)

- Internet Address Finder (www.iaf.net)

- SMARTpages.com (www.smartpages.com)

- Switchboard (www.switchboard.com)

- WhitePages.com (www.whitepages.com)

- WhoWhere (www.whowhere.lycos.com)

- Yahoo People Search (http://people.yahoo.com)

NOTE

If you are interested in finding out if your e-mail address is published in an International directory for a country other than the United States, the Web site called "My Email Address Is" (http://my.email.address.is/eiemail.htm) provides a list of searchable International e-mail directories that might be helpful.

Many of the preceding services obtain their lists of people and phone numbers from a third-party service called infoUSA.com (www.infousa.com), which provides opt-out instructions of its own. infoUSA purchases directory data from local telephone companies, and then resells the data to online services. If your phone number isn't listed with the telephone company, it probably isn't listed with infoUSA either. However, accidents can happen. I recommend you take the time to visit the listed Web sites and follow their instructions for removing your name, address, e-mail address, telephone number, or other personally identifiable information from their databases if you find it there. Don't forget to perform an e-mail search in addition to a phone number search, if the site offers it.

In addition to your name, address, telephone number, and/or e-mail address, US SEARCH.com (www.ussearch.com) provides additional personal information about you to the general public for a small fee. The types of information they provide include property ownership records (including dollar value and location), names and addresses of possible neighbors, and names and addresses of possible relatives. This service attempts to correlate several databases to make associations between you and data with which you might not otherwise be directly associated, and it provides much more comprehensive information than "typical" public records search engines. Therefore, I'm including it here as an especially notable service you should opt-out of. The databases searched by this service include FAA pilot records, Coast Guard records, marriage and divorce records, the Drug Enforcement Agency, bankruptcies and civil judgments, and the National Death Index. You can view a copy of a report or make corrections to the information they provide by sending a request by mail to:

> US SEARCH.com Inc.
> Attn: Legal Department
> 5401 Beethoven Street
> Los Angeles, CA 90066

US SEARCH.com also has an opt-out policy that allows you to prevent US SEARCH.com from giving out private information to others. If you decide to opt-out, public records—such as court cases, marriages, and so forth—might still be available, but private information—such as your home's dollar value—will be withheld from reports requested by members of the public. By default, private information is available to the public unless you opt-out. You should opt-out of this service to keep the amount of publicly available information in circulation about you to a minimum. To opt-out of the program, send your full name and address to their opt-out program at the following address. Be aware, when you send information to this service, they record it in their database. Provide only the bare minimum needed to identify any records to which you want the opt-out request applied:

> Opt-Out
> US SEARCH.com Inc.
> 5401 Beethoven Street
> Los Angeles, CA 90066

Unfortunately, there are also many public records search engines on the Web that offer no opt-out policy, because the records come from public sources, such as a county land records office or listed phone numbers from the telephone company. Those records are considered public whether the search engine makes them easily available to the public or not. You should be aware that your Social Security Number or other private information might inadvertently appear in these public records. You might want to review what those engines have to say about you, so I include a few of them here:

- **Docusearch (www.docusearch.com)** Investigative searches of all kinds.

- **Informus.com (www.informus.com)** ChoicePoint company that performs just about any kind of background check you could ask for.

- **KnowX.com (www.knowx.com)** Another ChoicePoint company that performs background checks from public bankruptcy, marriage, divorce, and license records.

- **Military.com (www.military.com)** Locates military personnel from public Department of Defense (DoD) records.

- **National Credit Information Network (NCI) (www.wdia.com)** Pre-employment screening, tenant screening.

Using the Direct Marketing Association's Opt-Out Service

The Direct Marketing Association (DMA) is a trade organization for businesses using direct marketing to reach their customers. Direct marketing includes contacting customers directly through postal mail, electronic mail, and the telephone. The DMA doesn't provide mailing lists to companies, but they do collect lists of people who do not want to be contacted by direct marketers. Member companies subscribing to the opt-out lists agree not to contact individuals who have requested this service. Adding yourself to opt-out lists helps reduce the quantity of mailing lists containing your personal information and the amount of junk mail with your address on it that requires shredding.

> **Opting out of telemarketing lists.** To opt-out of telemarketing services, you can register online (www.the-dma.org/consumers/offtelephonelist.html) for a small fee or print out the form. To avoid paying the fee, print out the online form, and mail it through U.S. mail to:

Direct Marketing Association
Telephone Preference Service
PO BOX 9014
Farmingdale, NY 11735-9014

Opting out of direct mail marketing lists. The form for opting out of direct mail marketing lists (www.the-dma.org/consumers/offmailinglist.html) is very similar to the telemarketing form. Again, to avoid the fee, use U.S. mail instead of the online form:

Direct Marketing Association
Mail Preference Service
PO BOX 9008
Farmingdale, NY 11735-9008

Opting out of unsolicited commercial e-mail lists. To opt out of e-mail direct marketing lists, there is no fee for registering online at www.e-mps.org.

Obtaining other consumer advice. For more information about how the DMA might be able to help you, you can contact them directly:

E-mail: consumer@the-dma.org
Telephone: (212) 790-1488

Digging Deeper...

The Power of Opting Out

As an example of the power of using the DMA opt-out service, consider the Bell South online white pages phone directory (www.real-whitepages.com). Information provided on this site comes from multiple sources, including Acxiom (www.acxiom.com). Acxiom collects demographic information, mail order buying pattern information, and survey information from yet additional sources, in addition to information from public records. Fortunately, Acxiom subscribes to the DMA opt-out lists, so the nonpublic information is suppressed from disclosure if you have requested to opt-out from the DMA. Acxiom doesn't provide that information to Bell South, which in turn doesn't display it on their Web site.

Protecting Your Computer

So far, we've discussed preventive measures you can take to protect private information by protecting your financial records from physical theft, and how to reduce the amount of private information you share with others as you go about our day-to-day activities. That still leaves some work to do to protect your private data using the computer. You need to assume that all your activities using the computer are *not* private unless you take specific actions to ensure that they are, as described in the next few sections.

Applications

As you download documents or new applications from the Internet, you risk the possibility of exposing your computer to a virus. Possibly, you could download a program written by someone intent on recording your online activities, stealing private files, or destroying data on your hard drive. In addition, when you're ready to sell that old computer, you need to erase any personal information remaining on the hard drive, lest your private data—especially any private information created by using financial applications, like Quicken or Microsoft Money—be sold right along with it.

In Chapter 2, we examine some protective tools like disk cleaners, antivirus software, strong passwords, and disk encryption.

E-mail

E-mail, by its very nature, is publicly available for others to view, copy, or store—similar to sending a postcard. An identity thief armed with your e-mail address and password might read your e-mail or impersonate you via e-mail. Mailing lists and Web sites that use e-mail to validate you when subscribing to their services are available to the identity thief if he has access to your e-mail. There are even several e-mail scams designed to trick the recipient into sharing bank account information or other private information with the sender. Lastly, e-mail is a common vehicle for spreading malicious programs on the Internet known as *worms*.

In Chapter 3, we take a look at ways you can protect your private information when using e-mail, such as using encryption or anonymous e-mail to keep e-mail conversations private.

Web Browsing

When you're online, you might perform research for school, keep in touch with friends and relatives, and make online purchases using information stored on

Web servers (computers designed specifically to make information accessible to you using your computer's Web browser software, such as Internet Explorer or Netscape Navigator). Most of our interactions on the Internet involve the Web. That's true for information thieves too. Credit card information and other private data are the most common types of information stolen from Web servers. Web site owners take steps to ensure that data theft doesn't happen, of course, but security accidents can let the occasional intruder slip through anyway. If a computer intruder manages to obtain credit card numbers from a Web server, he might use them fraudulently, distribute them for free on the Internet, or sell them.

Your private information can be exposed in other ways on the Web, too. Certain advertisers might track your online activities using hidden software or Web *cookies*. You might inadvertently give private information to a Web site that's not using proper security, thereby allowing your information to be viewed as it traverses the Internet.

In Chapter 4, we visit some changes you can make to your surfing habits, your Web browser software, and your computer's security settings to help avoid these kinds of situations.

Network

An identity thief can also steal private information from your home computer while it is connected to the Internet. Unless you take steps to protect your PC from being the target of a network-based attack, you risk leaving your personal information open and accessible for others to retrieve. You also risk allowing your computer to be used to launch a network attack against someone else.

Keeping your home network "locked down" as a measure to protect against identity theft is a bit like keeping your car locked to prevent someone from stealing the wallet you left sitting on the seat. The fatter the wallet and the more easily it can be seen from the outside, the more an outsider will be tempted to break in and steal it. Of course, if the car is hidden inside a garage, it's much less likely to tempt anyone who happens to walk by. Putting your home network behind a firewall hides what's stored inside in much the same way.

Chapters 5 and 8 shows you how to buy the right kind of firewall for your home and describes simple steps you can take to help prevent an outsider from intruding via your own network connection.

Your Family's Online Activities

If you share a computer with your family or other members of your household, your private data is exposed by your own online activities as well as by the activities of those with whom you share the computer. The people with whom you share the computer or network might be tricked into providing your private data to someone, might interact with a malicious Web site, or might inadvertently download a malicious program when you aren't monitoring their activities.

Chapter 6 discusses how home computers and networks work, and suggests some ways to safeguard and monitor the activities on your home computer system.

Summary

In this chapter, we examined the crime of identity theft from the perspectives of the criminal and the victim, which can be an individual or a business. Identity theft is a crime involving someone impersonating a victim for the purpose of financial gain or other personal gain, and so it is usually associated with another form of financial or cyber crime. Perpetrators of an identity theft are motivated by many reasons and might attempt to impersonate a victim for a short period of time for immediate personal gain or for a longer period of time in an attempt to hide their own identity for some reason. Criminals use a variety of methods to steal the information necessary to impersonate someone else's identity, including dumpster diving, shoulder surfing, social engineering, physical theft, online theft, and taking advantage of private information that is accidentally or intentionally made publicly available.

After taking a test to determine your risk factors, we examined some of the sources of private data that can be stolen and used by an identity thief, such as credit card numbers, bank data, and Social Security Numbers. Electronic forms of identification can also be stolen and used either directly to commit a crime or indirectly to obtain other data used in a financial crime. Many kinds of crimes associated with identity theft are reported to the Federal Trade Commission each year, such as credit card fraud, phone or utility service fraud, bank and loan fraud, and theft of government documents or services. Usually, the discovery of an associated crime results in a victim learning that he or she has suffered a theft of identity.

The best way to fight identity theft is not to let it happen in the first place. Your main focus must be to understand how to keep your private information private. You need to ask companies with whom you do business how they intend to use and protect the information you disclose during the course of conducting business with them. You can help yourself prepare for the possibility of identity theft by knowing your credit standing, keeping accurate records, guarding how you send and receive mail, and paying attention to how you manage credit cards, bank accounts, and government-issued identification.

One way you can keep your private information out of public view is to take advantage of every opportunity to resist disclosing it or remove it from circulation. You do not always have to disclose a Social Security Number just because someone asks for it. You can also make use of commercial opt-out programs to remove yourself from public people-search databases and telemarketing lists.

This chapter focuses on prevention steps that don't involve a computer, but much of your private information is actually stored electronically. When you use computers to make purchases or conduct other business online, you store and disclose private information that can be stored on another computer or sent across a computer network. In subsequent chapters, we review some ways to protect private data stored as the result of running computer applications, using e-mail, surfing the Web, and connecting to the Internet using a network.

Solutions Fast Track

Defining Identity Theft

☑ Opportunities for identity theft increase as the number of forms of identification you maintain increases.

☑ Someone might steal your identity for short-term financial gain or long-term need to hide his own identity.

☑ The Federal Trade Commission reports that the number of identity theft cases is on the rise.

☑ Methods someone might use to steal the private data necessary to impersonate your identity include dumpster diving, shoulder surfing, social engineering, physical or online theft, or taking advantage of private data inadvertently made public.

☑ You can determine your risk factors by reviewing if your financial management habits unnecessarily disclose private data.

Understanding What Electronic Information Is Private

☑ The 1999 Graham-Leach-Bliley Act placed restrictions on how financial institutions can share customers' private information with third parties. Financial institutions must disclose their privacy policies to customers and honor customer requests not to share private data.

☑ Information defined as private by the GLB Act is not all-inclusive. There is a substantial amount of data that is not defined as private yet can easily lead to the discovery of private, financial data, such as credit card numbers.

☑ People might not realize that certain identifiers—such as their computer's IP address, their e-mail address, or their ISP account information—can

also be used to obtain credit card numbers or other private data traditionally associated with identity theft.

☑ Recent technological developments can have undesirable affects on the
privacy of your data, which increases your risk of identity theft. Your
activities could be covertly recorded, revealing passwords or account
names you've typed online. Biometric data might be touted as the
ultimate identifier, but it also is vulnerable to identity theft.

☑ The Federal Trade Commission reports that 43 percent of identity theft
victims claim credit card fraud, such as unauthorized charges to existing
accounts or new accounts being opened in the victim's name.

☑ Unauthorized phone service accounts for 21 percent of identity theft
reports. This type of fraud involves someone opening phone service in
the name of a victim or using stolen phone service to have charges
billed to someone else's account.

☑ Bank and loan fraud accounts for 14 percent of identity theft reports,
involving unauthorized withdrawals from bank accounts or unauthorized
loans in the victim's name.

☑ Identity theft can involve theft of social security or military ID for the
purpose of obtaining a job or obtaining government benefits. It can
involve theft of medical services, theft of Internet or e-mail services, or
filing fraudulent tax returns.

Striving for Theft Prevention

☑ Understand how your private information will be used before disclosing
it during the course of conducting day-to-day business.

☑ Be familiar with your credit standing, so you can identify when something
unexpected shows up in your mailbox or on a credit bureau report.

☑ Keep accurate records, so you'll be prepared with account numbers and
other information if you should become a victim of identity theft.

☑ Lock down trash receptacles to discourage dumpster diving. Use a
shredder before discarding preapproved credit offers or other financial
documents.

☑ Carry as few credit cards as possible, in case your wallet is stolen. Avoid carrying any identification with your SSN on it in your wallet if possible.

☑ Choose a bank that supports the use of a password before making transactions.

☑ Keep financial records out of view from hired help, roommates, and relatives as a safeguard.

☑ Be aware of your surroundings when using an ATM or public Internet terminal. Others might be watching or listening. Be alert for someone sorting through your mailbox or trash bin.

Keeping Private Information Private

☑ Few laws actually regulate the use of Social Security Numbers as personal identifiers. As a result, SSNs have become de facto national ID numbers and are favored by some companies as a unique customer identifier.

☑ Government agencies must inform you if disclosure of your SSN is required; they must tell you how it will be used and what will happen if you refuse to disclose it. Other companies might provide this information even if they are not required to. Be sure to ask for information before disclosing your SSN to businesses or individuals.

☑ Many telemarketing services or people-search services offer the ability to opt-out of information sharing. It's a good idea to take advantage of opt-out programs whenever possible, to reduce the amount of private data that's "out there."

☑ You need to take steps to protect private data stored on computers. Private data sources include computer applications, e-mail, surfing the Web, or even just connecting a computer to the Internet.

Frequently Asked Questions

The following Frequently Asked Questions, answered by the authors of this book, are designed to both measure your understanding of the concepts presented in this chapter and to assist you with real-life implementation of these concepts. To have your questions about this chapter answered by the author, browse to **www.syngress.com/solutions** and click on the **"Ask the Author"** form.

Q: I received an e-mail from my Internet Service Provider stating that my credit card has expired, but it hasn't. What should I do?

A: Be careful; it could be a scam. Don't respond to the e-mail. Instead, call your ISP and ask if they actually sent the request. If so, then you can safely provide them with updated information.

Q: My employer requires me to wear a name badge that has my Social Security Number on it. How can I avoid wearing it if my employer requires it?

A: For one thing, don't wear the badge in public. Ask your employer if they will assign you an alternate number to display on the badge. Barring this, try putting a sticky note on top of the Social Security Number and remove it only when an official with your employer needs to see your number.

Q: I brought my tax return to work in order to print it out, because my employer has a much better printer than I own. I copied the return to my work computer before printing it and then I deleted it. Can my employer retrieve it, even after it has been deleted?

A: Your computer at work is the property of your employer. They can do anything they want to with it. They probably wouldn't be happy to know you were using their equipment to print your tax return anyway. Avoid using an employer's computing equipment for personal business.

Q: If someone steals my ATM card, do I have to pay for the purchases they make using it?

A: If you report the ATM card as stolen to your bank or financial institution within 2 days, your liability will be limited to $50. If you report a stolen card within 60 days, your liability will be limited to $500. Otherwise, yes; you might have to pay for all the purchases.

Q: Do the ATM card liability limits also apply to credit cards?

A: Yes. Federal law limits credit card liability to $50 for unauthorized charges made to your account.

Q: I never really thought much about keeping my telephone number private. Should I ask to have it unlisted with the telephone company?

A: Many of the online people-search engines get their initial data from the telephone company for phone company customers that allow their information to be listed. The search engines then use the list of names as a cross-reference to find additional data to add to records. In short, if you never appear on the telephone list in the first place, you probably won't appear on any of the search engines either. If your number is listed, and you decide to have it unlisted now, be sure to follow up with the search engines discussed in this chapter to ensure they stop publishing your number.

Chapter 2

Protecting Your Hard Drive

Solutions in this chapter:

- Know Your Computer
- Antivirus Software: Your First Line of Defense
- Updating Your Software
- Avoiding Account Sharing
- Using Disk and File Encryption
- Choosing Strong Passwords

☑ Summary

☑ Solutions Fast Track

☑ Frequently Asked Questions

Introduction

Using computers has become a way of life, but these new and useful tools of ours are also very useful to thieves who can use them to acquire information about us. Think of all the information your computer might contain. Chances are, you have entered your name, address, fax number, and phone number into programs to register them or provide information that can be available to others. Perhaps you did your tax return using software, so a file containing this private information is sitting on your hard disk. By accessing such information, identity thieves can get the data they need to impersonate you.

So, how do you protect yourself from something as new as cyber crime? By following an age-old adage—an ounce of prevention is worth a pound of cure. Taking a proactive approach to security can prevent most cyber criminals from accessing or destroying your data, and those who are more adept will generally move onto easier pickings. After all, there's always someone out there who hasn't taken the measures outlined in this book.

Identity thieves, hackers, and other cyber criminals will look for holes in the security of your system to gain entry to your data. Problems in your operating system or other software might allow them entry, so it's important that your systems are up-to-date in terms of the bug fixes we discuss in this chapter. Cyber criminals also commonly enter a system through poor passwords created by users, which is why we teach you how to create passwords that are difficult to crack. They might also use malicious programs to damage your data and possibly steal information about you. To protect yourself from such programs, you need to install antivirus software and carefully consider about deciding what programs you install on your machine. After you've taken these, and the other steps outlined in this chapter, you can rest more comfortably knowing that your data is safer.

Know Your Computer

Even the most experienced computer users might not know what's on their computer. While people try to keep their files organized, users of the computer and programs running on the system might save files to different locations. Many applications use different default directories to save files to the system, causing documents, spreadsheets, images, and other files to be scattered across dozens of folders. In other cases, such as tax programs, you might use the applications a few times, save important information to your hard disk, and never use it again.

Before taking steps to secure your system, you first need to understand what's residing on your hard drive.

It is a good idea to organize your important files together. Doing so makes it easier to manage files and take measures to protect them, and allows you to know where most of your private information resides on the computer. Windows 95/98/2000/Me/XP provide a folder (which is also called a *directory*) to store such files together. This folder is named *My Documents*. If you want to create a different directory to store your files, or you use a different operating system, you could create a new folder on your hard disk, and arrange your files together. By keeping your files together, you know where all your important data is located and can manage it more easily.

This same method of organizing documents can be configured into your applications. Many programs installed on your computer use default directories where files can be saved. Applications want you to save these files to the directory in which this program was installed or a common directory, like C:\Windows\ Personal. However, you can configure applications to save files to a particular folder. For example, let's say you created two folders called DOCS and SPREADSHEET in the My Documents folder. Microsoft Word could be config-ured to store all files in a folder called DOCS, while Microsoft Excel can be set to save spreadsheets in a folder called SPREADSHEET. To get these programs to all save to a common directory by default, you will need to go into each of these programs and reconfigure them. Reconfiguring your programs to do this might require different steps, but in a number of programs (such as those created by Microsoft), this is done selecting the **Tools** menu and clicking **Options**. After you're in the **Options** of the program, look for the **File Locations** of where your files are stored by default, and change the location so that each of the pro-grams save your files to a common location. Finding the default location of where files are saved by default also allows you to see where existing files are probably located. You can then move these existing files to your common direc-tory, so all the important data is gathered together.

For those who truly want to go the extra distance to protect their docu-ments, you can use utilities that will create a hidden virtual drive where you can store files. In reality, the virtual drive is a file on your hard disk, but it functions as a hard disk on your computer and will even appear in Windows Explorer as a drive letter (E:, F:, and so on). Security tools like BestCrypt create such directo-ries. While BestCrypt isn't free, a fully functional evaluation copy can be acquired from www.jetico.com. When BestCrypt runs, you use the virtual directory to view and store files. When it isn't running, or someone on another computer attempts to view the folders on your hard disk, the virtual directory can't be seen so the data appears invisible. Later in this chapter, we show you how BestCrypt also supports encryption to further enhance the security of your data.

Unfortunately, regardless of the method you use to organize your files, searching for your important files will generally require going through the various directories of your system and looking for familiar filenames. After these are found, you must then move your important data into folders or your hidden virtual drive. While this might be a long and monotonous process, the benefits of doing so will be seen if problems occur in the future. Not only will you know where your important files are stored, but (as discussed in the following sections), you'll now be better able to take precautions against losing your data or having unauthorized people access it.

The files you *choose* to save aren't the only ones on your computer, so you should also be aware of those that your system saves by default and where they are located. During the normal functions of your operating system and applications on your computer, a variety of files are saved to various locations. While many of these files might seem innocuous, there are some that might contain private information about you, show your browsing habits on the Internet, or contain data stored in personal files you've saved or worked on.

Temporary Files

Applications and your operating system will create what are called *temporary files*. Temporary files are created for numerous reasons. Some applications will use temporary files to store information until the next time you save. Operating systems like Windows 2000 will use temporary files when performing a specific operation. Generally, these files are removed when a task is completed, such as saving a document or spreadsheet, or your computer is shut down. However, if the application isn't designed to clean up such files, or problems such as an abnormal shutdown occurs, then these files will reside on your system indefinitely.

Many programs use the file extension *.tmp* to designate a temporary file. File extensions are used to determine what program is used to open a particular file, such as when your operating system knows to open Microsoft Word when double-clicking a file with the .doc extension. As mentioned, however, a common use for temporary files is to store information until the next time you save. For example, if you were working on a Word document, a temporary file for the document might be created in the same directory that the Word document was originally saved. The problem is that an unauthorized user or identity thief could open these temporary files using a text editor and view information contained within the document the temporary file is associated with. Even if they are unable to access the information in the file you've opened and you're working on, or you've moved the file off the hard disk, there is always a possibility that someone might be able to open the temporary file and view the information inside. For this reason, after closing a document you're working on, you should ensure that any temporary files for that document have been removed. If not, delete them.

The Temp directory is another place in which temporary files are commonly stored. On machines running Microsoft Windows, this directory is usually located in the root directory of C:\ or in C:\WINDOWS. This folder contains a variety of temporary files, including those that were temporarily used to set up programs you've installed, files that were created by the operating system or other software, and file attachments you've opened with your e-mail program. Even though these should be removed by software when no longer needed, a number of files will continue to exist in this directory. Operating systems might leave them if improperly shut down, setup programs might fail to include cleanup routines, or any number of other reasons might result in these files continuing to exist when no longer needed. The problem is that unless you positively know which files aren't needed by software, it can be difficult knowing which of these files to delete.

To remove such files on machines running Windows 98/ME/2000, and higher, you can use the Disk Cleanup tool. To start this tool, select **Start | Programs | Accessories | System Tools**, and click **Disk Cleanup**. When the program starts, you will see an interface like that shown in Figure 2.1. By selecting the disk to cleanup from the drop-down list, you then click **OK**. After the program starts, it will remove unneeded files from your hard disk, including temporary files, programs downloaded from the Internet, files in your Recycle Bin, and Temporary Internet Files.

Figure 2.1 Disk Cleanup Program

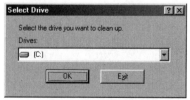

Temporary Internet Files

Temporary Internet Files are files that are downloaded from the Internet when you're browsing and stored to a directory on your hard disk. When viewing Web pages, the files making up that page (HTML documents, graphics, and so forth) are downloaded first to your hard disk, where the browser then reads them. On Windows machines, these files are stored in the Temporary Internet Files directory under your Windows directory. If someone were to look in this directory, they would see the pages you've visited. If you went to a site to read your e-mail (like www.hotmail.com), the e-mail messages would appear as HTML files stored in the Temporary Internet Files directory. This means that anyone looking in this directory would be able to view your private e-mails.

In addition to the Disk Cleanup tool, Internet Explorer provides the ability to remove Temporary Internet Files through the Internet Options dialog box. You can access this dialog box through the **Control Panel** or by clicking the **Internet Options** item on the **Tools** menu of Internet Explorer. In the "Deleting Hidden Information About You" section in Chapter 4, the **General** tab of this dialog box is discussed, which provides the ability to view and delete the files in your Temporary Internet Files directory.

The Temporary Internet Files section of the Internet Option's General tab provides a button called Delete Cookies. *Cookies* are text files that some Web sites use to store information about a user's visit to the site, or to obtain information about a user. Often, cookies are used to enhance a user's visit to the site. For example, e-commerce sites might use them to keep track of what you've put into a shopping cart to purchase. Because cookies can contain personal information about you, you should delete cookies to prevent this information from being viewed by others. In Windows, you can view cookies stored on your machine by looking inside the Cookies folder in your Windows directory.

Information on your Web browsing history can also be removed on the Internet Option's General tab. Your History is information stored in the History folder of your Windows directory that keeps track of Web sites you've visited. By looking in this folder, someone can see where you've gone on the Internet and determine any patterns to your browsing. The History section of Internet Options allows you to empty files in this folder, or adjust the number of days that Internet Explorer will store your history. We discuss deleting cookies and clearing your History in greater detail in Chapter 4.

While the task of removing unwanted files from your computer is filled with steps and can be time-consuming until you're used to it, a number of programs are available on the Internet that can automate this process. One such program is ZDelete, which can be downloaded from LSoft Technologies Web site at www.zdelete.com. This tool can be scheduled to permanently delete files in your Temporary Internet Files directory, Recycle Bin, Temporary Files directory, cookies, and history. ZDelete is shareware, so you will need to pay to register your copy after a 30 day evaluation period.

Other tools that can be downloaded to automate the task of deleting files can be found at Hideaway.Net's site (www.hideaway.net/e-mail/privacy_shareware/ privacy_shareware.htm). On this site, you can find Complete Cleanup, which is a shareware program that allows you to try its features before deciding to buy it. Complete Cleanup works with America Online, Internet Explorer, and Netscape, and it will delete Temporary Internet Files, history files, cookies, and other unwanted files that might be lingering on your hard disk.

Deleting Files Permanently for Privacy

When you delete a file from your hard disk, you might assume that it's gone for good. On Windows 95, Windows NT, and higher, when a file is deleted, it is sent to the Recycle Bin. This is a special type of folder residing in the root directory of each hard disk. The folder is called Recycled and is hidden so it isn't seen by default through programs like Windows Explorer. The Recycle Bin serves as a safety buffer, storing files you've deleted, so you can restore them if they were deleted by mistake.

To restore a deleted file, double-click the **Recycle Bin** icon on your desktop and right-click the file you'd like to restore. When the menu appears, select **Restore**, and the file will be returned to the exact location it was deleted from. If you want to restore the file to another location (such as the desktop), simply drag the file to where you'd like it restored to. In doing so, no damage is caused to the file, and it will appear as if it were never deleted.

After you've deleted a file, you can remove it from the Recycle Bin by selecting a file inside and pressing the key on your keyboard, or by right-clicking the **Recycle Bin** icon located on your desktop and selecting **Empty Recycle Bin** from the menu. You can also configure the Recycle Bin to immediately delete files by configuring its properties. To do this, right-click the **Recycle Bin** icon and then, when the menu appears, click **Properties** to view the dialog box shown in Figure 2.2. The dialog box will have one Global tab and a separate tab for each hard disk installed on your computer. To configure how files are deleted on each drive, click the **Configure drives independently** option, and then configure the tab for each drive. To configure all drives the same, select the **Use one setting for all drives** option. To delete files completely, so they're not moved to the Recycle Bin, ensure the **Do not move files to the Recycle Bin** checkbox is checked, or slide the slider bar below this so that zero percent of your hard disk is used for storing Recycle Bin files. If you'd like to have a dialog box appear when you delete a file so that you can confirm whether the file should be deleted, ensure the **Display delete confirmation dialog box** is checked.

Figure 2.2 Recycle Bin Properties

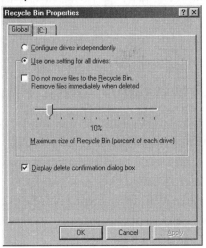

In addition to mistakenly thinking your files are permanently deleted when you delete them, you might make the same mistake with your e-mail. Many e-mail programs include a folder called Trash or Deleted Items in which deleted e-mails are stored. Until the e-mails are deleted from here, they remain viewable by anyone accessing the program and looking in this folder. In Outlook Express, you can empty the Deleted Items folder by right-clicking the folder, and selecting **Empty Deleted Items Folder**. You can also select individual e-mails in this folder and press the **Delete** key on your keyboard to permanently delete them. We discuss this in greater detail in the next chapter.

Even when files are "permanently" deleted in these ways, they can still be recovered from the hard disk. Even though the entry for the file is removed from the file system, the data continues to reside on the hard disk. Using tools that can read deleted data on your hard disk, such as Guidance Software's EnCase or any number of tools available on the Internet, someone with access to your hard disk can view and restore the files. Even though file systems like NTFS are more secure than FAT or FAT32, such tools can still access and restore these files. As shown in Figure 2.3, a free program called Disk Investigator allows the viewer to see the contents of a temp directory, where one file and one folder have been deleted.

Figure 2.3 Disk Investigator Shows Files Deleted on the Hard Disk

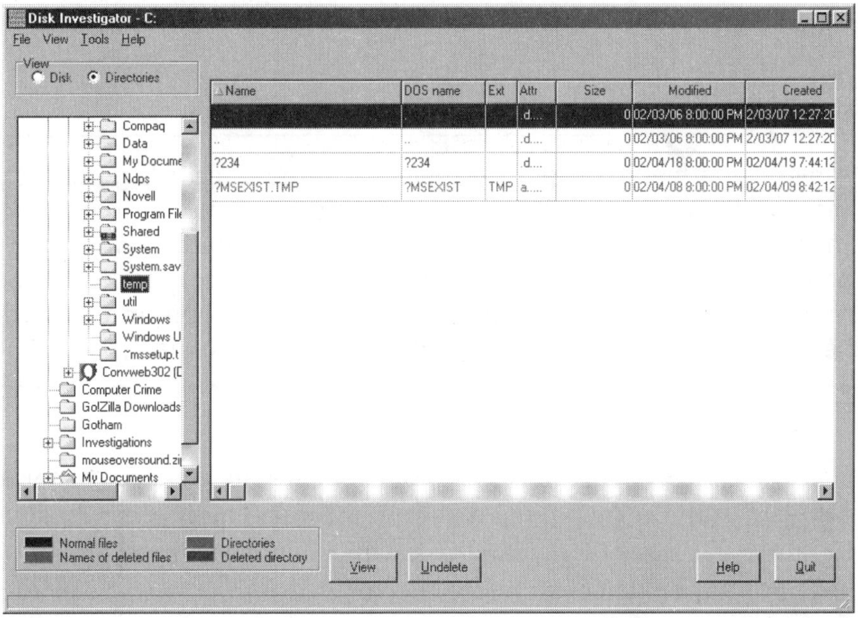

Digging Deeper...

File Systems

File systems are methods that dictate how a computer stores and retrieves files, how files are named, and possibly whether files can be stored more securely than others. Numerous types of file systems are available for different operating systems, including DOS, Windows, Macintosh, OS/2, and UNIX. You generally decide on the type of file system your computer will use when you format your hard disk.

The most secure file system for computers running Windows NT and Windows 2000 is NTFS. NTFS is short for the *New Technology File System*. It has support for long filenames and compression, and it allows you to determine who has access to a particular file.

To ensure the files you've deleted can never be recovered, you'll need to use a program that will wipe the deleted data from your hard disk. There are numerous programs on the Internet that can achieve this, which can be downloaded from www.download.com. Generally, these programs will overwrite the free space so that any deleted data on the disk is completely removed. Although this might be overkill in day-to-day use, it is useful if you're selling your hard disk or entire computer, and want to ensure that the buyer cannot recover any personal data on your computer.

NOTE

Many people feel that because they've deleted a file, it's gone for good. This isn't the case at all. When a file is deleted from your hard disk and emptied from the Recycle Bin of Windows computers, it is flagged so that it can't be viewed by the system, and the space it takes up can be overwritten. Until a file is written to the same location on the hard disk, the file can be viewed and restored by special software.

For a file to be permanently deleted from your system, you need to use software that will "scrub" or "wipe" the data from the disk. This is generally done by overwriting the free space on the hard disk with a random series of 1s and 0s. One such program is Eraser, which is available free of charge from www.hideaway.net/e-mail/privacy_shareware/privacy_shareware.htm.

Other Information that Might be on Your Computer

Beyond determining what files are lurking in the directories of your hard drive, you will also need to ascertain what private information exists on your system. You'll remember that when you first installed the operating system on your computer, you entered your first name, last name, and the organization you belonged to. When you installed other programs, you might have been required to enter your name, address, phone number, fax number, e-mail address, or other information. Such information might have been required for legitimate reasons (such as to register the application), but it might still reside on your system. Although you consider this information private, others might be able to view this information when sitting at your computer or over the Internet.

A major risk involved with information in the Registry exists when you consider shared folders. These are folders on your hard disk that are configured to be shared with other network users. In the case of shared folders used by Peer-to-Peer programs like KaZaA, files in specific directories can be shared over the Internet. While we discuss shared folders in greater detail in Chapter 5, you should realize that you should never share the root directory of your hard disk. By sharing the root directory, this means your entire C:\, D:\, and so on. If you were to do so, then someone could view your Registry remotely, or download the entire Registry and view it on their computer. Because your Registry might contain a significant amount of information about you, including passwords, it's important that you protect it by not sharing the root directory or Windows directory where it is stored.

You can view much of the information gathered from you by software by looking in the Windows Registry. To view the Registry, run REGEDIT from the **Run** command. To start the Registry Editor, click the item labeled **Run** on the Start menu, type **REGEDIT**, and then click **OK**. When the Registry Editor program appears, click the **Find** item from the **Edit** menu, enter your first or last name, and then click the **Find Next** button. As it searches for instances of your name, press the **F3** button on your keyboard to look for the next instance. You'll probably be amazed at how many times you'll find your name listed and personal information related to your name. Trojan Horse programs (which we'll discuss later in this chapter) and other malicious programs can access such information without your knowing. Such programs might transmit your information to an identity thief through e-mail, transmit it to a Web site, or provide other methods (such as creating a backdoor to access your system) so a hacker can access the information directly. Because of the detailed information that might exist in the Registry, it's important that you control the level of information that's added to it.

WARNING

Although it's possible to edit the Registry and remove the personal information stored there, it is *not* recommended that you modify the Registry unless you're certain what each entry represents and what effect it will have. To remove much of the private information stored in the Windows Registry, you can obtain software from the Internet that is generally safer than modifying the Registry through the Windows Registry Editor. One such program is Ownerfix, which is available free of charge from www.download.com. This tool allows you to modify owner and company registration information in Windows 95/98/NT/2000.

The level of information stored by an application and its ability to reveal personal facts to others will vary from program to program. An example of an application that might reveal a significant amount of personal data is ICQ. ICQ is an Internet chat program that allows you to meet and send messages to others online, and it can be acquired free of charge at http://web.icq.com. As shown in Figure 2.4, ICQ provides the ability to advertise details about yourself on the Internet. These details include your first and last name, home address, work address, phone number, birth date, gender, and other personal facts. While the level of information included in this program is optional, numerous ICQ users fill in as many of these fields as they can. In doing so, they risk an identity thief taking the information and stealing the user's identity. For this reason, you should examine the information stored in this and other software on your system, and remove as many personal facts from them as possible.

Figure 2.4 ICQ Details

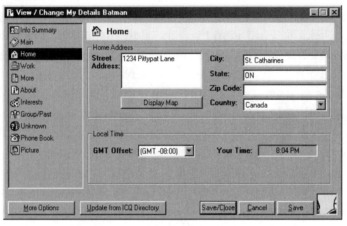

What Are You Protecting?

The first step in protecting data on your computer is deciding what it is you're trying to protect. You might not be interested in preventing others from viewing your weekly grocery list, but you would want to keep the information contained in your tax return private. By determining what it is you want to protect, you'll be able to determine the level of security needed to keep information safe.

As mentioned in the previous section, by organizing your personal files together in a single directory, you will be better able to manage them. Once you've decided on the files you want to protect, you can then determine the level of protection required. This involves backing up files, password protecting them, and deciding whether certain folders and files should be shared. In addition, you can protect the computer from other users who access the system.

Password Protecting Your Computer

Passwords are a useful tool for protecting your computer and its data from unwanted users. You can think of a password as a key to a lock. Without the correct key, it is difficult to bypass the lock. While we discuss how to create effective passwords later in this chapter, you first need to know how passwords can be used on your system, and how you would set up this protection.

If anyone has physical access to your computer when you're not around, the first step to getting into a system that's shut down is powering it on. With a Power-On Password, this person would need to enter a password before the operating system even starts. Without the correct password, anyone attempting to start your computer would be stopped cold.

Power-On Passwords are set up through your computer's setup program, which is used to configure hard disks, boot options, and machine passwords. On most computers, you can access the computer's setup program by pressing the **Delete** or **F10** key at startup. Because the type of setup program depends on the type of computer being used, the exact steps involved in setting up a Power-On Password will vary from machine to machine. However, all machines use this program to set up such passwords.

To prevent people from accessing this setup program and changing your Power-On Password, you can set a Setup Password that prevents people from accessing this program and changing your computer's settings. Setup passwords are set within the setup program just as Power-On passwords are set, so the exact steps vary from machine to machine.

Chances are, even if Power-On Passwords and Setup Passwords are set on your machine, you wouldn't want to shut down your computer every time you leave the room. For this reason, operating systems often provide alternate methods of password protecting your machine. One of these is password-protected screen savers.

Screen savers are programs that serve a number of uses on computers, which go beyond livening up the monitor with an attractive series of images. They protect your monitor from "burn in," where what's being displayed for a period of time is etched onto the screen, and also protect people from seeing what you're working on. Screen savers activate after a set time limit of inactivity and can be configured not to turn off until a correct password is entered.

Setting up password protected screen savers in Windows is done through the **Display** applet found in **Control Panel**. After the **Display Properties** are open, you then select the **Screen Saver** tab to see what's shown in Figure 2.5. On this tab, you'll see a section called **Screen Savers**, which has a checkbox labeled **Password protected**. Upon checking this box, a button labeled **Change** will become enabled. By clicking this button, a new dialog box will appear where you can enter the password you want to use for the screen saver. Once set, if anyone hits a key or moves the mouse while the screen saver is active, they will need to enter a password to disable the screen saver and access any programs that are running.

Figure 2.5 Passwords for Screen Savers Are Set through Display Properties

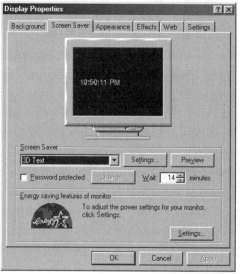

If the software you're using allows it, files created by the program can be password protected. If anyone attempts to view or modify the file, they are required to enter a password. Microsoft Word, Excel, Access and other applications provide this ability when the file is saved. In Microsoft Office programs (Word, Excel, Access, and so forth), password protection can be set by choosing **Save As** from the **File** menu, you can click a button labeled **Options**. This will display a dialog box where you can set a password to open the file and another password to modify it. Trying to crack these passwords using hacking tools can be a difficult process. Depending on the strength of the password (which we discuss later in this chapter), it can take days of running the hacking software on the password-protected file before getting the password. For this reason, unless a hacker knows there is something inside the file that's worth this work, they will often disregard the file and move onto easier pickings.

Programs and Files

For many people, the programs and files on a computer are what people are most concerned about protecting. If a virus or other malicious program makes its way onto your computer, important information like budgets, tax returns, resumes, and other files can be damaged or lost. Even if you have all the installation programs for software on your computer, reinstalling your operating system and every application will take a significant amount of time. Because of the concern over such data, you should take steps to protect your data.

Most operating systems provide some tool to backup files stored on your computer to a floppy disk, tape, another computer on your network, or some other media. In Windows 95/98/2000/Me/XP, you can find this tool by clicking **Start | Programs | Accessories | System Tools**, and then clicking the **Backup** icon. In Windows NT, such a tool is found by clicking **Start | Programs | Administrative Tools (Common)** and then clicking **Backup**. If you use a different operating system, you will need to check your operating system's manual or Help files.

When files are backed up, they are essentially copied in a compressed format, so that if anything happens to your system, they can then be restored as if nothing had happened. When making backups, you might find that your software offers several choices of backing up the data, including:

- Full backup
- Incremental backup
- Differential backup
- Daily backup

A *full* backup is sometimes referred to as a *normal* backup. When you make a full backup, all the files you select are backed up. When the file is backed up, the file is marked as having been backed up, which is useful when other types of backups are performed on your system.

An *incremental* backup backs up only those files that have been created or changed since the last time you made a full backup or incremental backup. As a file is backed up, it is marked as having been backed up, so that it isn't included in the next incremental backup (unless it is changed). Because only these files are backed up, it takes less time to perform an incremental backup because fewer files are involved in the process. Should you need to restore your files, you would need to first restore the last full backup you made and then each of the incremental backups you made.

A *differential* backup backs up only those files that have been created or changed since the last full backup. Unlike the previous methods, it doesn't mark files as having been backed up, so any files that were backed up this time, will also be backed up next time. The benefit of this is that when you need to restore the files, you only need to restore the last full backup you made and the last differential backup.

A final type of backup you might encounter is a *daily* backup. With this type of backup, all files that were modified the day of the daily backup are backed up. It looks at the date the file was created or modified, and if they match the current day, they are included in the backup. It doesn't mark these files as having been backed up.

What You Can't See Can Hurt You

Viruses and Trojans

Viruses are programs that are designed to cause a variety of activities on your system, such as corrupting and erasing files, reformatting your hard disk, or performing an action that is benign but annoying. Like a human virus, it can spread across your system, from one program or file to another. There are thousands of viruses with new ones appearing every month. They can be acquired through e-mail attachments, downloaded files, or through infected floppy disks and CDs.

Trojans are a different kind of program that's contained inside a seemingly harmless program. Sometimes called a *Trojan Horse*, it gets its name from Homer's *Iliad*, in which the Greeks gave the citizens of Troy the gift of a giant wooden horse. Once the Trojans brought the horse inside their city gates, warriors came out of the hollow horse, and killed the Trojan troops. Like this wooden horse, Trojans can also cause significant damage, such as damaging files or transmitting personal information obtained from a computer to an e-mail address.

Because viruses and Trojans can be so destructive, it's important that you install antivirus software on your computer and keep its antivirus signature files up-to-date.

Antivirus Software: Your First Line of Defense

New viruses come out all the time, threatening to damage your system and/or destroy your data. To protect yourself from these malicious programs, you need to install antivirus software on your computer. Antivirus software is a type of program that searches your hard disk and removable media (such as floppy disks, CDs, and so forth) for known viruses. When a virus–infected file is found, it can then repair the file by removing the virus's code, or delete the file to prevent other files from becoming infected.

The way antivirus software can perform these actions is through signature files, which are also sometimes called *virus definition files*. These contain information used by the antivirus software to identify known viruses, and they contain information used by the software so it can effectively clean any infected files. Without signature files, the antivirus software wouldn't be able to function properly.

Numerous antivirus software programs are on the market that can help protect your data from viruses. We look at several of the most popular software packages and show you how you can update your signature files and software to keep up-to-date with the viruses that are out there.

NOTE

Viruses can have a wide variety of effects on your system. Some viruses are downright silly, playing music over your speaker repeatedly. Others can be a major problem in terms of identity theft. One such virus is PWSteal.Coced240b.Tro, which is designed to steal passwords. It is sent to you as an e-mail attachment named 26705-i386-update.exe, claiming to be a patch sent to you from support@microsoft.com. Once it's activated on your system, it sends password information on your machine to an e-mail address. While there are numerous password stealing viruses, this one is used to illustrate how a virus can do more than cause damage to data.

What You Might Not Know about Antivirus Software

Antivirus software is only effective against *known* viruses. In other words, if information about the virus isn't included in the signature file, the antivirus software can't do anything to protect you. There are a number of reasons why your antivirus software might not know about a particular virus.

One of the major reasons your antivirus software can't detect a virus is because it is so new that the antivirus company isn't aware of it or the company hasn't updated its signature files yet. Programmers write new viruses every week, for a variety of reasons. Some are for malicious reasons, where the programmer wants to cause problems for as many people as possible. In other cases, the programmer might want to infect a specific computer, such as that of an enemy or those in a particular institution. For numerous other programmers, they might write the virus for educational reasons, wanting to see if they can actually do it. If the last reason is true, the virus is accidentally released or someone with access releases it for them. Whatever the reason, after the virus is initially released to other computers, no antivirus will be able to help the first infected systems.

Another type of "virus" that antivirus software can't protect you from are hoax viruses. Hoax viruses aren't actual viruses, but they can be just as damaging. They are generally warnings that are distributed through e-mail, often encouraging recipients to perform some action. Some might tell the reader to check their hard disk for a specific file, and, if it exists, it tells them it is a virus that should be deleted at once. Unfortunately, the file in question is usually one installed by the operating system and is supposed to be there. The recipient finds the file, deletes it, and their operating system or other software fails to work properly. Because the warning seems so helpful, you might find friends or family sending you these warnings. If you find one, the best advice is to do nothing until checking whether antivirus manufacturers like Norton, McAfee, and so forth advise similar action. You can view a list of hoax viruses and find more information about them by visiting Symantec's Hoax page at http://securityresponse.symantec.com/avcenter/hoax.html.

Finally, the most common reason antivirus software can't protect you is because of user error. The user might fail to configure his antivirus software to constantly search for viruses, or he might fail to regularly scan the hard disk for viruses. Worse yet, the user might fail to download signature updates to ensure that the antivirus is searching for the latest viruses. Failing to use the antivirus software properly can be as damaging as not running the software at all.

NOTE

Many new computers come with software preinstalled, possibly with antivirus software already installed. When you purchase a new computer with antivirus software installed, ensure that it is configured correctly and has the latest antivirus signature files. If you choose to have antivirus signature files automatically updated, then you will need to ensure that the antivirus signature files are actually being updated.

An example of a problem of antivirus software improperly set up on new computers was seen with the Hewlett Packard Pavilion computers, which came with a slim version of McAfee installed. This version wasn't the full-version available from their Web site (www.mcafee.com), which provides the auto-update feature. Instead, when people clicked on the McAfee icon in the system tray, a Web page was displayed enticing people to sign up for a fee.

You should install a full version of antivirus software on your system, and update your signature files regularly. Later in this chapter, we show you how to update them manually and discuss automatic updates, as well.

Why Update?

Updating your antivirus software is vital to its ability to adequately scan, detect, and clean viruses. Like any other application, software updates are required to fix vulnerabilities and bugs in the program. Updating your software might require installing a simple patch or getting the latest version of the program. However, a more frequent update that's required by antivirus software is signature files.

Many people make the mistake of installing the antivirus software and thinking that no further action is required. However, because signature files contain information used to detect and clean viruses from your system, your antivirus software will be unable to detect any viruses that appeared after this software was released. Every week to every few weeks, new signature files become available and need to be installed for your software to work at peak efficiency.

What Kinds of Software Are Available?

Numerous antivirus software packages are on the market, for a variety of systems. Choosing the right one might seem confusing and scary, with an incorrect choice leaving you vulnerable. In choosing the right antivirus software, you should look at the reputation of the manufacturer and how long they've effectively been providing services.

One of the most popular software packages is Norton Antivirus, and it is obtainable from Symantec's Web site at www.symantec.com. Versions of this software are available for both Microsoft Windows and Macintosh systems. Norton Antivirus is well-respected and provides antivirus solutions for networks, including Novell NetWare and Windows NT/2000. Not only can Norton Antivirus scan for viruses on demand, but it also has the ability to check for viruses in the background.

Another popular manufacturer of antivirus software is McAfee, and its products can be acquired from www.mcafee.com. It runs on versions of Microsoft Windows and Macintosh computers, and it can scan for viruses on demand as well as in the background. McAfee has been in business for years and is a well-respected antivirus software manufacturer.

Another popular antivirus software package is F-Prot, which is available from Frisk Software International's Web site at www.f-prot.com. Platforms supported by F-Prot consist of all Windows desktop and server versions, Linux, and legacy DOS systems. In the business of antiviruses since 1989, it is well-respected. F-Prot also has the ability to scan for viruses on demand and scan in the background.

Manually Updated Signatures

To update the signature files on your system, you might be required to manually download them and install them yourself. The method in which they are installed will vary from product to product. McAfee and Norton use self-extracting executable files that search for your installation of the antivirus software and then copy the signature files into that directory.

Automatically Updated Signatures

An easier method of updating signature files is to set your antivirus software to do it for you. For this, your system needs to be connected to the Internet. When online, the software will regularly check the manufacturer's site. If an updated signature file is detected, the software will either inform you of the update or download the file in the background. Upon downloading the file, the software automatically updates itself. This saves you from having to visit the manufacturer's site and perform the tedious task of updating the files yourself.

Web-based Software

With so many people connecting to the Internet, it is a small wonder that many antivirus programs provide the ability to scan incoming and outgoing e-mail and content (such as scripts and applets) downloaded with your browser. This is an important feature for antivirus software. Anyone who uses the Internet will be mainly exposed to viruses through e-mail attachments and malicious programs on Web sites. The ability to scan such files before they're able to execute the virus protects your system from becoming infected.

Performing Signature Updates

Signature files must be updated regularly to be effective. As mentioned, this update can be performed manually or by using features included in the software itself. This section looks at how to perform signature updates of three of the most popular antivirus software packages—McAfee, Norton, and F-Prot.

McAfee

McAfee provides the ability to perform signature updates both manually and automatically. To perform a manual update, you will need to follow these steps:

1. Use your Internet browser to visit McAfee's Web site at http://software.mcafee.com/centers/download/default.asp.

2. Upon reaching this Web page, you will see a listing of links. Some of the links are for security updates and patches for McAfee software, while one will state **Antivirus (DAT) Files**.

3. Click the link labeled **Antivirus (DAT) Files**. You will see a page offering antivirus updates for a variety of McAfee VirusScan versions. If you are using versions 3.x or 4.x, then you will be redirected to a page for upgrading to version 6.x. If you are using other versions, then click the link associated with the version of McAfee you're currently using.

4. A new page will appear with a button stating **Download**. Click this button, and your download will begin.

5. When the download is complete, open the file. It is a self-installing executable that will automatically update your virus signature files.

McAfee also provides the ability to update antivirus files automatically when you're connected to the Internet. On the **File** menu, you will see an option titled

Update VirusScan, which will automatically connect to the McAfee Web site when you're connected to the Internet and (depending on the options you choose) will update either your signature files or the software itself.

Norton

Norton Antivirus provides the ability to perform signature updates both manually and automatically. To perform a manual update, you will need to follow these steps:

1. Use your Internet browser to visit Symantec's Web site at http://securityresponse.symantec.com/avcenter/download.html.

2. Upon reaching this Web page, you will see a listing of links. Some of these are for security updates to Symantec software, while one will state **Download Virus Definitions (Intelligent Updater Only)**.

3. Clicking the link labeled **Download Virus Definitions (Intelligent Updater Only)**, you will see a page asking you to choose the language you'd like to use.

4. After clicking a language, a new Web page will load asking you to specify the antivirus software you're using. What you choose here depends on which software package you've purchased.

5. After selecting the antivirus software you're currently using, another Web page will load offering you different choices for downloading the signature files. Some of these are several files that will fit on a floppy disk, while others will specify the antivirus software the signature files are for. Click the link that suits your needs.

6. At this point, Windows users are presented with a window that will enable you to choose where the file will be downloaded. You can choose to save the file to disk, if you're upgrading more than one machine, or choose to open the file after it's downloaded.

7. Upon opening the downloaded file, the Intelligent Updater program asks whether you would like it to update your signature files. Click the **Yes** button. The updater program will search your system for Norton Antivirus and begin copying the new signature files to your system.

If you don't like the idea of performing a manual update, Norton Antivirus also provides a feature called *Live Update*. This feature allows you to check Symantec's Web site for signature updates whenever you're connected to the

Internet. It is the easiest solution for users who aren't comfortable performing a manual update or who don't want to check Symantec's site regularly for updates.

F-Prot

F-Prot also has the ability to perform manual and automatic updates. To perform a manual update, follow the following steps.

1. Use your Internet browser to visit F-Prot's Web site at www.f-prot.com/ f-prot/download/.

2. Upon reaching this Web page, you will see options for downloading trial versions of the software, buying full versions, and downloading signature files. To download the latest signature files, click the link labeled **Signature files for Application/Script Viruses and Trojans**.

3. If you're a Windows user, you'll be presented you with a window that will enable you to choose where the file will be downloaded. You can choose to save the file to disk, if you're upgrading more than one machine, or choose to open the file after it's downloaded.

4. To open the file, you will need to use WinZip and extract the files to the directory in which F-Prot was installed. These files will overwrite the existing signature files, upgrading them in the process.

5. Return to your browser, and click the link labeled **Signature files for Document/Office/Macro Viruses**.

6. If you're using Windows, you'll be presented with a window that will enable you to choose where the file will be downloaded. You can choose to save the file to disk, if you're upgrading more than one machine, or choose to open the file once downloaded.

7. To open this file, you will need to use WinZip and extract the files to the directory in which F-Prot was installed. These files will overwrite the existing signature files, upgrading them in the process.

F-Prot also provides an updater utility in the antivirus program that connects to Frisk Software International's Web site when you're connected to the Internet, and updates the signature files. This feature is only included with the Windows version of F-Prot, so users of other versions will need to manually update their signature files.

Is Your Antivirus Software Working?

After you've installed your antivirus software, you should check to see if the software is actually working. Don't install it and just assume it functions normally. Although you won't really be able to determine if the software is working until you get a virus, which is unwanted, you can check whether the software appears to work properly.

Because most antivirus software will run in the background while you're working, determine if a small icon for the program appears in the lower right-hand corner of the Windows taskbar or on the control strip (control strip modules folder) if you're using Macintosh.

You can also check is whether the signature update was applied correctly. To do this, open your antivirus software and look for the date of the signature file. As shown in the Figures 2.6 and 2.7, this information is provided in the program for your reference. If the date matches that of the file you updated to, then it shows the latest signature file has been applied. This information might appear slightly different from program to program. Notice that while Norton Antivirus Corporate Edition shows the version number and date of the signature file, McAfee VirusScan will also inform you of how many days old the signature file is (see Figures 2.6 and 2.7).

Figure 2.6 The Version and/or Date of a Virus Signature File Appears Within the Program After It's Applied

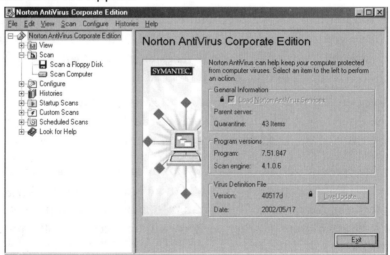

Figure 2.7 McAfee Virus Scan

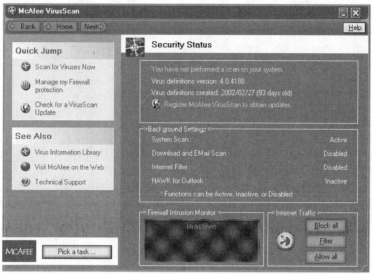

Finally, you should run the software and scan for viruses on demand. Open the program and start a scan of your hard disk, and monitor whether it appears to scan for viruses. If it does, be content with the fact that your antivirus software is functioning properly until the next update and upgrade.

Digging Deeper...

Viewing Hidden Programs

Hidden programs are programs that run on your system without your being aware of them. Some of these programs are called *spyware*, which is software that secretly gathers personal and organizational information from your computer, monitors your Internet activity, and/or obtains other information about you. After obtaining this information, it sends it over the Internet, where it is then relayed to advertisers and other parties. Because it might be installed with a legitimate software package you install or secretly programmed into the code, you might not be aware that this information is being gathered, why it's being gathered, and who is viewing these facts about you.

Continued

Another type of hidden program can be a Trojan. One such Trojan is Backdoor.Sdbot, which a portable executable that copies itself to your Windows System folder, and runs as a service in the background. This Trojan allows hackers to gain control of your computer through Internet Relay Chat (IRC), and can update itself to newer versions over the Internet. While antivirus software can remove it, you will also need to make changes yourself, because it writes entries to your Windows Registry.

You can see if hidden programs are running on your system using Task Manager on systems running Windows XP/NT/2000. You can start Task Manager by pressing **Ctrl + Alt + Delete** at the same time, and then clicking the **Task Manager** button on the screen that appears. When Task Manager appears on your screen, click the **Processes** tab. This will list all processes running on your system. Most of these need to run, but, if you know one shouldn't be there, you can select the process you want to stop and then click the **End Process** button. On Windows 9x and Windows Me, the two processes that definitely need to be running are SYSTRAY and EXPLORER. To determine the programs that absolutely must be running on your operating system, check the Web site of the operating system's manufacturer.

Updating Your Software

Just as updating your signature files is important, updating your software is also important. Software updates are also sometimes called *fixes*, *patches*, *security packs*, *service packs*, or other similar names. These need to be installed to fix security vulnerabilities, bugs in the program, or other problems that have been found to exist. If these vulnerabilities aren't fixed, then viruses, Trojans, and hackers can exploit the software and access or destroy data on your system. Software updates need to be applied not only to your operating system but also to antivirus software, server software, Internet browsers, and other applications.

In some cases, manufacturers might decide not to release an update, because they are planning to release a new version (also called an *upgrade*) of the software. New versions include or do not require the updates for previous versions, because they don't have the same features or vulnerabilities, or they have the "fix" code already included in the upgrade. This does not however mean that you don't need to continue your vigilance in monitoring a manufacturer's Web site for updates. With every new version, new updates might become available. As such, you should ensure that you're using the latest version of software and that you monitor the manufacturer's Web site for updates for the upgraded software.

Digging Deeper...

Update Vs. Upgrade

The terms *update* and *upgrade* can be confusing to some people. After all, when you download and apply the latest signature files, you are performing an update even though the software hasn't been modified in any way. In the same light, if you install a bug fix to your antivirus software, this doesn't mean that your signature files are up-to-date. An update is anything that brings elements of your system up-to-date. Signature file updates, which are discussed earlier in this chapter, apply to only the antivirus signature files themselves, while software updates actually modify the programming code to fix any issues that are known to the manufacturer.

Upgrades take place when major changes occur in a system, and a new version of the software is released. Upgrades might be minor (such as when Windows 3 upgraded to Windows 3.1), or they might be significant and easily identifiable (such as when Windows 3.1 upgraded to Windows 95). Compared to software updates, which are generally made available at no cost on the manufacturer's Web site, upgrades are generally infrequent and costly.

You should read information associated with an update or upgrade to see what changes are being applied to the software. Software updates will fix problems with the actual software, while other types of updates (such as antivirus signature file updates) will only bring limited aspects of the system up-to-date.

The Number One Mistake People Make

The most common mistake people make is installing software and then thinking that's all that's required. As we mentioned regarding antivirus software, failing to apply updates to signature files will leave you unprotected from the latest viruses on the Internet. The same logic applies to other software on your system.

When programmers write software, they can make mistakes or run behind schedule. For this reason, certain bugs might exist in software that's been released by a manufacturer. In some cases, the manufacturer might even know the bugs exist and decide to release an update to the software at a later date. However, if people don't update their software, they won't be able to benefit from the repairs and enhancements provided through the update.

Updates are released on an ongoing basis, so it's important to check the manufacturers Web site with regularity. Even knowledgeable users might install the latest update but fail to regularly check for updates that improve the functionality or security of an operating system or application. By not performing updates, you are taking a risk that your software might not work as well as it could, and that viruses and hackers might now have the ability to take advantage of vulnerabilities in your software.

Functionality versus Security Updates

Some updates are released to improve the functionality of the program, while others are released for security reasons. When functionality is the issue, a manufacturer might have received complaints that under specific situations, an application or operating system behaves erratically. In other cases, the manufacturer might try to meet a certain release date and decide not to have a feature included or known bugs to be fixed. To deal with the known issues, the manufacturer releases an update to the program at a later date.

Security updates are released to deal with vulnerabilities in the program. Microsoft released an e-mail security update to protect Outlook from viruses that are designed to attack the software and redistribute the virus through an address book. In the case of Windows NT 4, operating systems that don't have Service Pack 2 or higher installed have a vulnerability that allows hackers to use the Guest account to acquire Administrator rights. Using this vulnerability, a hacker could access any information on the system and make any modifications he or she desired. By installing security updates, you ensure that you're protected from known issues that could compromise the security of your system.

Installing Security Patches

You can install security patches on your system in a number of ways. The method used often depends on the software involved and the operating system being used. Most software manufacturers provide patches on their Web site, allowing customers to download and install them. As times changed and more customers gained Web access, manufacturers have come up with new and more efficient ways of getting updates to their customers.

Microsoft offers the Windows Update site for its customers. Users running the Windows operating system and Internet Explorer can access this site by selecting **Windows Update** from the **Tools** menu of Internet Explorer. An alternative method is using your Internet browser to visit http://windowsupdate.microsoft.com. Once here, you can click the hyperlink labeled **Product Updates** and launch a program that will check your system and determine what updates are required. After this information is obtained, a list of uninstalled updates is displayed. This saves users from having to remember which updates they have and haven't installed.

Another useful tool provided by Microsoft is the Critical Update Notification tool, which can be acquired from the Windows Update site. When users connect to the Internet, this tool will check Microsoft's site for new updates and patches that haven't been installed on your machine. If a new update or patch exists, the Critical Update Notification tool will inform you of the update, so you can then visit the Windows Update site and apply the upgrades to your system.

Windows Me and Windows XP users can also benefit from the Automatic Updates feature, which checks the Microsoft Web site for the latest updates and patches, downloads them automatically, and then asks if you'd like to install them. If you choose **Yes**, then the updates are installed on your system immediately.

In using these tools, Microsoft states that no personal information is acquired from your computer. This maintains your privacy and prevents unauthorized individuals from viewing information about you residing on your system.

While we'll discuss a number of popular software packages in this section, you should know that these aren't the only programs you'll need to update. Operating systems like Windows, Macintosh OS, Linux, and others might provide updates through their Web site. Application suites like Microsoft Office or individual applications might require updates to fix problems or enhance security. Even security-related software like your firewall and antivirus program might have updates that need to be installed. For this reason, you need to take an inventory of the software installed on your system and check each of the manufacturers Web sites for any updates or newer versions that might be available.

Internet Explorer

As mentioned in the preceding section, Internet Explorer can be updated automatically using the Windows Update Web site, the Critical Notification tool, and the Automatic Updates feature in Windows Me and Windows XP. In addition to these methods, you can manually look for updates by visiting Internet Explorer's

Web site at www.microsoft.com/windows/ie. On this site, you'll see a listing of security updates that can be downloaded and installed on your system as well as a link to download to the latest version.

Outlook

Outlook is e-mail software that is manufactured by Microsoft. It can be manually updated by visiting the Outlook Web site at www.microsoft.com/office/outlook/downloads. Here you will find links to download the latest security patches and other items related to Microsoft Outlook.

Microsoft also provides an Office Update site, which allows you to install updates to programs that are part of Microsoft Office. Because Microsoft Outlook is part of the Microsoft Office line of products, you can update Outlook in addition to traditional Office products like Word, Access, and Excel as well as Outlook. Because Outlook is so integrated with these products, you should update any other Office programs using the Office Update site at the same time.

By visiting the Office Update site at office.microsoft.com/productupdates, you will see a link that will allow Microsoft to analyze your installation of Office and determine what updates and patches haven't been installed. After this analysis is complete, a listing of suggested updates are displayed on a Web page, allowing you to choose which ones you'd like to install on your system.

IIS

Internet Information Server is Web server software for Windows NT Servers, while Internet Information Service is a Web server service for Windows 2000 Servers. Internet Information Service is an evolution of the Internet Information Server, and it achieved the name change when IIS 5 was released with Windows 2000. IIS provides Web services for intranets (Web sites for local networks) and the Internet.

Because IIS 5 is a service that's integrated with Windows 2000, it can be updated using the Critical Update Notification tool or the Windows Update Web site. Visiting the download section for Windows 2000 at www.microsoft.com/windows2000/downloads, you will find links for security patches and other software for Windows 2000 and its Web services. Here, you can obtain the files need for performing manual updates.

Netscape

Netscape is a popular browser that can be downloaded from the Netscape Web site at wp.netscape.com/computing/download. At the time of this writing, Netscape doesn't offer security patches and updates, so you need to make sure you have the latest version to ensure you've got the most recent bug fixes and, therefore, the most secure version available.

Opera

Opera is an Internet browser that can be downloaded from www.opera.com/download. At the time of this writing, Opera doesn't offer security patches and updates, so, as with Netscape, you need to make sure you have the latest version.

Beware of the Free Stuff

Looking a gift horse in the mouth is good advice when it comes to free programs that you find on the Internet or receive through e-mail. Free programs might contain viruses or be malicious programs designed to obtain information or damage data. Even though it might be free upfront, the cost of using the program might be high in the long run.

Virus-infected files are commonly transmitted as file attachments to e-mail messages. Some viruses will go through an address book and send a virus-infected message or file attachment to each person on the list. For this reason, even though the message appears to have come from someone you know, it might actually be a virus. As such, if you're not expecting a file being sent to you from a specific person, ignore the attachment and delete the message. If the message is from a friend, family member, or colleague, then contact them to see if they sent you a file before opening it. If they didn't send you anything, delete the message immediately.

Another type of free program might obtain information, damage data, or even go so far as reformat your hard disk. Malicious programs can be written to perform a variety of tasks. Once executed, the code can then perform various functions that are undesirable and dangerous.

In other cases, the malicious code might be secretly included in a seemingly legitimate program. This is common with spyware, which is software designed to gather information about you and transmit it to a specific source. Advertisers and other parties use spyware (which is also called *adware*) to determine what sites you visit or acquire other information about you. Because you don't know what information is being gathered, installing this software can be dangerous.

To protect yourself from spyware, you can turn to a number of tools on the Internet that will prevent such programs from sharing information about you and your browsing habits. One tool is AdAware, which can be acquired from LavaSoft's Web site at www.lsfileserv.com. This tool acts like antivirus software and uses updateable files containing information on known adware programs. It will scan your system for spyware and remove any that are found. Another tool is SpyStopper, which can be acquired from InfoWorks Technologies Web site at www.itcompany.com. When SpyStopper is used it will block any spyware, cookies, advertisements, and so forth, protecting your information from being sent out over the Net. In Chapter 4, we address spyware again and discuss how it is associated with browsers.

Avoiding Account Sharing

Accounts are used to ensure that a particular person has certain access to a system. On computers like Windows 98, accounts can be used so that each person can control her display settings, background picture, and so forth. On network operating systems like Windows 2000, accounts are used to control access to files and folders on the hard disk as well as specify which programs and network resources can be accessed. In addition, other types of accounts exist, such as accounts used on the Internet. E-mail accounts allow you to access your e-mail from your Internet Service Provider's mail server, while Internet connection accounts are used to access the Internet itself.

Sharing accounts is a major security risk for both home users and businesses. By sharing accounts, you allow others to access your personal information, desktop settings, files on a network, or other resources. If the information they acquire includes your employee number, address, financial records, or other information you assumed was secure, then the damage could be significant. By acquiring the power of your account, another person has the ability to access data that might enable them to steal your identity.

NOTE

The identity of a user on a network or the Internet is based upon who has access to the account. If more than one person is using your e-mail, Web site accounts, or other accounts, distinguishing you from others is almost always impossible. Such power allows others to send e-mail in your name, apply for credit online, and perform other tasks that can damage your credit and reputation.

Common Reasons, Risks, and Deterrents for Sharing Accounts

Many people share accounts because of financial reasons, personal reasons, or because it's easier than setting up a separate account for every person in the house or business. Unfortunately, by sharing accounts, you are taking a great risk with others accessing your information and being able to modify files and your computer.

People often share accounts because there is a level of trust between them. You might trust a friend, family member, or coworker enough to share your username or password with them. In doing so, they can access everything you can, modify your data, and change whatever settings you have access to. If that person shares your account with another person that they trust but you don't, then personal information can easily fall into the hands of this individual, putting your identity at risk of being stolen.

In the case of accounts used to access the Internet, many home users and businesses might find it too expensive to purchase separate accounts for each person. However, even though it might be financially unfeasible to get a different Internet account for each person, you should still set up separate e-mail accounts. Additional e-mail accounts can be purchased from an Internet Service Provider for a low price. By setting up separate e-mail accounts on e-mail programs, you're preventing another person in your house or business from viewing private information that might be transmitted through e-mail messages.

A common reason that colleagues in businesses might share their accounts is because it's easier than having security settings changed or new accounts set up. A business might have one person temporarily performing the job of another person, or a temporary employee might be hired to perform certain tasks. To do this, they need the same network security access. Rather than putting in a request to the network administrator to set up a new account or change the existing security settings of the temporary employee, employees give their username and password to the person. Unfortunately, even after the temporary employee moves onto another job or leaves the company, the person still has the necessary information to access your account.

A number of risks are involved in account sharing. Depending on the type of account, someone could access personal files saved to a network server, change the environment settings of your computer, or send threatening or unsuitable e-mail messages to other people. When you share your account with someone, they not only have the ability to access the same information as you but they also have the ability to pose as you.

Creating accounts for each person who uses a computer or network is the best method of controlling who can access what. By providing an easy and efficient policy for new employees, and creating accounts in a timely manner, you create an atmosphere that encourages people to acquire their own accounts. You can also create a Guest account with limited access, which enables people who have yet to acquire their own account limited access to the system.

A common method many networks use is to set a policy that forces each user to change their password after a set period of time. For example, a company might force users to change their passwords every 90 days. If anyone has access to an account, they won't be able to use it after the password changes.

When deciding whether to pay for additional Internet and e-mail accounts with others in your home, you should realize that the benefits of multiple accounts far outweigh the costs. Using an e-mail account that's separate from one your child or spouse uses will keep any messages you receive private. It will prevent others from responding to messages with your account and posing as you. The last thing you want is your child sending a nasty message to your boss, using an e-mail account that show's your name as the sender. Using separate dial-up connections will also enable you to maintain an element of privacy and prove which sites were visited by you. As we discuss in later chapters, your Internet account can be used to show which sites you visited and when. If your teenaged child decided to use an Internet connection provided by your company, you wouldn't want to explain why an account meant for you was being used to access inappropriate sites.

While we fully discuss the risks of sharing accounts in Chapter 6, you should understand that multiple accounts can be created for Internet connections, e-mail accounts, and even accounts used by your operating system. This is handy in your work environment as well as within your home.

Creating Multiple Accounts in Windows

Microsoft enables you to make separate accounts for people through different versions of the Windows operating system. The level of security these accounts will provide depends on the version of Windows being used.

Windows 98 has the ability to create a multiuser environment, but creating accounts for this operating system will only allow users to control their own display settings, background, and other environmental changes. It doesn't allow you to decide whether certain users can open specific files, use certain programs, or view different folders on the hard disk. The accounts are used to control environment settings, not security settings on the computer.

To create accounts in Windows 98, double-click the **Users** icon in the **Control Panel**, and follow the steps of the wizard that appears that allows you to enter a username and password. While this won't deter users with different accounts from accessing data throughout the computer, it will hide documents stored on the desktop from other users and allow users a certain freedom in defining their own environmental settings. In other words, Windows 98 won't prevent any user from viewing files stored in a folder on your hard disk. If a document is saved by you to the desktop, another user won't see it on the desktop when he or she logs on. If that person decided to use Windows Explorer to navigate through the folders on your hard disk however, they would still be able to open it. As mentioned, Windows 98 provides minimal security compared to other systems like Windows NT or 2000.

Windows XP, however, provides you with the ability to set up individual user accounts for your computer with different levels of security. The levels of access in Windows XP are:

- Restricted

- Standard

- Administrator

Restricted accounts are also referred to as *Guest* accounts, and they have the ability to use installed software and save documents. Standard accounts are also called *Limited* accounts, and they have the abilities of a Restricted account as well as being able to install most programs and change their own passwords. *Administrator* accounts have all these abilities as well as being able to create user accounts, change system files and settings, read other user account files, change their passwords, add and remove hardware, and install any programs.

Setting Up an Account in Windows XP

To set up an account in Windows XP with any of these security levels, you must follow these steps:

1. Click **Start menu | Settings | Control Panel.** In the **Control Panel**, double-click the icon labeled **User Accounts**

2. Click the **Users** tab, and then click the **Add button**.

3. Enter a name for the account, your full name, and an optional description of the account. If your computer is part of a domain, enter the domain name. If it is not part of a network or is part of a peer-to-peer network, leave the domain entry blank. Click **Next** to continue.

4. Enter the password for the account, and then enter it a second time to confirm it. Click **Next** to continue.

5. Select the level of access for this account (that is, **Administrator**, **Standard**, or **Restricted**), and then click **Finish**.

Setting Up an Account in Windows 2000

Windows 2000 Professional enables you to make local user accounts, which have varying degrees of access to the system and folders and files on the computer. You create users for the computer using the **Users and Passwords** tool in **Control Panel** with an account that's a member of the Administrators group. If you double-click the **Users and Passwords** icon, a dialog box opens with a button labeled **Add**. Click the **Add** button; you will be able to create a new account by adding information for the account. For greater control over users, you can use the **Advanced** tab of **Users and Passwords** by following these steps:

1. In **Users and Passwords**, click the **Advanced** tab and then click the button on this tab labeled **Advanced**. Microsoft Management Console with the Local Users and Groups snap-in will appear.

2. In the right pane of Local Users and Groups, click the folder labeled **Users** to display a list of users in the right pane.

3. In the right pane, right-click an empty space to display a menu, and then click the **New User** item from the menu. This will start the New User wizard.

4. Enter the account name for the user, their full name, and an optional description of the user. Below this, enter the password for the user twice (once to specify it, and a second time to confirm it).

5. Click **Create** to create a new account

Creating Multiple Internet Connection Accounts

Microsoft makes it easy to create new Internet connections by providing wizards that take you step-by-step through the process of setting up a new account. By following the instructions provided on each screen of the wizard, you should have little to no problem setting up accounts in whatever version of Windows you're using. If you're using an operating system other than Windows, you should also have the ability to create multiple Internet accounts on your machine. To do this, check the Help files of your operating system.

Setting up Multiple Internet Connection Accounts in Windows 98

In Windows 98, you create new accounts using the Make New Connection wizard. After you complete setting up an account with the wizard, a new icon will appear in Dial-Up Networking. To create a new account, follow these steps:

1. Click **Start | All Programs | Accessories | Communications | Dial-Up Networking**. In Dial-Up Networking, double-click the icon labeled **Make New Connection**.

2. When the Make New Connection Wizard appears, enter the name the connection will appear as in Dial-Up Networking. From the drop-down list below, select the device that will be used to connect to the Internet. Click **Next**.

3. Enter the area code and phone number to call to connect to your Internet Service Provider. From the drop-down list, select the country your ISP is located in. Click **Next**.

4. Click **Finish** to complete the setup of your account.

Setting up Multiple Internet Connection Accounts in Windows XP

Windows XP also uses a wizard to set up multiple Internet accounts. The wizard walks you through setting up new accounts. You access this wizard through the **Control Panel** on the **Start** menu, and then you follow the instructions on each screen. To create a new account, you would follow these steps:

1. Click **Start | All Programs | Accessories | Communications**. In **Communications**, double-click the icon labeled **New Connection Wizard**.

2. Click **Next** when the first screen appears, welcoming you to the wizard.

3. Select the option labeled **Connect to the Internet**. Click **Next**.

4. When the next screen appears, you have the options of **Choose from a list of Internet service providers (ISPs)**, **Set up my connection manually**, or **Use the CD I got from my ISP**. If you choose the first option, a list of ISPs will be provided that you can select from. If you choose the second option, you will continue answering questions that will enable you to set up your new connection. The third option is used if your ISP provided a CD that is used to install software and automatically configure settings. For this section's example, we continue with the steps needed to set up a connection manually. Click **Next**.

5. The next screen provides three options that are used to configure your account—**Connect using a dial-up modem**, **Connect using a broadband connection that requires a username and password**, and **Connect using a broadband connection that is always on**. While these options are self-explanatory, your choice will depend on the type of connection you're using to get on the Internet. For the remaining steps, we assume that you're setting up a dial-up connection. After making this choice, click **Next**.

6. Enter the name for this connection, and then click **Next**.

7. Enter the phone number for the ISP and then click **Next**.

8. When the next screen appears, you can decide who will have access to the account. If you wanted to allow any account in Windows to use this connection, you would select **Anyone's use**. For the connection to only be available to the account you're currently logged in with, select the option called **My use only**. Because we are setting up an account that can only be used by you, select **My use only**, and then click **Next**.

9. In the field labeled **User name**, enter the username provided by your ISP for this account. In the other two fields, enter your password. To prevent those who shouldn't have access to this account from using it, deselect the checkbox labeled **Use this account name and password when anyone connects to the Internet from this computer**. To ensure this is deselected, verify that a checkmark doesn't appear in the checkbox. Click **Next** to continue.

10. Click **Finish** to complete the setup of your account.

Setting up Multiple Internet Connection Accounts in Windows 2000

Windows 2000 provides an Internet Connection Wizard built into it that's similar to the one found in Windows XP. This wizard can be launched through **Internet Options** in the **Control Panel**. To set up a new account in Windows 2000, follow these steps:

1. Click **Start | Settings | Control Panel**. In **Control Panel**, double-click the icon labeled **Internet Options**.

2. Click the tab labeled **Connections**. On this tab, you'll see a button labeled **Setup**. Click this button to launch the wizard.

3. When the Internet Connection Wizard appears, you will see three options that allow you to sign up for a new account, transfer an existing account to the computer, and set up an account manually. For the instructions that follow, select **I want to set up my Internet connection manually, or I want to connect through a Local Area Network (LAN)**. Click **Next**.

4. The next screen provides to options **I connect through a phone line and a modem** and **I connect through a local area network (LAN)**. For the instructions that follow, select the first option of connecting through a phone line. Click **Next**.

5. Enter the area code and phone number to call to connect to your Internet Service Provider. From the drop-down list below, select the country in which your ISP is located in. Click **Next**.

6. Enter the username and password for the account. Click **Next**.

7. Enter the name for this connection. Click **Next**.

8. The screen that follows allows you to set up a new e-mail account. If you decided to create a new e-mail account, you would choose **Yes**. Because we discuss creating new accounts in the next section, you should choose **No** for this instruction. Click **Next**.

9. Click **Finish** to complete the setup of your account.

Creating Multiple E-mail Accounts with Outlook Express

Outlook Express provides the capability for multiple e-mail accounts to be used and keeps any messages and contacts for each account separated. In other words, each member of your family can have their own account set up in Outlook Express, and configured so they can't see one another's e-mail or contacts. To configure Outlook Express in this way, you would set up a different *identity* for each e-mail account.

Before setting up any identities in Outlook Express, you should obtain the following information from your ISP:

- E-mail address of the new account (such as. username@domainname.com)

- Names of the mail servers used for incoming and outgoing mail

- Account name and password for the e-mail account

Without this information, you might have difficulty setting up a new identity in Outlook Express. To save yourself from experiencing problems, ensure that you have this information handy.

Identities can be set up in Outlook Express by clicking the **File** menu, selecting **Identities**, and then clicking the menu item labeled **Add New Identity**. Upon clicking this menu item, a screen will appear, asking you to enter the name for the identity. To prevent others from viewing the e-mail and Address Book contacts of this new identity, ensure the checkbox labeled **Require a password** is checked. You then enter a password for the identity, which anyone attempting to access this account will need to enter. Upon clicking **OK**, you'll be asked if you want to log on as the new user. If you choose **Yes**, then you will be prompted for information about the new e-mail account. If you choose **No**, you'll still be able to configure the account the first time this identity is used. The Internet Connection Wizard is invoked the first time a new identity is used, requesting information to set up a new e-mail account, as shown in the following steps:

1. The first screen prompts you to enter the name of the person who will use the account. The name entered is what will appear in the From field in an outgoing message. Click **Next**.

2. Enter the e-mail address to be used for the account. Click **Next**.

3. On the screen that appears next, enter the name of the mail server used by your ISP for incoming mail. Below this, enter the name of the mail server used by your ISP for outgoing mail. Click **Next**.

4. Enter the username and password for the e-mail account. To require the user to enter his or her password each time this account checks for new e-mail, ensure the checkbox labeled **Remember password** is clear. Otherwise, check the checkbox to allow e-mail to be downloaded from the server, and new e-mail to be sent without having to enter a password. Click **Next**.

5. Click **Finish** to complete the setup of your account

What You Can't See Can Hurt You

Hidden Data about You

User accounts might contain varying degrees of information about a user. Some accounts, such as those on networks, provide the ability to put personal information including addresses, phone numbers, Social Security Numbers, or other data that can be useful to identity thieves. Most systems, like Windows 2000, provide the ability to control who can view the information and generally restrict access to members of an Administrator group. For this reason, you should limit who has Administrator access. Routinely granting high-level access to users of a computer or network can have the same effect as having no security at all.

Using Disk and File Encryption

Encryption is the process of scrambling data so that it can't be viewed by anyone who shouldn't have access to it. If anyone gains access to your system remotely or by physically accessing your computer, he or she won't be able to view the encrypted data. For example, let's say someone steals your laptop and starts the computer in the hopes of viewing private information stored on your hard disk. Because you've encrypted the data on the disk, they would be unable to view it without a password or encryption key. An encryption key is an algorithm or mathematical code that's used to encrypt and decrypt the data. Without this key, the person attempting to view the data is essentially locked out.

Encrypting data can be performed in a number of ways. Some operating systems have native support for encryption, so you don't have to install any third-party programs on your computer to encrypt data. Using this feature, you can encrypt files and folders on your system. Other operating systems don't provide this support, meaning that you need to install programs available from the Internet. Some of these programs create a virtual disk, which is an encrypted file on your hard disk that appears like a normal drive letter. We discuss each of these in the paragraphs that follow. In Chapter 3, we discuss encryption further by looking at how e-mail and file attachments can be encrypted using tools like Pretty Good Privacy.

Windows XP and Windows 2000 provide the ability to encrypt data on hard disks formatted to use the NTFS file system. NTFS provides encryption through the Encrypting File System (EFS) that allows you to encrypt files or folders. If you encrypt a folder, all files within the folder are also encrypted. EFS uses a unique encryption key that is available to people who are authorized to view the data, and it controls the encryption/decryption process. This goes on in the background, however, making the process transparent. You're not even aware that a file is encrypted unless you're not authorized to view the data.

Encrypting data in Windows 2000 and Windows XP is done through Windows Explorer. In Windows Explorer, navigate through the folders to find the file or folder you want to encrypt. After you've decided on what you want to encrypt, follow these steps:

1. Right-click the file or folder, and then click the **Properties** item on the menu that appears.

2. When the Properties dialog box appears, select the **General** tab, and then click **Advanced**.

3. Click the **Encrypt Contents To Secure Data** checkbox. Ensure that a checkmark appears in this checkbox to indicate that the file or folder is to be encrypted.

4. Click **OK**.

Decrypting data in Windows 2000 and Windows XP is equally simple. The same procedure you used to encrypt data is followed, except that you clear the **Encrypt Contents To Secure Data** checkbox. After this checkbox is cleared, the file or folder in question will be decrypted after you click the **OK** button.

EFS does have some limitations, and it will not allow you to encrypt every file on your system. If compression is used on files and folders, you can't encrypt them. You have the choice of either compressing or encrypting files and folders, but you can't do both. You also can't encrypt files with the System attribute, because this could cause problems with your system. Finally, and most importantly, EFS can only be used on hard disks using the NTFS file system. If you're using any other file system, then EFS won't be available to use. Aside from these limitations, you can encrypt any other files and folders on your system.

Other operating systems might not have native encryption support, but they can still benefit from third-party encryption tools. One such tool is BestCrypt, which can be downloaded from Jetico's Web site at www.jetico.com. BestCrypt supports Windows 3.1/9x/Me/NT/2000/XP as well as DOS and Linux. It uses several encryption algorithms, including Blowfish, Twofish, Rijndael, and GOST, which ensures that your data is protected. Using the control panel shown in Figure 2.8, BestCrypt creates a virtual drive on your hard disk that (as far as other programs on your computer are concerned) functions as an actual drive on your computer. Files saved to the virtual drive are automatically encrypted.

Figure 2.8 BestCrypt Control Panel

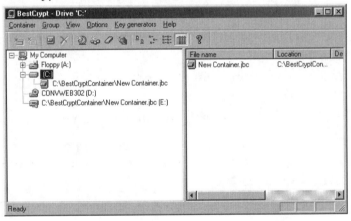

BestCrypt's control panel is used to create a container on your hard disk. This container is an encrypted folder that is mounted using BestCrypt and then appears as another hard disk. When looking at Figure 2.8, C:\ is the actual hard disk on the computer, D:\ is a CD-ROM, and E:\ is the mounted virtual drive. Although E:\ can be used as an actual encrypted drive, it is really a file called *New Container.jbc*, which is stored in C:\BestCryptContainer. When configuring the container used for this drive, you can specify both the size and encryption method used. Any data saved to the container is encrypted, and any data removed from the folder is automatically decrypted. To access any data in the container, you need to use a special password created with the control panel.

Digging Deeper...

The Cipher Tool in Windows 2000

Windows 2000 provides an additional method of encrypting data on your computer. A tool called cipher.exe can be used from the command prompt to display, encrypt, and decrypt data. To encrypt or decrypt data, you type **CIPHER** with any command line switches and the name of the file or directory being encrypted. The switches used with this tool are:

- **/E** Encrypts the data
- **/D** Decrypts the data
- **/S** Performs the command on any subdirectories and files in those directories
- **/I** Continues performing the command after errors have occurred
- **/F** Forces encryption on directories, even if they are already encrypted
- **/Q** Reports the most essential information

While the cipher.exe option exists, encrypting and decrypting files and folders through Windows Explorer is considerably easier, as described earlier in this section.

Choosing Strong Passwords

Passwords are a series of characters that are used to identify whether a person has the authority to access specific resources. This might sound like technobabble, but it's really not that difficult to understand. You've probably seen old war movies, where a sentry asks, "Hark! Who goes there?" and then follows up with the question, "What's the password?" When the sentry asks who is approaching, the person answers with his or her name. This is the same as the field on a login screen that asks for your username or account name. While this identifies you,

you might not be who you say you are. That is why a password is required. The password is a code that helps to prove your identity, and it establishes that you have authority to enter and use certain resources.

Poorly chosen passwords are regarded as the most common threat to network security. Once a person accesses a computerized system using your account and password, the system will accept that person as if they were you. The impact of this will often depend on what the password is used for. For instance:

- Someone with your computer or network password could access your files, including financial records, e-mail messages, stored lists of other passwords, and other information you want to remain private.

- Someone with your online banking password could withdraw money, apply for credit cards and loans, or purchase items online billing them to your account or new accounts they've set up in your name.

- Someone with seemingly less critical passwords, like chat programs, could be a major problem, because someone impersonating you could damage your reputation and be a source of embarrassment.

While the preceding are just a few examples, they show how stolen passwords can affect you in a variety of ways. Unfortunately, as with many of the tactics used in identity theft, you won't be aware that your password has been stolen until after the damage is done. This is why you should be proactive about protecting your identity.

Avoiding Weak Passwords

Because passwords play such an important role in security, you should avoid weak passwords. Weak passwords are passwords that are easily guessed or cracked with a hacking tool. The following is a list of commonly used weak passwords. Look them over, and see whether you've made the mistake of using a weak password:

- The words *PASSWORD, SECRET, PAYDAY, BONKERS,* and *GOD.* These are commonly used passwords, therefore easy to guess.

- The first, middle, or last name of yourself, your significant other, or child.

- Birthdays or anniversaries.

- Your username, part of your username, or your username spelled backwards. For example, if your username was JOHNDOE, don't use JOHNDOE, JOHND, EODNHOJ, or similar variations.

- Repeated characters, such as AAAAAAA or 666666.

- Consecutive letters or numbers, like ABCD or 1234.

- Adjacent characters on your keyboard, such as QWERTY.

- Words that describe your duties or tasks, such as MANAGER or DEADLINE. Many people use such words that describe their job or are stress related.

- Words that describe your ethnicity, religion, or group affiliations, such as ITALIAN, CHRISTIAN, or WRITERSGUILD. People commonly use such elements of themselves for their password.

- The current month or season of the year, such as FEBRUARY or WINTER.

- Words related to their favorite sport or team. For example, MAPLE-LEAF or HOCKEY would be easy to guess if people knew you were a sports fan.

- Obscene or sexual terms.

- Words found in the dictionary. This not only includes the English dictionary, but the dictionary of any language. Because software is available that will hack your password by trying every word in the dictionary, even the most obscure word serves as a weak password.

In addition to avoiding these pitfalls, you should remember to change your password on a regular basis. If someone has your password, changing it will remove his or her ability to use the password from that point on. Microsoft recommends you change your password every 45 days, but it is common for passwords to be changed every 90 days. While you should do this on your own with all your passwords, some networks might be configured to force you to change your password after a period of time.

When changing your password, you should come up with a new password each time. Many people make the mistake of recycling several passwords over and over. If someone knew what your password was three months ago, they might try it every so often to see if you're reusing it. Many companies realize this and force users to use different passwords for a certain number of changes. For example, an enterprise might require users to change to a new password a dozen times before a password can be reused.

You should also avoid variations of previously used passwords. A common mistake is to use the same password, add a number to the end, and increment it. For example, if you had the password BonGO1, you might be tempted to change it to BonGO2, BonGO3, and so forth for future passwords. However, if someone knew that your previous password was BonGO1, he or she might try incrementing the numbers until they get it right.

A final mistake to avoid is using the same password in more than one place. For example, you might be tempted to use the password for your Internet account, network login, and e-mail. You might even use this password for different Web sites, such as auctions, banking, or sites that offer other services. If an identity thief gets one of these passwords, then he or she could access multiple accounts. For this reason, you should use a different password for each account.

Protecting PINs

A PIN (short for Personal Identification Number) is a form of password that's numerical in nature. If you've ever used a debit card or credit card at an ATM machine, or perhaps used online banking, you were required to enter a series of numbers to prove you're authorized to use the accounts. In this case, your debit or credit card number was your user ID and your PIN is your password.

Because of the convenience of debit and credit cards, many people get so comfortable using them that they become lax protecting their PIN. If you don't shield the keypad when you enter your PIN, you might allow others to see your PIN as it's entered. You might not even think to shield your credit card from a person behind you in line who could view the credit card number. Criminals do something called *shoulder surfing*, a technique in which the thief looks over and memorizes your number. If they can memorize your credit card number, they can order items with it by phone, over the Internet, or through the mail. If they obtain your debit card and PIN, they can purchase items or withdraw money from your accounts.

As with other passwords, there are common mistakes that are made when a person creates a PIN. Some people repeat numbers in their PIN, such as 3333, or use consecutive numbers like 12345. These are easy for thieves to see when shoulder surfing or to guess if entering random numbers in an attempt to guess a PIN.

Another use for PINs is online banking. With online banking, you are required to enter the number on your debit card or your bank account number as your user ID and a PIN (or personal access code) as your password. Many banks set up access to online banking over the phone, and have their customers enter a multiple digit code by pressing numbers on the keypad of their phone. In addition to making the previously mentioned mistakes for PINs, customers commonly use the first or last part of their debit card or bank account number as their personal access code. For example, if your debit card number was 1234567890, you might choose 1234 or 67890 as your PIN. Because many criminals know the common mistakes people make, they know which numbers to try as possible PINs.

Some people are worried about forgetting their PIN and subsequently create a security threat by writing PINs down. A person might jot down a PIN on a piece of paper and carry it in her purse or wallet, so she can refer to it as needed. In some cases, people have gone so far as to write the PIN on the debit or credit card itself. Unfortunately, if his card is lost or stolen, the criminal not only has the card but also has the PIN.

Similar to this problem is one where people share their PIN with others. For example, you might ask a friend, family member, coworker, or acquaintance to purchase something on your behalf, and then you'll hand over your card and PIN to purchase the item. In doing so, you are giving the person the ability to empty your bank account or max out your credit card. Because the person has your PIN and access to your card and/or account number, he now has potential access to your finances anytime in the future. Remember the level of trust you're bestowing on this person and make an informed decision about whether the person is worthy of your trust.

Tradeoffs: Using Password Storage

You know the old saying, "You can't have everything." When security is an issue, there is a tradeoff between defense and convenience. The more secure your password, the more difficult it will be to use. The easier your password, the less secure it will be. It is up to you to find a balance between that two that's both comfortable and secure.

One way to help keep track of your passwords is to evaluate the information you're accessing. Some sites that require passwords, such as logging into your company's network, will allow you to access network files, e-mail, and other services. In such cases, you should use a password that's difficult to guess or crack. Other sites provide low security information and wouldn't really require a strong password. If you visited a site that allowed you to view the weather in your area, Web casts, or news articles, significant password security wouldn't be necessary. In such cases, there would be little harm in using a generic password that's used for multiple sites. The exception would be if you had to fill out a form with personal information to set up an account on such sites. Because you wouldn't want an identity thief accessing this information, a more secure password would be needed.

Some software makes it easier to remember passwords by storing them and entering them as needed. Internet Explorer 6 provides an AutoComplete feature that allows you to save entries made into Web pages. For example, if you entered a username and password on a certain Web page, the dialog box shown in the Figure 2.9 would appear. By clicking the **Yes** button, your entry is saved. The next time you go to this page and enter your username, the password will automatically be entered. This saves you from remembering every password you use for each Web site. However, if multiple users use your computer, then anyone who visits that Web site and enters your username will have the password appear automatically. This means they will be able to access the site as if they were you. This is a particular problem if you use e-mail sites like Hotmail, because people will be able to view your messages and compose new ones as you. If the password were saved for an auction site, they could make bids in your name. Most importantly, if you saved the password or PIN used for an online banking site, then they could perform online transactions, apply for credit and loans, and any other services you could do yourself.

Figure 2.9 AutoComplete Feature in Internet Explorer 6

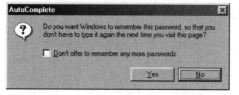

Information saved with the AutoComplete feature is stored on your computer and saved in an encrypted format. This prevents Web sites and hackers from obtaining your passwords through this feature. However, despite these measures to protect your privacy, remember that the only way to be 100 percent secure on the Internet is to never to go on the Internet at all. The most secure method of storing a password is in your own memory, not on computers. As such, you should use your best judgement when deciding what passwords will be stored with this feature.

Because of the possible danger of someone obtaining information from the AutoComplete feature, you should consider the value of information you're accessing before you choose to allow Internet Explorer to remember the password. For example, if you are accessing an online magazine and don't care if anyone else uses your password to view it, then you might allow IE6 to remember the password. If you are entering your online banking site, then you would probably click the **No** button, so that IE6 doesn't save the password and AutoComplete it the next time someone visits the Web site.

If you don't want to use the AutoComplete feature at all, then you should consider disabling it, so that IE6 doesn't offer that option when you fill out entries on an online form. To disable AutoComplete, do the following:

1. Click the **Tools** menu in Internet Explorer and select **Internet Options**.

2. When the Internet Options dialog box appears, click the **Content** tab.

3. In the **Personal Information** section of the **Content** tab, click the button that's labeled **AutoComplete**. This will display the dialog box shown in Figure 2.10.

4. When the **AutoComplete Settings** dialog box appears, clear the checkbox for **User names and passwords on forms** in the section labeled **Use AutoComplete for** (see Figure 2.10).

5. To clear any entries that AutoComplete has already stored, click the button labeled **Clear Passwords** in the section labeled **Clear AutoComplete history**" (see Figure 2.10).

Figure 2.10 AutoComplete Settings in Internet Explorer 6

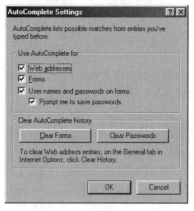

If you decide to not use the AutoComplete feature and to rely on your own memory, you might be tempted to write down your password. Many people make the mistake of writing passwords on a sticky note and posting them on their monitors, beneath keyboard trays, or under their desks. The problem is that so many people do this, thieves know to look in these places. If you're worried about forgetting your usernames and passwords, and you are steadfast in your decision to write them down, then store the document with your passwords in a safe place. Many companies make a list of administrator passwords, seal them in an envelope, and lock them in a safe. If you don't have a safe, consider getting a safety deposit box and keeping your passwords in there. If you forget one, you can refer to it, while being assured that they're secure.

In addition to the AutoComplete feature in Internet Explorer, there are numerous tools on the Internet that allow you to manage your passwords. These tools have varying degrees of security, but might be useful to keep track of all the passwords you might use. We discuss these in Chapter 4 of this book.

Digging Deeper...

Writing Down Passwords

Despite the importance of keeping passwords private, many people display their passwords in plain sight. On one occasion, a manager complained that when he used an Internet dial-up account from his computer, someone else in the office always seemed to be using it already. This prevented him from going online, and he wanted to get a second dial-up account for the office.

While fixing a computer, the technician noticed a sticky note on the monitor of an office computer used to access the Internet. This Internet terminal was in the center of the office and in a major traffic area. The words *Internet Password* were scrawled at the top of the note, and the username and password of the dial-up account were written below. It was never established how many people had set up the account on their home computers and laptops, but usage of this account dropped significantly after the password was changed.

Creating Strong Passwords You Can Remember

The best method of maintaining your passwords is to never document them and never rely on tools to remember them for you. The trick is to find a balance between having a password that you can remember and having a password that's difficult to crack or guess. By keeping passwords memorized, you increase the security of your identity.

Passwords have a number of common elements that must exist if the password is to be considered strong. A well-chosen password will consist of combinations of the following:

- Uppercase letters like A, B, C, and so on

- Lowercase letters like a, b, c, and so on

- Numerals like 1, 2, 3, and so on

- Special characters, such as symbols and punctuation. These include ({}[].<>:'"?/|\`~!@#$%^&*()-)

You should use at least three of these different types of characters in your password. The more combinations you use, the more difficult it will be for hacking programs to crack your password.

You should also use six or more characters in your password. The more characters used in your password, the more difficult it will be for thieves to determine your password when shoulder surfing or using hacking tools. The limited length of your passwords will depend on the limits set by whoever created the program you're entering a password into. Some Web sites might have an eight-character limit, while operating systems like Windows XP and Windows 2000 allow passwords that are up to 128 characters in length.

The length of passwords and characters you use will also depend on the Web sites you visit. Many sites differ in the number of characters you can use for passwords, what characters can be used, and the order the characters appear in your password. For example, one site might limit your password to eight characters, not allow you to use special characters, and require it to begin with an upper or lowercase letter. When visiting sites, you should follow the instructions provided regarding what's expected of the passwords you use.

After you know the components of creating a strong password, the next trick is remembering your passwords. One method that has been used by people for years involves coming up with a phrase that describes the site, and then using the first letter of each word. For example, if you went to Cisco's site, you would see that they make routers for networks. A sentence you could use to describe this site might be *Cisco makes routers for networks*. By taking the first letter of each word, your password becomes *Cmrfn*. Another option, so that you are sure to remember exactly which words are in your phrase, is to use a phrase from a familiar song, poem, or movie dialogue. While this seems simple enough, you'll notice there is a problem with this easy-to-remember password—it only uses two of the categories used to make strong passwords (uppercase and lowercase letters), and it is less than six characters in length.

To strengthen the password, you need to add numbers, special characters, or both to the password. A common method is to take a number you're familiar with, such as a birth date, and interlace it with the word. If the date was January 1, 2002, then you could put each number of the date after each letter. By doing this, the numbers 01-01-2002 and Cmrfn becomes C1m1r2f0n02.

While this is a common method of creating strong passwords, there are alternative methods that I've suggested to people over the years. A simple method of creating a strong password that's easy to remember is to combine the name of a company or a product that's offered on a site with the date that you first registered. For example, if you registered on January 1, 2002 with a site that provides an online magazine about widgets, your password might be Widget#112002. You could further strengthen your password by putting the date inside of the word itself. For example, if you decided the date would be after the second letter in the word, it would become Wi#112002dget. To aid in remembering the dates you registered, you could document the site and date for future reference. Although the document serves as a list of passwords, it wouldn't be obvious to anyone reading the list.

Another simple method of creating easy-to-remember passwords that combine letters and numbers is based on a child's game. As a child, you might have passed "secret" messages in which the letters were converted to numbers, based on their respective places in the alphabet. As shown in Table 2.1, writing the message required knowing that A was the first letter in the alphabet, B was the second, and so on. Breaking the code involved changing 1 to A, 2 to B, 3 to C, and so on. Using this code, the word *widget* would now become 23947520. By combining the word and number together, and adding a special character to separate it, you now have an incredibly strong password. For example, if you went to Cisco's site, you could use a password that is a combination of the name Cisco, the numerical representation of this name, and a symbol, such as an exclamation mark after the second letter. This means your password would be Ci!sco3919315. While the password is complex, knowing how it was created makes it easy to remember.

Table 2.1 Converting Letters to Numbers

A 1		N 14	
B 2		O 15	
C 3		P 16	
D 4		Q 17	
E 5		R 18	
F 6		S 19	
G 7		T 20	
H 8		U 21	
I 9		V 22	
J 10		W 23	
K 11		X 24	
L 12		Y 25	
M 13		Z 26	

One drawback of using this method is that it is only feasible to use with company names, products, or other words that are small. Converting longer words, like Microsoft or HackProofingIdentityTheft, into a numerical equivalent would be more difficult. Despite this, it does provide you with an alternative to creating passwords you can remember.

While each of these methods are useful in remembering strong passwords, they aren't viable when remembering PINs. As mentioned earlier, PINs are numerical, so many people use simple combinations (such as 1234) or difficult combinations that they write down to remember. Each method is a security risk, which makes it easy for criminals to obtain your PIN.

An easy way to remember your PIN is to associate it with a word. If you look on the keypad of your phone, you'll see that many of the numbers have letters associated with them. Before creating the PIN for your debit card, you could look at the keypad of a telephone and come up with a word. For example, if you thought of the word *JARS*, you would see that the letters on the keypad of a phone are associated with the numbers 5277. If you have an existing PIN that you're not ready to change, you could use this method and look at the keypad to come up with a word. For example, if your existing PIN is 4475, you would see that these numbers make the word *GIRL*.

If you absolutely must write down your PIN (which we strongly discourage), you should at least make it very difficult for anyone to identify it as a PIN. One method is to disguise the PIN as a phone number in your personal phone book. For example, if you needed to note the PIN for your bank, in the B section of your phone book (B for *bank*), you might write down *Bob*, followed by your PIN within a fake number. If your PIN is 9934, then "Bob's" number might be 905-555-9934. Anyone reading the number would think it's your friend's phone number rather than the PIN for your debit card.

Summary

A significant amount of information might reside on your computer, which might be vulnerable to various forms of attack. You should be aware of the data existing on your computer and where data might exist (such as the Registry), and you should make efforts to protect your information. By managing your files under a single directory structure (such as the My Documents folder), you can identify what information resides on your computer, limit the possibility of the data being accidentally shared, and make it easier to back up the files.

In addition to files you want to keep on your system, there are also files you should remove. Certain files exist in your Temporary Internet Files folder, Cookies folder, History folder, and Temporary folder that could allow cyber criminals to view private information about you or conclude certain facts about your browsing habits. In addition, temporary files created by software on your machine could allow culprits to acquire data that you wanted to remain private. While operating systems provide tools to delete these files, a number of tools are available on the Internet that you can schedule to delete such files automatically.

A variety of viruses, Trojans, and malicious programs can wreak havoc on both your computer and your personal life. Such files can be downloaded from the Internet, attached to e-mails, or acquired through a variety of other methods. To protect yourself, resist the urge to open any files you weren't expecting to receive in e-mail, or downloaded from less-than-reputable sites. To protect your data, install antivirus software and be careful of the programs you install on your machine.

Updating software is just as important as updating the signature files used with your antivirus software. When operating systems and other software programs are released on the market, they might contain bugs that make them function unpredictably. They might also contain vulnerabilities that could be exploited by hackers, viruses, Trojans, and other malicious programs or cyber criminals. To ensure that any problem code in a program is fixed and your system is as secure as possible, you should check the software manufacturer's site and ensure that you have all the latest patches, bug fixes, and other updates installed on your machine.

You can create accounts to identify yourself and provide you with access to resources. This includes accounts that can be used to access the operating system, network, Internet, and e-mail accounts on your computer. By creating new accounts, you can control access to information that is accessible through the different accounts. Unfortunately, if you share your account information, you allow others to have the ability to view your data and impersonate you on the Internet or corporate network. You should avoid sharing accounts whenever possible.

Passwords are vital to security. Strong passwords decrease your chances of someone accessing your account. By using a combination of uppercase and lowercase letters, numbers, and special characters, you decrease the chances of someone guessing or cracking your password.

Solutions Fast Track

Know Your Computer

☑ You should organize your personal files so they are in subdirectories under a single directory. Not only will this prevent accidental sharing of folders containing important information, but it will also make it easier to back up important files.

☑ Don't enter any more information than necessary when filling out registrations for software. This information might continue to reside in the Registry, and it might be accessible to unauthorized users and programs (such as hackers and Trojans).

☑ Back up important files on your computer, so you don't lose information if your system is infected by a virus or malicious programs downloaded from the Internet.

Antivirus Software: Your First Line of Defense

☑ Install antivirus software on your system and ensure that it is running constantly in the background while you work.

☑ Update signature files so you're protected from the latest viruses.

☑ Signature files can be installed manually, or you can purchase subscriptions to have your software update automatically.

Updating Your Software

☑ Install any patches, fixes, or service packs that the manufacturer releases for your antivirus software. Doing so will protect you from vulnerabilities in the software.

☑ Microsoft provides a variety of methods for updating your application and operating system, including the Windows Update Web site, Office Update, Critical Notification tool, and Automatic Updates. You can also manually download updates and apply them to your system.

☑ Check the manufacturer's Web site on a regular basis to determine whether new updates exist for software.

Avoiding Account Sharing

☑ You should avoid sharing your accounts with anyone. Doing so allows others to impersonate you on the Internet and can result in people using your personal information to steal your identity.

☑ Everyone who uses the Internet should have his or her own e-mail address. Sharing an e-mail account allows others to send e-mail using your name, jeopardizing your reputation and possibly your finances.

☑ Set up accounts for everyone who uses your computer or network. Doing so will limit their access to aspects of the system. Depending on your operating system and network, you can control what data they can access.

Using Disk and File Encryption

☑ Encryption prevents unauthorized persons from viewing data. It scrambles the data so that it can't be viewed, thereby protecting your information.

☑ Encrypting File System (EFS) is a encryption system that is native to computers running Windows 2000 and Windows XP.

☑ Tools like BestCrypt can be used to create virtual encrypted drives, which are actually encrypted folders on the hard disk. Files stored in this container are encrypted.

Choosing Strong Passwords

☑ Use a combination of uppercase and lowercase letters, numbers, and special characters to create your password.

☑ Avoid documenting your passwords, because others might be able to view the document and obtain your passwords.

☑ If a password has been compromised, change it immediately.

Frequently Asked Questions

The following Frequently Asked Questions, answered by the authors of this book, are designed to both measure your understanding of the concepts presented in this chapter and to assist you with real-life implementation of these concepts. To have your questions about this chapter answered by the author, browse to **www.syngress.com/solutions** and click on the **"Ask the Author"** form.

Q: I tried to encrypt data in Windows 2000, but I noticed that some files won't encrypt. What am I doing wrong?

A: Nothing is wrong. EFS will not work on System files, because your computer could become unstable if files with this attribute were encrypted.

Q: My company provides me with a dial-up account, and my child uses it to surf the Web. Should I be concerned about this account being used for nonwork-related Internet browsing?

A: Check with your company to find out what the policy is about nonwork-related activities. Because the company pays for your connection time, they probably have a policy stating that using the account for anything other than work is prohibited. If this is the case, you could be risking your job or face disciplinary action. As such, you should set up a second dial-up account for when you're using the Internet for anything other than work.

Q: I think someone looking over my shoulder at work has seen my network password. What should I do?

A: Contact the network administrator, and tell him or her your concern. Arrange to have your password changed immediately.

Q: My accountant has sent me an executable file in an e-mail message. Should I be concerned?

A: If you weren't expecting a file from someone, don't open it. Instead, contact the person and ask if they actually sent it to you, and, if so, what the program does. Many malicious programs and virus infected files are sent via the Internet. Even if a file attachment comes from a friend, family member, or colleague, a virus might have accessed their address book and sent virus infected files to everyone in it.

Q: My antivirus says that it has found a virus on my system. What should I do?

A: If a virus has been found, then the antivirus software has this virus included in its signature file. Therefore, the software has the ability to remove it from your system. To ensure no other virus-infected files exist on your system, run a scan on all hard disks on your computer.

Chapter 3

Keeping Your E-mail Private

Solutions in this chapter

Introduction

Many people are attracted to the Internet for its anonymity and are surprised to find that they're not as anonymous as they thought when surfing the Web. Hidden information exists in e-mails about you and your e-mail provider, programs might acquire your e-mail address and add you to bulk e-mailing lists, and other people might be able to access and read your e-mail without your knowing. As discussed in Chapter 2 and further discussed in this chapter, Trojans and other viruses can be used to damage data on your machine, distribute viruses using your e-mail address, and even reveal personal information about you and your computer. While you might have started thinking there was a level of anonymity when you started using the Internet, you'll find that information might not be as private as you thought.

In this chapter, we discuss methods you can use to keep your e-mail private as well as aspects of your identity. We also discuss a number of common scams involving e-mail and the Internet, and we show you how you can identify these scams by certain indicators. While antivirus solutions are discussed in the previous chapter, we expand on the discussion by looking at antivirus protection for e-mail in this chapter. By the end of this chapter, you'll have a good understanding of how e-mail works and the problems related to e-mail, and you'll be able to take steps to safeguard your digital identity.

E-mail Privacy Is Not Just about Spam

Privacy is an important issue when it comes to the Internet and e-mail. Many sites provide *privacy policies* that outline their rules on what is done with information that's provided by you or obtained through other measures. These privacy policies might explain whether you could be added to mailing lists, if employees can routinely access your personal information, the rights of individuals under a certain age (such as children), or if your information is shared with the government, law enforcement, or other organizations and individuals. By reading privacy policies, you might find that your e-mail privacy is limited or even nonexistent.

Some of the reasons Web sites and Internet Service Providers (ISPs) release information related to your e-mail addresses are legitimate. An example of a legitimate circumstance would be a criminal investigation. If someone sent threatening e-mail or distributed illegal material, like child pornography, the people investigating the case could obtain information about the person (via subpoenas, warrants, court orders, or similar documentation) from the Web site or ISP.

Unfortunately, many sites gather information about you and then sell the information to businesses, for no reason other than to make money for themselves. This information might include registration information that you had entered at a given site, such as your name, address, phone number, e-mail address, gender, Social Security Number (or Social Insurance Number, in Canada), or any other items that identify you. The site might take your information and then sell it to advertisers or other third parties.

Another way your e-mail and personal information might be distributed is through databases that allow people to search for others online. Examples of such services are Yahoo! People Search (http://people.yahoo.com) and US SEARCH (www.ussearch.com). Using these search engines, you can enter bits of information about a person and acquire his or her address, phone number, age, and e-mail address. For a fee, US SEARCH will even go so far as to perform a background check and provide you with information about real estate ownership and value, bankruptcy, tax liens, court judgments, and more. As you can see by this, you never truly know who might be viewing the information you considered private. A more detailed discussion about these databases appears in Chapter 1.

How E-mail Services Work

Before we go too far, let's look at how e-mail is sent and where it goes. The term *e-mail* is short for *electronic mail* and is, quite simply, an electronic letter that's sent over the Internet. *Mail clients* are programs that are used to create, send, receive, and view e-mails, and most current mail clients allow messages to be formatted in plain text or HTML, like Web pages. In other words, your e-mails can be simply textual in nature, or they can include formatted text, images, sounds, backgrounds, and other Web-page-type elements.

When you send an e-mail message, you might think that it simply goes from Point A to Point B, but many more stops occur along the way. As shown in Figure 3.1, when you send an e-mail, it first goes to the mail server belonging to your ISP. When it reaches your ISP, the mail server looks at the address you're sending the e-mail to. This e-mail address is in the form of *mailbox@domain* and ends by denoting the top-level domain (such as .com, .net, .org, .ca, and so forth). For example, if the e-mail address was mybuddy@fakedomainname.com, then the mail server would see that the top-level domain is a .com domain.

The mail server needs to use a number of servers to find the IP address of the recipient's domain. An IP address is a unique number that identifies computers on the Internet, and it is similar to a street address in that it is used to ensure messages get to the correct destination. Because the sample e-mail address (mybuddy@fakedomainname.com) is a .com domain, the ISP's server would contact a .com server to find the IP addresses of name servers for .com domains. After the ISP's mail server knows where to find name servers, it sends out several requests to the name servers to find the IP address of the recipient's domain (in this case, *fakedomainname.com*). After your ISP's mail server has the IP address of the recipient's mail server, it can then send the message. When the mail server at fakedomain.com gets the e-mail, the message will be placed in the recipient's mailbox.

Figure 3.1 How E-mail Gets from Sender to Recipient

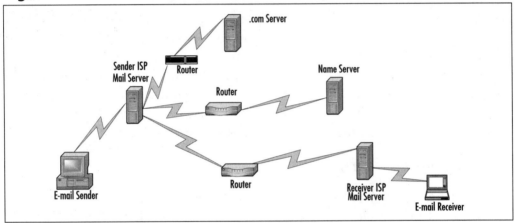

To make the e-mail process a little clearer, think of e-mailing in terms of sending interoffice mail from one department to another. You give your mail to the delivery person, who looks at the envelope's destination. From the address, the delivery person knows that the recipient is on the third floor. He goes to the third floor and asks someone where the department is. When he finds the department, he contacts the department to find where the department's mailroom is. When he finds the mailroom, he places the message in the recipient's mailbox. To deliver the mail, several steps must be taken to locate the recipient.

In terms of e-mail, the process is a little more complicated. The e-mail is broken into smaller pieces of data called *packets*, and the packets might be routed through numerous devices called *routers*. Routers are used to find the fastest route between one point and another, and packets making up your e-mail might travel along different routes before finally reaching their destination. Upon reaching the destination, the computer (in this case a mail server) puts the packets back together, so the e-mail achieves its original form.

While this seems to be an incredibly long and arduous process, anyone who has sent e-mail can testify that an e-mail can travel from Point A to Point B in seconds or minutes. While multiple steps are involved, the process itself takes very little time.

Because e-mail travels across multiple routers, servers, and lines, more parties than just the recipient might be able to access the messages or data attached to an e-mail. For instance, a copy of an e-mail is on your computer; therefore, anyone who can access your computer can read your message. Because your e-mail is also sent to your ISP, other people can view your messages that are sent onto the Internet. People with software called *sniffers* can grab e-mail packets off routers and lines on the Internet. The recipient's ISP can look at the e-mail received by the person the e-mail is meant for. Finally, the person receiving the e-mail will have a copy of the e-mail when he or she downloads it from the mail server.

To protect yourself and your data, you should consider using *encryption*. Encryption scrambles the contents of a message and attachments, and then puts the contents back together on the recipient's end. Anyone attempting to view the data in between will generally be unable to decipher the content. We discuss how to encrypt messages in the section later in this chapter entitled "E-mail Encryption Made Simple."

What You Can't See Can Hurt You

E-mail Envelopes

Sending an e-mail is similar to sending a postcard through the mail. Anyone with access to the postcard can read it, just as anyone who accesses your e-mail has the ability to view its contents. For more important mail, you would protect your mail by putting it inside an envelope before sending it. Likewise, you might want to provide additional security for your e-mail.

To protect e-mail, you can encrypt it before sending it onto the Internet. You can use a variety of methods to encrypt e-mail. For instance, Pretty Good Privacy (PGP) and Secure Sockets Layer (SSL) are common methods, which we discuss later in this chapter.

Big Brother and Your E-mail

When it comes to privacy, you might harbor a certain level of fear and paranoia about "Big Brother" monitoring what you do on the Internet, what you're writing in e-mails, and what is being done with your information. However, you can rest easy if you take a moment to consider the logistical problems of any law enforcement agency monitoring every computer system. To store all of the information that everyone sends over the Internet would take an equal or greater number of computers than are being used as Internet servers. To make this even more difficult, you would have to have a huge population of civil servants reading every e-mail, looking at every picture, and documenting every issue that is worth attention. In short, it can't be done.

However, while Big Brother probably isn't watching you, others might be. As you saw in the previous sections, methods exist in which your e-mail might be intercepted, read on a mail server, or accessed in other ways. Criminals might seek your information to obtain credit card information and other financial data, personal information with which to steal your identity, or any number of other facts they can use for monetary gain.

With home computers and other machines that are used by multiple people, you might have the problem of people opening your e-mail program and viewing your e-mail. As discussed in Chapter 2, putting password protection on your e-mail browser is a sound method of keeping others from viewing your e-mail. If the e-mail program on your computer supports passwords, you can set one and ensure that anyone who doesn't have the password will be prevented from viewing your e-mails. The ability to place passwords on an e-mail program, or accounts used by the program, are available in many e-mail packages, including those used by corporate networks.

Another major weak link in e-mail security is simply forgetfulness. Many people access their e-mail and then walk away from their computer when they're done reading their messages. They forget to close the e-mail program and log off. This is a particular problem in corporate networks (both with and without Internet access), where control of e-mail often depends on the account used to log onto the network. When this happens, anyone who uses the computer after you will have access to your data. This not only means they can open any of your files on a server, but they might also be able to view your e-mail. By opening any internal e-mail programs, they will be able to see what you've written, the files you sent, and any e-mails that you've received. If your network has Internet access, they might decide to browse the Internet, causing any firewall logs to show that it was you who visited the sites. As mentioned in Chapter 2, a sound way to protect data when you're away from your computer is to use password-protected screen savers and other password-protection methods to lock out intruders from physically accessing your computer's data. As discussed in Chapter 5, you can also use personal firewalls to disable Internet access during certain periods of the day or after the system has been idle for a set period of time. By disabling Internet access, another person will be unable to browse the Internet under the guise of your connection, and they will also be unable to send e-mail with your account.

Companies routinely monitor Internet connectivity and e-mails being sent from computers in the workplace. A survey conducted by the American Management Association (www.amanet.org) found that almost 63 percent of major companies in America monitor their employees by checking their Internet connections, while 47 percent store and review their e-mail. This is done to ensure that employees are following the policies outlined by the company regarding proper usage of these technologies.

What You Can't See Can Hurt You

Carnivore

While Big Brother probably doesn't care what you're writing in your e-mail messages, the government isn't powerless to find out. Because those involved in organized crime, espionage, drug trafficking, and other serious crimes might use e-mail to communicate their actions, the FBI needed a method to perform surveillance on the e-mails involved. The result was the *Carnivore program*.

Carnivore is software running on a computer that is used to intercept Internet communications. It has the ability to discern e-mails coming from a particular source. Carnivore can also be configured to limit the type of information being intercepted. For example, they can grab a suspect's e-mail between the person and another particular individual and ignore other communications.

Little information about the specifics of Carnivore is available, and for good reason. If the public were knowledgeable about exactly how the program worked or had access to its code or the program itself, hackers and security experts might be able to fashion devices or soft-

Continued

www.syngress.com

ware to block it. However, significant information is available about what is required before agents can use Carnivore, and what would happen if they used it inappropriately.

Before Carnivore can be used for e-mail surveillance, a high-level official from the Department of Justice first needs to give authorization. When this authorization is given, an order can then be filed with federal district court judges. Even when it reaches this point, there is no guarantee the FBI can use Carnivore. Applications to intercept e-mail are only approved for investigating specific federal felony offenses, and the FBI must indicate that other techniques are too dangerous or would not work. If a court order is given, it is limited to 30 days. If the information being sought is acquired within this time, then e-mail interceptions must stop. In many cases, to ensure privacy is being protected, judges might require agents to submit reports, updating the court on their progress. Generally, these reports must be filed every week to 10 days. In addition, the ISP that the suspect uses must be informed, so Carnivore can be installed.

If Carnivore is used inappropriately, the penalties can be swift and severe. Evidence acquired with the tool can be excluded, and persons using the tool can face civil penalties and criminal prosecution. Because the system is complicated to install and requires assistance from an ISP, a level of expertise and cooperation is required to install, run, and operate the program.

How E-mails Can Get Lost

Generally, e-mail is a reliable method of sending messages. However, at times, Murphy's Law seems to take effect (especially when you're sending an important e-mail!) and a message can take a considerable amount time to reach its destination. The reasons vary, but delayed e-mail can be frustrating and even scary when important data is delayed for a significant amount of time.

In many cases, the reason a message takes a long time to travel from your machine to the recipient's machine has to do with the mail servers involved. If you send e-mail to your ISP's mail server, and the mail server experiences problems and can't send mail, then your messages will be stuck in that machine until your ISP fixes it. In some cases, the e-mail you sent will be completely lost and will never reach its destination. The same can occur when mail reaches the mail server of the recipient's ISP.

As addressed in the previous section, e-mail goes through multiple hops as it travels across cyberspace. Just as the recipient can save an e-mail to his machine, a message can also be saved at any hop along the way. This can be a major problem if information in the e-mail is private and considered valuable by you or the recipient. If someone at one of the mail servers stores your e-mail and doesn't pass it along to the proper recipient, the e-mail can appear lost. As discussed later in this chapter, the way to avoid e-mail being read by anyone other than the proper recipient is to encrypt the message and any file attachments sent along with it.

Packets of information might also get lost and bounce around cyberspace. This happens more often than you'd expect, but generally, after a set amount of time, the lost packets are re-sent and the information reaches its destination. At times however, the unexpected happens, and data is sent but never received. Problems with the mail servers, routers, or other hardware and software involved in the process might cause the information to be lost.

In still other cases, an e-mail is never able to find the recipient. The name servers might be unable to find the recipient's domain, causing the e-mail to sit on your ISP's mail server for a significant amount of time. When this happens, a message is generally sent to the sender, stating that the mail could not be sent.

Similar problems might occur if the recipient's mailbox is improperly configured. If something is wrong with a person's account, the recipient's ISP might send a message back to you stating that the specified mailbox could not be found. In such cases, the recipient will need to contact her ISP and inform them that a problem exists.

When important information appears to be lost, you should wait a reasonable amount of time before becoming concerned that the e-mail hasn't reached its destination. In some cases, this can mean waiting until the next day. If you were expecting e-mail or a reply from a recipient, send another e-mail asking if the previous e-mail was received. In many cases, the e-mail was actually received, but the recipient failed to respond immediately. When all else fails, ask for an alternate e-mail address to send the message and/or attachments, so that your e-mail can get there sooner than later.

Have you ever changed your phone number and started receiving phone calls meant for the previous owner of that number? The same can apply to e-mail. When someone discontinues his or her Internet account and e-mail with an ISP, the particular username is generally up for grabs. For example, let's say that John Doe had the e-mail address jdoe@fakedomainname.com. John decides he doesn't like the service provided by the ISP, cancels his account, and gets a new Internet account and e-mail with a different ISP. After John Doe leaves, a new user named Jane Doe gets an Internet account and e-mail with the fakedomainname ISP, and she is issued the same e-mail address that John Doe used to have. When this occurs, e-mail that was meant for John Doe might now be sent to Jane.

When you change e-mail addresses, send out e-mail to everyone you deal with (including colleagues at work, customers, friends, family, and so forth) informing them of the change. Internet Service Providers are under no obligation to forward your e-mail after you leave.

On the other end of the spectrum, instead of getting lost, some messages remain visible to the public for long periods of time. Message boards and newsgroups allow you to post messages that are visible to anyone who uses the board or group. Messages posted this way are like the bulletin boards that you might see at your local grocery store, where anyone can view the message you post. If messages aren't purged after a period of time, the information you write to message boards and newsgroups can stay online indefinitely. For this reason, you should take extra care when posting messages to these forums.

What You Can't See Can Hurt You

Verifying the Safety of Attachments

Attachments are files that are included within e-mail messages. You can think of an attachment as an enclosure to a letter that you send through snail mail (*snail mail* is normal mail sent through the postal service). Attachments can be pictures, documents, or other items that you include with your messages.

When you receive e-mail with attachments, you should be especially careful. They might contain viruses, malicious programs designed to damage your data, Trojans designed to send your personal information to an e-mail address, cookies meant to acquire your e-mail address or other information, or any number of other problematic files. If you're not expecting a file from someone—even someone you know—delete it. If the e-mail is from someone you trust, then contact him first to ensure that he actually sent an attachment to you. The results of not taking these precautions can be devastating if you open the wrong type of file from within your mailbox.

Understanding Spam

Spam is unsolicited mail, much like the advertisements and other junk mail that that frequently stuffs many home mailboxes. This is garbage mail that rarely has any interest for you, is never asked for, and is sent by someone you don't know.

Where spam got its name is ambiguous at best and goes back to the early days of the Internet and BBSs (Bulletin Board Systems run on individual computers that people dialed into directly). Some believe it comes from computer users at the University of California who made a rather derogatory comparison between the processed lunchmeat product made by Hormel to e-mail that nobody wants or asks for. Others believe the term comes from the song by British comedians of Monty Python, which was about the ubiquity of Spam. Whatever the exact source, spam is something that isn't likely to disappear from the Internet.

Spam often comes from lists of e-mail addresses or software that sends thousands or millions of messages. While it might appear that the e-mail was sent directly to you, it is actually from e-mail addresses or software that automates the sending of mass e-mails. Most legitimate businesses avoid soliciting customers in this way, because so many people find spam irritating. Also, many Internet Service Providers find bulk mail to be a violation of the contract between them and their customers, so they are apt to shut down sites or discontinue customers who are sending such mail. Furthermore, the Federal Trade Commission warns that many states have laws regulating the sending of unsolicited commercial mail, making spamming illegal.

You can deal with spam in a number of ways. One method is to look over the spam message and see if there is a method of having you removed from their list so you don't receive further e-mails from them. Usually a hyperlink or information dealing with removal is located toward the very top or bottom of the message.

Another method to avoid receiving spam is by disabling cookies. Cookies, as we discuss in the next chapter, are small text files that are sent by some Web sites, contain information about you, and are stored in a folder on your computer. Cookies are commonly associated with Internet browsers, which access Web pages, but, because most e-mail programs allow you to accept messages in HTML format, HTML e-mails can contain cookies as well. (*HTML* is Hypertext Markup Language, and it's used to write Web pages. If you receive a solicitation in e-mail that's in HTML, it might look just like a colorful active Web page.) Cookies are sometimes used to track your spending habits, and they help to generate new spam based on those habits. For this reason, plain-text messages are safer than HTML messages, because plain-text messages aren't capable of storing cookies and other content that could be dangerous. Chapter 4 and the Appendix describe how to disable and delete cookies.

You can also contact companies you routinely deal with and inform them not to share or sell your information. Generally, privacy policies outline whether companies share or sell client information. If they do share or sell information, then you might have to decide whether you really want to use their site.

Spam filters are programs that analyze the contents of a message to see if it has the common elements of spam. If a message contains some of the common elements, the spam filter deals with the message in a specific way. For example, you might configure the filter to add the word *spam* to the subject line, so you know that the message is spam when you look in your inbox. You can also configure it to delete the suspected spam, so that you never see it. One such program that you can use is EmTec Software's *Spam Detective*, which runs on Windows systems and is available at www.emtec.com/spamdetective. However, before investing in such software, you should visit the Web site of your Internet Service Provider. Many ISPs offer spam detection and elimination services to customers, in which spam-like e-mail is deleted on the server. This saves them the cost of using bandwidth to send you e-mail that you don't want anyway.

E-mail Attacks Are Not Just about Viruses

The most common method of e-mail attack involves viruses, which are programs that, once executed, can damage your data and possibly transmit your information to others. While viruses are discussed in Chapter 2, this isn't the only type of e-mail attack. You can fall victim to other common methods of attack, including worms, interceptions, impersonations, scams, and Denial of Service (DoS) attacks.

A worm is a program or computer algorithm that self-replicates, making copies of itself and distributing the malicious programming across multiple systems. Essentially, it "worms" its way through a system, eating up memory and using resources along the way. An e-mail worm traditionally replicates by taking e-mail addresses from your address book and sending itself to other people's systems.

Some e-mail worms might go a step further and scan your mail messages. It will look through your e-mail and take elements of your messages to create a message that appears to be coming from you. When someone sees the e-mail message, information in the subject line or body of the message will show that it's from you, making the person confident that it's okay to open the message. Upon doing so, the worm is activated and attacks the system.

To prevent worms from attacking your system, antivirus software should be installed. See the "Using Antivirus Protection for E-mail" section later in this chapter. To avoid worms, remember that worms will propagate because of attachments that are opened, or improperly shared hard disks (as discussed in Chapter 5). If you don't know the person sending an e-mail attachment to you, or you aren't expecting an attachment from someone you do know, don't open it. It's always better to be safe than sorry.

Malicious content can also be transmitted through HTML messages that you receive with your e-mail software. E-mail messages can be either plain text or HTML. As mentioned earlier, HTML is Hypertext Markup Language, which is used to create Web pages. When you view an HTML message through your e-mail software or a browser, you are viewing a Web page that could have hyperlinks, cookies, scripts, and applets. Viewing an HTML e-mail with such content can be just as bad as visiting a Web site with this content. For safety's sake, only accepting e-mail messages in plain text will avoid this problem.

E-mail attacks can have a widespread effect on the Internet and public in general. When a mail server is attacked, the server can go down. When a server goes down, e-mail can't be retrieved from it, and e-mail to other systems can't be sent. When e-mails are intercepted, or accounts and passwords are retrieved from databases on the mail servers, both system security and personal information security is at risk. If spam or viruses are involved, the effects of hitting one server can be spread across multiple systems.

E-mail Attachments

E-mail attachments are commonly used to distribute viruses, but many people are becoming aware that attached files can be dangerous. These days, many people take steps to avoid opening them. If someone won't open the file, the virus remains dormant on the system. Using social engineering, a user can be enticed to open an e-mail attachment, even though they know better. For example, the "I Love You" virus, which is also known as the "Love Bug" or "Love Letter" virus, is an example of how social engineering is used to get people to open virus-infected attachments. In 2000, many people received messages with the sentence *I Love You* in the subject line, thinking they had received e-mail from someone who loved them. Upon opening the attachment with the e-mail, they were infected with a virus. Because the virus then used the person's e-mail program's address book to distribute itself to others, other people received messages that seemed to come from you also stating "I Love You." By playing on a natural desire people have to feel loved, the virus was distributed to an incredible number of systems.

In early 2001, the "Anna Kournikova" virus also hit a massive number of systems. Anna Kournikova is a professional tennis player with a large number of fans, and she is a very attractive woman. With this in mind, a virus was sent out as a file attachment called AnnaKournikova.jpg.vbs. People receiving this file thought it was a picture of her, and they opened the file to see it. With the virus released, the damage was done. Like the I Love You virus, the Anna Kournikova virus used a recipient's address book to distribute the virus to others, making others think you had sent them a picture.

How Your E-mail Can Be Hijacked

One method of e-mail attack is a Denial of Service (DoS) attack. When a hacker attempts to attack a server in this way, she sends a massive number of requests to the server. DoS attacks involve sending an enormous number of requests for Web pages or files, or sending a huge number of e-mails to a mail server. With each request, more processing, memory usage, and hard drive activity occurs. In addition, the bandwidth of the connection to the Internet becomes overwhelmed, because the server tries to send all the files being requested and attempts to fulfill every request. Any legitimate user trying to view a Web page, download a file, or send and receive e-mail from the swamped system will be denied service, because too many requests are already being processed by the system. Eventually, the server goes down and is unavailable to anyone attempting to access it.

A DoS attack can affect you in a number of ways. If you need to access a particular Web page, send or receive important e-mail, or access any other services being provided by the downed server, you'll be unable to complete your task. If you need to perform these tasks as part of your job, then this will prevent you from doing your work. Should the person who performed the DoS attack have your e-mail address, then he or she would be able to use your e-mail address and impersonate you by using a different server. While you're prevented from sending e-mail, that person can freely pose as you online.

E-mail Interceptions

Other attacks on mail servers can be geared toward intercepting e-mails. A number of methods can be used to intercept data on the Internet or a network.

In doing so, a cyber criminal is able to view any important data that might be contained within an intercepted e-mail.

This type of attack involves software or access to a server. Software might be used to grab packets of data off a network and view the packets' contents. If a person has access to the server, he would simply view the e-mails residing on the server, just as you would read files saved on your computer. If hacking is involved, a hacker would access the e-mail on the server to get information that he desires. After the e-mail is read, the person might then find usernames, passwords, personal data, and financial information being sent via e-mail to other accounts. Using this information, he could then perform other crimes like credit card fraud, loan frauds, or illegally accessing other systems.

A *Man in the Middle* attack, which is also called *TCP Hijacking*, is an example of this type of attack. Using special software, a cyber criminal removes packets of data being sent from a server to you or from you to another server. The cyber criminal can then view the data for any relevant information. For example, if you made an online purchase, the thief could acquire the confirmation message sent by the e-commerce server to you, and he could view a credit card number that's part of the message. After getting this data, he then puts the data back onto the Internet, so you are unaware that anything is amiss. The cyber criminal could also modify data, tampering with its authenticity and integrity, before he resends it back onto the network.

A Man in the Middle attack relies on data to be unencrypted. As you can see later in this chapter, if the data is encrypted, the data will be unreadable by a cyber thief, preventing her from viewing or modifying the information. Because of this, you should encrypt sensitive data being sent over the Internet and check the security of e-commerce sites before you supply private information.

When talking about spam in the previous section, we noted a number of ways that spammers can get your e-mail address and send you e-mail. The tricks we listed aren't the only tricks thieves can use to send unsolicited mail to the public. Frequently, spammers use someone else's e-mail address as a return address. When the e-mail is sent out, the person sending the spam uses a stolen e-mail address but includes a legitimate link in the e-mail so people who are interested in their product can still contact them. Stolen e-mail addresses are used for spam because many ISPs check to ensure that a return address is valid before putting a message in a customer's mailbox. This practice cuts down on the amount of spam being submitted to customers, but, because the stolen e-mail address is valid, the spam manages to bypass this protection.

Stolen e-mail addresses might also be used to avoid messages that bounce back to the sender. If any of the spam reaches an unreachable address (such as one that is no longer in service) the ISP might return a message stating that the mailbox cannot be found. Depending on how many e-mails are sent in the bulk mailing, this can result in thousands of "unreachable address" messages bouncing back to your e-mail account. If enough e-mails are sent to an ISP's mail server, the server might register it as a DoS attack (even if it isn't meant as one). If the server associates this as being a DoS attack, it might shut down, resulting in anyone using the ISP being unable to send his or her own e-mail.

Digging Deeper…

Account Thefts in the News

As cyber crime becomes more prevalent, news stories about account thefts appear more frequently in the news. Criminals with computer expertise have been known to hack systems, obtain usernames and passwords, credit card information, and any number of other details. After a person has access to your network account and password, she might then have the ability to read your e-mail, view your data, and obtain the information needed to commit other crimes using elements of your identity.

In this section, we mention how sending massive numbers of e-mails to a server can result in Denial of Service attacks. In Anchorage, Alaska, in January 2000, Scott Dennis performed three such attacks against the U.S. District Court for the Eastern District of New York. Dennis overwhelmed their mail server with e-mail messages. A former system administrator for the U.S. District Court of Alaska, he claimed that he wanted to prove it was vulnerable to outside attacks. He was sentenced to three months in jail, three months home confinement, and one year of supervised release. In addition, he must have authorities monitor his computer activity, perform 240 hours of community service work, and pay restitution.

Assuming the mail server doesn't shut down, your mailbox will be filled with bounced messages and complaints from recipients of the spam. If enough of these messages come in, actual e-mail that's meant for you might be unable to get through. ISP's often have a limit on hard disk space used by each account, and the mail server might refuse messages after this limit is reached. Also, as you download hundreds of complaints, it will be almost impossible to find all of the e-mail that is actually meant for you.

While you're contending with the massive number of messages you're receiving, people receiving the spam will complain to your ISP. Many ISPs have specific policies dealing with spam, and the ISP could decide that you've violated their service agreement by sending out spam. In this case, they could cancel your e-mail account and refuse to provide you with Internet services.

As you can see from all this, the problems associated with a spammer using your e-mail address are numerous. If you find that someone's stolen your account to send spam, contact your ISP immediately, and explain what you think has happened. Generally, the only way you'll realize this has occurred is after you've begun experiencing the symptoms of it (such as bounced messages and angry replies from recipients asking you to take them off your mailing list). In many cases, you will be limited in what solutions are available to fix the problem, and you will generally have to get a new e-mail address.

Recognizing Mail Scams

Mail scams have probably been going on since the postal service was invented. When e-mail began to attract people to communicate online, criminals followed. Online con artists use the same scams that had proven to work when faxed to phone numbers, advertised in magazines, or sent through the post office. The difference with e-mail is that they can reach an immense group of people with one message. The more e-mails sent, the more potential victims.

Every day, people go on the Internet for the first time, with a number of them looking for ways to make money with their computer, find a way to work at home, or to find something needed in their life. You might know someone like this—a family member, friend, or colleague at work. Having never been online before or been exposed to a criminal element, they might receive mail scams and think their lucky day has arrived. Wanting to believe the promises offered in an e-mail message, the latest technology on the planet makes them fall victim to some of the oldest scams around.

One way to recognize an e-mail scam is to recognize urgency in the message. Mail scams often claim that their offer is time sensitive, making you believe that if you don't act today, right now, immediately!, you'll lose out on a great opportunity. This is a common sales trick. If you fear you'll miss out on a great deal by waiting, you'll be much more likely to buy now. It prevents you from sitting down and thinking it over, to determine rationally whether the offer is as good as they say or if it might be a scam.

Another way to recognize a scam is that it offers something that's too good to be true. Getting a "legitimate" university degree without going to school, items and services at outrageously low rates, or medical cures that even your doctor doesn't know about are just a few of the scams available on the Internet. Remember, if it seems too good to be true, it probably is.

A red flag can appear in a mail scam that can allude to how the e-mail got to you. For instance, the message might state that your name was "taken from a list of lucky winners" or "a friend" referred your name. There is never any mention of which friend referred you or how your name ever appeared on the list. By mentioning this, they are hoping to build your confidence in the scam.

Another way to identify a scam is that the name of an actual company isn't mentioned in the e-mail. This prevents you from investigating the business through the Better Business Bureau (www.bbb.org) or finding information about who actually owns the company and where they're located. By failing to provide this information, you're prevented from making an informed decision.

One of the best ways to recognize a scam is to investigate opportunities that come your way. Chances are, you're not the first person who has received such offers, and the scam is actually one that's been around (in one form or another) for years. By going on the Internet and looking for others who might have been defrauded by similar e-mails, you can determine the level of risk involved in accepting an offer. By becoming knowledgeable about common e-mail scams, you'll be better able to avoid them.

Solicitations and Chain Letters

Everyone would like to get rich quickly, find miracle cures, win free vacations, or have other wonderful things happen in their life. The answers to these wishes aren't found in e-mails, advertisements, and letters you receive. After all, if someone had the secrets to become rich, live longer, or go on fabulous getaways, why would they bother wasting their time sending e-mails to you?

Anyone who has an e-mail address has received solicitations and chain letters, which promise great things and deliver nothing. Many are old scams that have been simply sent out over the Internet. They're designed to get your money, personal information, credit card numbers, or anything else that might be of value. Becoming involved in such schemes, you might wind up losing your money, your identity, or, in some cases, your life. Here are a few of the common scams:

- **Chain letters offering the potential to make money** You are asked to send a small amount of money to names on a list and then add your name and address to it. After forwarding out the mail, others will then send money to you. In doing so, you will lose your money and break the laws dealing with chain letters that ask for money (Title 18, United States Code, Section 1302, of the Postal Lottery Statute).

- **Work at home scams** In a work-at-home scam, you are offered the chance to make money by working at home. The work involves stuffing envelopes, crafts, or other labor. To get started, you must pay for supplies and equipment, but when you submit your work to get paid, it is considered "below their standards." While they make money off of the equipment and supplies you buy, you make nothing.

- **Pyramid schemes** Pyramid schemes require a person to pay to join a group and recruit new people who will also pay into the pyramid. There is generally no actual product that's sold or genuine investment involved in the scam, although some pyramids might involve members buying products at inflated prices and in quantities that are greater than could ever be sold. Generally, the only people buying these products are those involved in the pyramid itself. Pyramid schemes often have no product, however, and rely on people to invest money and recruit new people who will also bring revenue into the scam.

- **Ponzi scheme** A Ponzi scheme is similar to a pyramid scheme. It also involves recruiting members who pay into an "investment" expecting a high rate or return. Because there is actually nothing that will return an investment on money put into the scam, the person running it takes money from new recruits to pay investors that have been in the scam for a long period of time. Eventually, the scam collapses in on itself, and the investors lose their money.

- **Fake health and weight products** Fake health products might offer miraculous results, but in actuality, they don't work and could be detrimental to your health.

- **Free vacations or prizes** Free vacations and prizes might be offered to you via e-mail. A small fee is then required, or not everything in the vacation is included (such as airfare, hotel, and so on). In the end, you pay more than if you'd gone through a legitimate travel agent.

- **Surveys** Surveys are another method of acquiring information about a person. By creating a fake survey that is mailed, e-mailed, or made available online, you might be asked to provide information about yourself. This might include your name, address, Social Security or Social Insurance number, credit card information, e-mail address, or even your Internet password. If you fall for this scam, the person who created the survey doesn't need to do any work to steal your identity, because you give all your information directly to them.

The rules-of-thumb to protect yourself from such scams is "buyer beware" and "don't believe you'll get something for nothing." People have lost considerable amounts of money on these scams. Due to the embarrassment of being defrauded, people will feel foolish and not report the crime. This is a mistake, because it allows a criminal to get away and defraud others.

One of the most dangerous scams to get involved in is what many people call the "Nigerian 419," or "Nigerian Letter Scam." The Nigerian 419 scam is named after a section of the Nigerian penal code that addresses frauds, this scam has bilked many people out of their life's savings. An old scam, it has moved from enticing victims through letters, to faxes, and now through e-mail.

Nigeria 419 Scam

The scam begins with an e-mail from a civil servant, representative of a foreign government or agency, which is traditionally Nigerian. In this e-mail, the official offers to transfer millions of dollars into your bank account. The e-mail might claim this money was acquired by over invoicing contracts, from a fallen government's funds, or any number of other seemingly plausible reasons. Because this money is being held up overseas, they need your personal bank account to transfer the funds into. For doing nothing more than allowing this money to be deposited into your account, you will receive a commission of upwards to 30 percent.

To rope in the victims for this scam, e-mails are sent out en masse, with hundreds or thousands of people receiving them. The more people who receive the e-mail, the better the chances are that someone will respond to it. After all, it isn't costing anything is it?

As the scam unfolds, the victim might be requested to provide blank company letterhead, bank account numbers, telephone and fax numbers, or other personal information. The con artist claims that the letterhead and other information are needed to complete the transaction and begin the process of having the money released to the account. However, the information provides the con artist with information that could be used to commit other frauds. Throughout this, the victim is lead to believe that they are involved in a legitimate business deal, receiving official looking documents sent from the countries in question.

Eventually, the victim is required to supply money. This might occur at any point in the scam, beginning as small amounts and growing as the scam progresses. In other cases, one large up-front payment is required to free the money into your account. The reason for the money being needed includes bribes, fees to transfer the funds, attorney fees, taxes, and so on. For each fee that's paid, the victim is assured that this is the last time they'll need to pay any money. Eventually, the victim has paid out so much money that they desperately need the promised funds to recoup their losses.

At some point in this scam, the victim is usually required to visit a foreign country to complete the arrangement, so the money can be transferred. At this point, the scam can become particularly dangerous. An American man was murdered in Lagos Nigeria in June 1995, while he was traveling to Nigeria to complete such a transaction.

As is the case with many victims of fraud, many people don't report becoming victimized by this scam, even though it has cost them large amounts of money. Some people have lost their businesses, homes, and life savings because of this scam. Although fear of violence or embarrassment might prevent numerous victims from reporting the crime, the U.S. Secret Service reports that advance fee schemes, like the Nigeria 419 scam, gross millions of dollars annually.

Although we've covered the common elements of the Nigerian 419 scam, a con artist might use variations of it to get new victims. Figure 3.2 contains an excerpt of an actual e-mail that makes a similar offer of funds in a foreign country, and requests your assistance in obtaining it:

Figure 3.2 Excerpt of a Nigerian Scam E-mail

```
Dear friend,

I am the first wife of the late UNITA leader who was recently killed in
Angola.

The main motive of my mail to you is that am looking for assistance in your
country. I need a trustworthy individual to deal with who has a legitimate
and profitable business and would like to go into partnership with me,
because I am in possesion of some of my husband's wealth and I want to
utilize this opportunity to invest it. There is a box containing precious
```

Continued

Figure 3.2 Continued

```
stones that I want to move out of our country now, and I am so worried that
I don´t even know what to do , but my immediate problem now is a huge sum
of money lodged with a security company in Europe for which I require your
assistance.


Please try as much as you can to get in touch with me through my e-mail
address so that I can know if there is any business opportunity.


I look forward to your response,


Thank you


Mrs Mariam Savimbi
```

If you're the victim of such a scam, you should contact your local police department and report the fraud. The Secret Service has also created *Operation 4-1-9,* to combat this particular type of fraud, and can be contacted by mail at:

> United States Secret Service
> Financial Crimes Division,
> 950 H Street, NW,
> Washington, DC 20223.

You can also contact the Secret Service by phone at (202) 406-5850 or through their Web site at www.secretservice.gov.

Spam as Social Engineering

As mentioned earlier in this chapter, spam is another method of social engineering, as people responding to the e-mail might provide information if the offer seems legitimate and/or provides a product they're interested in. They might order products through a spam message, thereby providing their name, address, city, state/province, credit card information, and other data that is useful in identity theft. Therefore, you should avoid responding to e-mails that are obviously unsolicited mail, and verify the legitimacy of messages that you're not quite sure about.

A good example of spam being used to gather information about people can be found in fraudulent e-mail that claimed to be from American Online (AOL). As shown in the following e-mail, this scam made it appear that AOL had been hacked, and AOL needed you to resubmit your credit card information. If you didn't comply with this request, then your account would be removed from AOL. However, if you did supply this information, AOL would give you 10 hours of Internet connection time for free. Unfortunately, those who fell for the ploy soon found that the following message was not from AOL:

```
Hello AOL members,

You are receiving this e-mail because of a recent attack by a hacker on
your billing or password information.


We have made a contract with SYI--Secure Your Information--to upgrade our
account databases on to their Web servers.


Please goto http:..16bit.at/aol and fill out the information requested.


Failure to do so within a week of receiving this will cause your AOL
account to be suspended until further notice.


If you comply to this e-mail and upgrade your account information on the
site, you will receive 10 hours of free AOL time.


If this is a child or teenager reading this e-mail, please notify your
parents or the account holder to update the account information.


We are sorry for the inconvenience.


If you have received this e-mail before and have already submitted your
information on our secure servers, you have done so in error.


Please resubmit your information so we can provide you with the best
security the Internet has to offer.


Please do not reply back. Go directly to our site.
```

As you've probably guessed, people who complied with the request and sent their credit card information soon found unauthorized charges on their credit account. Because criminals use numerous tactics to get information needed for identity theft, you need to be suspicious of requests for personal and financial data.

Using Antivirus Protection for E-mail

As discussed in Chapter 2, viruses are rampant on the Internet, and they are often distributed through e-mail. To ensure that you're protected when you open the e-mail you receive, and to prevent the spread of viruses, you need to purchase antivirus software that checks your e-mail for the presence of viruses. Popular antivirus software packages include McAfee VirusScan (www.mcafee.com) and Norton AntiVirus (www.symantec.com).

Viruses are generally spread through e-mail as attachments, which are files included with an e-mail message. They might be compressed files (such as ZIP files), programs (such EXE files), or documents. Once the file is executed, the virus is released. Executing the file can be done by opening or viewing the file, such as by installing and/or running an attached program, opening an attached document, or uncompressing a file.

Most e-mail software provides a preview pane that allows you to view the message contents without actually opening it. This can be a problem if you are viewing an HTML e-mail, which appears as a Web page and can contain malicious content. Viewing HTML documents in the Preview pane has the same effect as opening the HTML message itself. Your computer can then fall prey to any scripts, applets, or viruses within the message. To protect yourself, you should set your e-mail software to view plain-text messages.

Antivirus software should provide real-time scans of your system, and it should check e-mail attachments on a regular basis. For example, Norton AntiVirus will scan every four seconds for new e-mail messages that have attachments. If HTML content is included as part of the message, real-time scans can also detect any viruses embedded in the message. By checking your system regularly, the chance of being infected with a virus decreases dramatically. For more information about e-mail software that will scan for viruses in the background, check the section called "What Kinds of Software Are Available" in Chapter 2.

Antivirus software is important because of the damage that can be caused by viruses. One of the most infamous viruses to be propagated through e-mail is the Melissa virus. In 1999, a file called list.zip was posted to a newsgroup called alt.sex. The file was supposed to contain a listing of sexually orientated Web sites, and the usernames and passwords required to access them illegally. However, when people downloaded the file, opened it, and ran the program inside, they became the first to be infected with the Melissa virus.

When the Melissa virus infected a system, it exploited a security vulnerability in Microsoft Outlook e-mail software. The virus accessed the address book and sent the virus to every address listed. It is estimated that Melissa crippled computers at approximately 300 companies and cause nearly $400 million in damages.

In time, the creator of this virus was arrested. In December 1999, David Smith pleaded guilty to federal and state charges, and he was sentenced to five years in prison. Even though antivirus programs are able to detect and remove this virus, it is interesting to note that it continues to infect systems and be distributed. The reason is because it still reaches people who don't have antivirus software on their system with updated signature files.

Even if antivirus software is installed on your system, there is no guarantee that it will actually catch the virus. As seen in the case of the Melissa virus, when people downloaded the file called list.zip from the alt.sex newsgroup they were infected with the virus. Regardless of whether these people had antivirus software installed, the signature files for the software didn't have any data on the Melissa virus. Why? No one had been infected with it before, so antivirus software manufacturers had no way of dealing with it. Until a virus is known to them, and an antivirus solution is created, the virus can infect any computer using antivirus software.

A common reason a computer with antivirus software is infected with viruses is because the signature files haven't been updated. Antivirus software manufacturers release new signature files on a regular basis, and it's up to you to download and update them on your computer. To make this easier, many of the manufacturers provide features to automatically update the signature files.

Digging Deeper…

Spam Filtering

Spam-filtering software analyzes e-mails for elements that are common to spam. This includes elements such as keywords in the subject line and body, whether the message came from free e-mail services, and so on. However, because viruses have been sent out through spam messages or messages that have elements in common with spam, spam filtering might also have the benefit of removing a number of virus-infected e-mails before they are downloaded into your inbox.

NOTE

When you install antivirus software on your system, ensure that it starts up automatically each time your computer starts. An icon should appear in the lower right hand corner of your Windows toolbar, and on Macintosh computers will appear on the control strip (control strip modules folder). You should also run a scan of your hard disk to ensure that the software is checking files for viruses.

Hiding Your E-mail Identity

When using the Internet, you probably take advantage of some of the methods used to meet and communicate with others. Perhaps you engage in chats using Internet Relay Chat (IRC), visit newsgroups, use messenger services like AOL Instant Messenger and ICQ, or simply send e-mail. When using these services, you probably entered the e-mail address provided by your ISP to allow others to send messages and files to you. However, others can use some of the search tools mentioned in Chapter 1 to find information about you.

To protect yourself on the Internet, you need to know how certain information is stored in e-mail, whether your e-mail is private, and how to prevent others from gathering personal data through your e-mail information. In this section, we discuss these issues and see how you can use *anonymous* e-mail to hide your identity.

Knowing What's in Your E-mail Headers

When you look at your e-mail, you might think that the only information contained in the e-mail is your e-mail address, the recipients e-mail address, the subject line, the body of the message, and any files you might have attached. Looking at this information, there is no way for anyone to determine any significant information. However, e-mail messages are sent using the Simple Mail Transfer Protocol (SMTP), and it uses headers that are hidden in the message. Reading these headers, people can find out more about you than you ever intended. Before explaining these headers let's first look at the following sample e-mail header:

```
Date: Fri, 24 May 2002 19:30:14 -0500 (EST)
To: "Buddy Smith" <mybuddy@fakedomainname.com>
```

```
From:   "John Doe" <johndoe@fakedomainname.com>
Subject: Test
Cc: info@fakedomainname.com
```

Headers also follow standard SMTP. Because e-mail programs use this standard in the format of headers, it is fairly routine to decipher their meaning. In the preceding example, the first line shows the date and time the e-mail was written. In this example, the e-mail was written Friday May 24, 2002 at approximately 7:30 P.M. Eastern Standard Time (EST). The next line shows the name and e-mail address to whom the e-mail was sent. You can see that the mail was sent to Buddy Smith, and his e-mail address is mybuddy@fakedomainname.com. The next line shows the name and address of the e-mail sender. In this case, you can see that John Doe sent the e-mail message, and you can also see his e-mail address. Beneath this, you see the subject of the e-mail. Finally, the last line shows that the message was also sent to another e-mail address, using the carbon copy (Cc) line. This is used to send additional e-mail messages to people, and semicolons can be used to separate multiple recipients. If you are sending carbon copies, but don't want people to see who else the e-mail was sent to, you can use a Blind Carbon Copy (Bcc). When you fill out an e-mail message, you can enter e-mail addresses into the Bcc section of the e-mail, and copies of the e-mail will be sent to these addresses. When the mail server gets the e-mail, it will look at the Bcc line and remove the additional e-mail addresses from the message. The recipient will receive the message but won't be able to determine who else received a copy of the message.

In addition to these basic e-mail headers, extended e-mail headers also appear in messages. To understand these headers, let's look at another sample header, as follows:

```
Return-Path: johndoe@fakedomainname.com

Received: from mail.fakedomainname.com (mail.fakedomainname.com
[209.190.xxx.xxx]) by mail2.fakedomainname.com (8.9.2/8.9.3) with ESMTP id
MAA19047 for <mybuddy@fakedomainname.com>; Fri, 24 May 2002 19:30:33 -0500
(EST)

Received: from LOCALNAME (user-37bs269.dial-up.fakedomainname.com
[208.144.xxx.xxx]) by mail2.fakedomainname.com with asmtp (Exim 3.22 #1) id
179pjC-0003rl-04; Mon, 24 Feb 1997 19:30:34 -0500 (EST)

X-Sender: johndoe@pop.fakedomainname.com

X-Mailer: Microsoft Outlook IMO, Build 9.0.2416 (9.0.2910.0)
```

The first line in this header is the *Return-Path*, which is used to specify where replies to this e-mail should be sent. Mail servers will also use this line when bouncing back the message if it is undeliverable. In some e-mail programs, this line might appear as *Return-Errors-To* or *Reply-To*.

The next line is *Received*, which specifies how the e-mail was received. When looking at this line, you can see that on Friday May 24, 2002 at approximately 7:30 PM, the mail server mail.fakedomainname.com passed the e-mail to mail2.fakedomainname.com for delivery to mybuddy@fakedomainname.com. While the e-mail address has been blanked out in this entry with Xs, it also shows the IP address of the mail server. This can be useful when determining the location of the e-mail server, who owns it, and more.

The line after this shows where the e-mail originated. When reading this line, you can see that the user used a dial-up PPP account with an IP address of 208.144.xxx.xxx. A mail server called mail2 in the fakedomainname.com domain received the e-mail and stamped the e-mail with the time it was received.

Below this are two lines that begin with *X*, which is extraneous information that many e-mail programs add to the header. The first of these here is the *X-Sender*, which shows the account and mail server that is used by the sender to receive his messages. The other is *X-Mailer* which shows the e-mail program that was used to send the e-mail. While these aren't necessary to effectively send the message, the e-mail program adds this information to the header.

If these examples were to show e-mail that you sent, you would have seen your name, e-mail address, the server you use to acquire your mail, the name and IP address of the mail server that sent the mail (which can be used to obtain further information), and even the program you used to write the e-mail. This doesn't even include the information that could be obtained by viewing what you actually wrote in the body of the message itself. As you'll see in sections that follow, anonymous e-mail can be used to hide such information from people. This doesn't however protect you from what can be viewed in your workplace.

If cyber criminals review this information, they could determine a considerable amount of information about you. They could find the mail server you used to send the mail, the IP address that was issued to you by your ISP when you sent the e-mail, the software you used to create the e-mail message, and numerous other pieces of information. Using this, they could exploit vulnerabilities in the software you used to write the e-mail, steal your e-mail address, and use the mail server to mimic your e-mail account and possibly acquire the information you supplied to your ISP when you set up the e-mail account. While the chances of this occurring might be somewhat remote, you should realize that each little piece of information can be compiled and then used to steal your online identity.

What You Can't See Can Hurt You

Your Identity at Work is Not Private

Many people think that e-mail is their private business, and anything they write in these messages is their intellectual property. However, the acid test is where you write the e-mail. Assuming you're doing nothing criminal, the e-mail you write on your home computer, using your own equipment, is nobody's business but yours and the person you're sending it to. If you're writing this same e-mail on a computer in your workplace, the parameters change drastically.

Because you're using your employer's computer, software, network connections, Internet connections, and other property belonging to the workplace, the e-mail messages you write at work actually belong to the business. Because of this, you can be fired for sending personal e-mails or using Internet technologies inappropriately at work. This might seem unfair, until you consider it from the employer's point of view. Companies pay a significant amount of money for computers, network infrastructure, and software, and they expect this to be used for work. A person using his or her computer for personal reasons is considered to be the same as someone taking a company car across the country on vacation. Quite simply, the company bought the equipment for work, not play.

Many companies have policies regarding conduct and the appropriate use of network and Internet technologies in the workplace. When an employee doesn't abide by these rules, the effects can be serious. The American Management Association (www.amanet.org) conducted a survey, and found that 27 percent of the companies have fired employees and 65 percent have taken disciplinary actions for inappropriate use of office e-mail or Internet connections. Examples of companies firing their employees for such conduct are plentiful. The New York Times fired 23 employees in 1999 for attaching pornographic images to e-mail messages, Xerox fired 40 employees for using work computers to view pornographic Web sites, and Dow fired 24 employees and disciplined 235 employees in 2000 for e-mailing material that was sexually explicit and/or violent.

Knowing What Your Chat Says about You

While social engineering has been traditionally associated with hacking, it is also used for acquiring personal information used in identity theft. Remember that once a person has enough tidbits of data about you, he has the opportunity to use the information for impersonating you. By limiting what information is made available about you, you make it more difficult for your identity to be stolen.

This can be more difficult than you think when you consider the elements of a conversation. Any conversation is an exchange of ideas, interests, and facts, which results in two people knowing more about one another. You generally start by introducing yourself (providing your name) and then exchanging information about you job (showing where you work), whether you're married and have kids (providing information about your marital status, sexual preference, and family structure). Even in a short conversation, a considerable amount of data might be given.

Commonly, people engaging in social engineering will slowly fish information out of you by asking one question after another. While each question seems innocuous and might be useless on its own, asking numerous questions can result in the person compiling a complete profile on your identity.

On the Internet, many people engage in conversations through chat rooms, in which people type messages back and forth using software. As discussed in Chapter 2, some programs used for exchanging messages allow you to enter a significant amount of information about yourself. To prevent others from viewing more information than you're comfortable revealing, you should ensure that there is minimal information entered in the program.

In chat rooms and messaging software, you generally use aliases or nicknames, so that your actual name isn't provided to people. When you enter a chat, the first question that is generally asked of you is "Age/Sex/Location" or "a/s/l." You might be hesitant to reveal such information, but there is a logical reason about it. First, mentioning your age shows whether you're a child or adult, so they know how to speak to you and make an informed decision as to whether they want to. Imagine not knowing this, and accidentally telling a risqué joke to a child or complaining about age-related problems to a 19 year old. The second part of the question asks your sex, which means your gender. This also helps people decide whether to speak with you. While it might not be politically correct, many women like talking with other women about issues that interest them, just as many men like talking with other men about women. Also, as cybersex (the exchange of sexual dialog between people online) is common in chat rooms, people might not want to talk with others of the same gender. Finally, the location is used to determine the country you're from. Some people make the mistake of entering their address, city, and state/province when this is asked. The location is asked to help in discussions, because it can lead to general conversations on culture, news items about your country, or other topics.

By keeping information simple and vague, others will be less apt to use this information in a negative way. For example, if someone asks what you do for a living, you could mention your position but not your workplace. Also, feel free to mention that you're not comfortable answering a question and sharing specific information. After all, the person you're talking to is a stranger, so they should understand. If they don't, find someone else to chat with.

Setting Up Anonymous E-mail

For a number of reasons, you might want to keep your e-mail address and other information contained in e-mail messages private. People often use programs to chat with other people on the Internet, but they might want to keep the level of familiarity to a minimum. In other words, while typing messages back-and-forth is fine, you don't want them sending e-mail to your home or workplace.

You can find free e-mail services on the Web, which you can use to set up an account to send and receive e-mail. However, when you log onto Web sites like Hotmail to compose an e-mail message, the IP address the machine you're using is included in the e-mail message. Using the IP address, someone can backtrack and find the ISP you're using, and she could possibly find your account name and other information. While free e-mail services provide a level of anonymity, they don't fully protect your information from being viewed by others.

To prevent people from viewing such information, you can use anonymous re-mailers. Anonymous re-mailers provide you with an e-mail address. When e-mail is sent to the address, the message is modified slightly so that the e-mail address you sent it from is replaced with the e-mail address you set up with the re-mailing service. The re-mailer then resends the message to the receiver's e-mail address, which you specify in your message. When the recipient receives the message, the header information in the e-mail will now show the IP address of the re-mailer, the re-mailer's mail server, and the new e-mail address that points to the re-mailer service. Any information that specifies who you actually are is removed from the e-mail and replaced with information pointing to the service. This revised information creates a barrier between cyber criminals and you.

A number of anonymous re-mail services are available on the Web, with varying levels of security. Some provide additional protection by using Pretty Good Privacy (discussed in the section "Using Pretty Good Privacy with Microsoft Outlook" later in this chapter) but many do not. Also, some e-mail re-mailers charge for their services, so check to see if the security and price is right for your needs.

Digging Deeper...

Degrees of Anonymity

Even though anonymous e-mail provides you with a degree of anonymity, don't assume that you are completely anonymous. If someone were to use the re-mailer for illegal purposes—such as sending death threats or harassing e-mail—the operators of the service would either assist authorities or be forced to with a subpoena, warrant, or court order. In most cases, the police will still be able to determine who sent the e-mail and where it was sent from.

Free Anonymous E-mail

While some anonymous e-mail services charge for achieving a level of privacy, a number of free services on the Internet might suit your needs. In the past, many people avoided anonymous e-mail providers, because they had the habit of shutting down after a period of time. Because it costs money to maintain a site, people had to periodically find a different anonymous re-mailer. This is less of a problem today, because many sites either sell advertising space on their site or provides additional services for a fee. In many cases, the sites that offer anonymous e-mail for a fee will also provide free anonymous e-mail for a limited time, allowing you to try before you buy.

Free anonymous e-mail is particularly useful if you're concerned about your privacy but don't want the added expense of paying for the services of an anonymous re-mailer. If most of your e-mail doesn't contain sensitive information, but you occasionally have the need to send a message anonymously, then this is an option that will be useful to you.

subDimension.com is an excellent anonymous e-mail service that can be found at www.subdimension.com/free-mail. When signing up for a free account, very little information is required. All that they insist on you providing is the account name and password you'd like to use.

Stealth Message is another service that allows you to set up a new account quickly, by simply entering a username and password. After the account it set up, you can login and immediately begin sending e-mail. With this service, you can send encrypted messages, so any unauthorized parties will be unable to view the contents of your message. You can visit their site at www.stealthmessage.com.

NOTE

After signing up for anonymous e-mail, send a test message to yourself, and check the information contained in the e-mail's header. Look at the contents, and try to find any information that reflects the name or IP address of your ISP's mail server, the normal e-mail address you use, or anything else that might reveal who you are. By looking at this information, you can ensure that any e-mail that's being re-mailed is indeed anonymous.

E-mail Encryption Made Simple

Encryption has been used for centuries by businesses and military forces to keep important information private by using coded alphabets, words, and names. When the Internet became a new method of communication, new encryption methods were subsequently created to keep the data transmissions private.

E-mail encryption is a process of scrambling the data in your e-mail messages and any file attachments you might include, so that only the intended recipients of the messages will be able to view them. An encrypted e-mail message is coded using a mathematical algorithm, which mixes up the bits of data in the message and makes it virtually impossible for a thief to turn the data into a usable format. In other words, your data is protected because anyone who tries to intercept the data will find it completely useless.

When e-mail isn't encrypted, it is called *plain text*. A plain-text message can be viewed by anyone with access to the e-mail message, because it can be opened with common programs that exist on most systems. For example, if you sent an unencrypted e-mail message and I managed to intercept it, I could open the message and view it using a standard text editor, my e-mail program, or any number of readily available programs.

When e-mail is encrypted, it is called *ciphertext*. When a ciphertext message is accessed by anyone other than the recipient, it appears as a useless jumble of data. This is because it needs to be decrypted back into a plain text message. After it's decrypted, the person receiving the message can read it in its original format. It sounds complicated, but all you need is encryption software to do the work for you.

Two common methods of encryption are private key and public key. You can think of a *key* as programming code that works like a key for a lock. Without it, the e-mail would remain locked up and unusable. A private key is an encryption code that is known only to the people who will exchange encrypted e-mails between one another. Traditionally, a key is shared between a sender and receiver, but, the problem with this is that if the key is lost or stolen, the security is lost. To prevent this from occurring, a combination of private and public keys might be used. A public key is encryption code that is held by a designated authority. The authority serves as a middleman between a sender and receiver, and allows recipients of encrypted e-mail to acquire public keys through them. A public key combined with a private key can be used to encrypt/decrypt messages and digital signatures.

Digital signatures are used to verify that a sender actually sent an e-mail. Digital signatures are used to verify your identity and whether you actually sent a message. When an e-mail is digitally signed, code is added to the message that uniquely identifies you as the sender.

Different standards are used for encryption and digital signatures, but, in this chapter, we look at two ways that are commonly used to secure e-mail—Secure Multipurpose Internet Mail Extensions (S/MIME) and Pretty Good Privacy (PGP). S/MIME allows you to sign and encrypt e-mails that you're sending. This ensures that a message wasn't tampered with after the message was initially sent.

Pretty Good Privacy also enables you to encrypt and sign your e-mail, but it allows you to perform the tasks of encryption within a single software package. With PGP, you can create your own key, send the public part of this key to a PGP server, and get public keys from other users. OpenPGP is based on PGP, which combines public-key and symmetric cryptography.

Obviously, your needs for encryption will vary in the types of e-mail you send out. Encryption should always be used when transmitting sensitive data over the Internet. Encryption isn't necessary when your e-mailing a friendly message or exchanging non-vital data, like recipes. In contrast, encryption should definitely be used if your message contains personal or financial information. For example, an e-mail message containing your phone number, address, credit card number, or other sensitive materials are prime candidates for encryption. How you choose to use encryption is a decision you need to make with every e-mail you send, but you should evaluate your messages from the perspective of a cyber criminal by identifying what information, if any, a criminal could use against you.

Digging Deeper...

What's a Digital Signature?

Chapter 2 describes how hoax viruses can be used to get people to delete files on their computer. In a hoax virus situation, people receive an e-mail that sounds genuine and informs them to search and delete a file with a certain name. When the person searches, they find the file-name, and do as they're told. After all, how would the person sending the e-mail know that such an obscure sounding filename existed on their machine? The answer is because your operating system or other common software on your machine installed it.

Social engineering is what causes people to act on hoax viruses. Hoax viruses play on the fact that people will often believe what they're told, especially if it sounds like its coming from an authoritative source.

A digital signature is a code that's added to e-mail, so that people receiving the e-mail are ensured that the e-mail actually comes from you. In this way, adding a digital signature is similar to signing your name to a letter, to let the receiver know that it actually came from you. With digital signatures, it's also possible to ensure that the contents of a message or file attachment haven't been changed since it was originally sent. Digital signatures can be used regardless of whether encryption is also used.

In the sections that follow, you can see how Pretty Good Privacy and S/MIME can be used with many e-mail clients as well as some Web-based e-mail available on the Internet. Your choice regarding which of these you use will generally be based on personal preference and the features available on your e-mail software and Web-based e-mail sites.

Using Pretty Good Privacy (PGP) with Microsoft Outlook

Pretty Good Privacy (PGP) is encryption software that can be used to encrypt e-mail messages and files. Freeware and commercial versions of PGP are available on the Web, and can be downloaded and/or purchased from www.pgpi.com. When the software is installed, plug-ins for Microsoft Outlook and Outlook Express can then be installed, allowing you to encrypt, decrypt, and sign messages sent through these e-mail packages.

As discussed in the preceding section of this chapter "E-mail Encryption Made Simple," PGP uses a combination of public and private keys to secure your e-mail. It uses public key cryptography, which uses a "secret key" to encrypt and decrypt a message. The sender uses the recipient's public key to encrypt the message, while the recipient deciphers it using his own private key.

When PGP is run on Microsoft Outlook, Outlook will also validate a digital signature with public keys that are stored on a "key ring." This is a collection of public keys already installed in PGP, and used to decrypt the digital signature. If it can't find the proper public key to verify the digital signature, you will be prompted to acquire the public key from a key authority. If it already has the public key, then it will verify the digital signature, which validates the authenticity of the message. The message itself is decrypted using your own private key. It's important to realize however that once decrypted, the e-mail message will remain decrypted while its stored on your machine.

Pretty Good Privacy is a well-respected method of encrypting e-mail. Plug-ins are available for both Microsoft Outlook and Microsoft Outlook Express, so you can send, encrypt, decrypt, and digitally sign any messages sent or received with this software. Once PGP has been installed on your system, using Pretty Good Privacy with either of these e-mail programs is quite easy.

When the PGP plug-in is installed, it is integrated with your installation of Outlook or Outlook Express. When you open or send a message, you'll see several new buttons on the right of your toolbar: the Encrypt Message, Decrypt PGP Message, and Launch PGPKeys buttons (see Figure 3.3).

When you click the Launch PGPKeys button, the PGPKeys tool is invoked. Using this tool, you can perform a variety of tasks, including creating new keys that are used for encrypting and decrypting messages. This is the same Key Generator that was used when you first installed PGP, allowing you to create a key that's necessary for the encryption/decryption process.

Figure 3.3 Microsoft Outlook Express 6 Toolbar with Pretty Good Privacy Buttons

When the Encrypt Message button is clicked, the e-mail and any attachments will be flagged as needing to be encrypted. Upon hitting the Send button, PGP will encrypt the message and place it in your Outbox to be sent. When the e-mail is encrypted, it will change in appearance to anyone viewing the message. Similar to the following example, the e-mail becomes coded, so that no one can make sense of it until it is decrypted:

```
-----BEGIN PGP MESSAGE-----
Version: PGPfreeware 7.0.3 for non-commercial use <http://www.pgp.com>

qANQR1DBwU4D4CaG0CSbeWcQB/9u1esxSM0NZw71D9fNArA3W4RcdRlwdYen/nwt
M91KTo3SuSnogNEJ9I1lGtePDFQ6zBGW696SVOE8fUuMh1mnKfOMaTuQuhMnP+jJ
/c0TKk3Wn3cKz86G/Dok1pdHpAXxLJXWAmBDKLBzGcjeDWJP4Yo3nJ3vWE0OwMcj
Wq5SlNWy2xQJsodT+jKMkfjqxa8zwtQZxFlpnmA1DQ4UxJV0LC74WOegGk5MAUFr
3D1fDM1PgBaJyb7+YZkLVI/13weW7putZQkqfp/0FE7Qq7Y8wAMf5YGOUpN6bcb7
kili2eeecpyiyWuVlhcklIs+vbIpJYTlZRBKmrYzs6AL/TQnB/9JeOVEahqdlrir
5T6yW5cE3QLN0GDqXRqiO5uxar7J75w/O9ngIq9YayYIwPj7BeH4umTlAbXpsOw2
3kIAw+9AsC3leG1b01WD4A0XgPLkH5pxFDxxZtlKnMbLrTAJIrgeD07zpk/nTOOM
g72tARUY3CqSO00YkomAEbz9+mkcgCV2fGDWnK02nqFM+IdZTuY/PBO1XH2QEfFD
9r98rKqUJoCdu0AtIqOboz5u+nOubEXoCk1qwM7AyxRDPDM4sRm3hB+cI4xjead0
UlaoKt8CRSujBOrE03z13FO2gDRKKDiCSuWIhVBT/1aQbpQOk3HzvmMaFeZGY4fF
v/Zrguc9yTaZZ+Ybw1xunBKq0uLn6pWi5fwLOEViMmvj/N5Z5eSF0/4Bhkt7UspK
guXjVwXBpb7/vSfIjCE=
=X7eE
-----END PGP MESSAGE-----
```

If you were the person to receive such a message encrypted with PGP, you would need to decrypt it before it could be read. Upon opening the message, click the Decrypt PGP Message button, and a dialog box appears asking you to enter a password. This is the password that you chose when setting up PGP on your machine. At this point, PGP has validated you (the recipient) and can decrypt the message using your private key. This protects the e-mail from being read by just anyone who sits at the machine using your e-mail program. Once the correct password is entered, the message and any file attachments will be restored to their original format. You can now save the unencrypted message and any attachments to your hard drive. PGP has not necessarily validated the sender though, unless the message also includes a digital signature. You will need to have the public key from the person who sent the e-mail in order to validate the sender using digital signatures, which will be discussed later in this chapter.

Using Personal Certificates with Netscape

Personal certificates are used to digitally sign e-mail, receive encrypted mail, and identify yourself to Web sites that use certificates for authentication. As discussed in the "E-mail Encryption Made Simple" section of this chapter, digitally signed e-mail ensures that a message is actually from the person it claims to be from, and that it hasn't been tampered with during transmission. Personal certificates serve as an electronic form of identification, in the same way your driver's license is used in day-to-day life to authenticate your identity. Personal certificates are issued by an organization called a certificate authority (CA) that is sanctioned to issue certificates. An example of a CA is VeriSign (www.verisign.com), whose site you can visit with your browser, enter some information, and download certificates.

Personal certificates can be used for authentication for certain Web sites, such as e-commerce sites or sites that require enhanced security. They can be used to confirm your identity and also the identity of the site. Because a cyber criminal could post a Web site that looks like a legitimate e-commerce site and then prompt you for personal and financial information (such as a credit card number), certificates can be used to ensure that you're exchanging data with a legitimate Web site.

If you're using Netscape, you can use personal certificates for e-mail and browsing security. You can acquire a personal certificate for Netscape by visiting http://verisign.netscape.com/personal/index.html and following the online instructions. On this site, you will see that the certificates are free for 60 days, but you need to purchase them after the trial period. After you've gone through the process of installing a personal certificate, you can then being using it with Netscape Messenger.

Managing certificates and controlling how they are used is done through the Preferences dialog box. To access this dialog, click the **Edit** menu, and then click **Preferences**. When the dialog shown in Figure 3.4 appears, expand the **Privacy and Security** folder in the right pane, and click **Certificates**.

The top section of your Security Preferences is used to control how Netscape selects certificates. Your choices are to **Select Automatically**, which causes Netscape to select a certificate from among those currently on the computer. When this option is selected, you won't be asked which certificate to use. To have Netscape enquire which certificate to use, select the option labeled **Ask Every Time**.

Figure 3.4 Security Preferences in Netscape 6

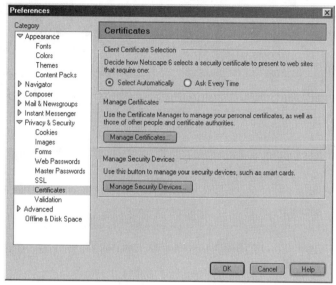

Below this section, you can see the Manage Certificates section, which allows you to manage the certificates installed on your system. By clicking the **Manage Certificates** button, you can view which certificates are installed and delete certificates that are no longer needed. A Certificate Manager dialog box appears, listing your certificates and buttons to view, delete, and back up your installed certificates.

Certificates might need to be deleted for a variety of reasons. If you no longer use a particular site or deal with a particular individual or company anymore, the certificate for them might no longer be required. Also, certificates expire after a period of time. By selecting a certificate in **Certificate Manager**, and then clicking the **View** button, you can view the date the certificate was issued, when it expires, and other certificate details.

Verifying E-mail Senders in Outlook

Using PGP with Microsoft Outlook or Outlook Express, you can also digitally sign messages and attached files, so a recipient is ensured of the information's authenticity, and that the data hasn't been intercepted and tampered with. As mentioned earlier in this section, PGP adds a number of buttons to your Outlook toolbar. While we looked at using some of the buttons to encrypt and decrypt messages in Outlook, this section looks at the buttons used to verify e-mail senders.

When you create a new message, you will see a button called Sign Message. When the Sign Message button is clicked, your message is flagged to indicate that you want it signed using PGP. Upon clicking the Send button, you are then required to enter the password for your key. Upon entering the correct password, your e-mail is signed, and your message is slightly altered. For example, let's say you entered a single sentence in the body of your message stating *Sing, sing a song...* Upon sending the message, the body of it would now look similar to the following:

```
-----BEGIN PGP SIGNED MESSAGE-----
Hash: SHA1

Sing, sing a song ..
-----BEGIN PGP SIGNATURE-----
Version: PGPfreeware 7.0.3 for non-commercial use <http://www.pgp.com>
iQA/AwUBPO6a6VUj3i6+E9uzEQJQkgCfXSmMotrHXuUQdnA1hjklMana8gsAn3Hi
M7rY9z9x3D68XAflv1LPOXy+
=Yzef
-----END PGP SIGNATURE-----
```

When you receive a message that looks like the previous message, you can use Outlook or Outlook Express with PGP installed to verify whether the message was tampered with. Upon opening the message, click the button labeled Decrypt PGP Message, and you will be able to determine who sent the message, when it was signed, when it was verified, and what the status of this verification was. For example, if you decrypted the previously signed message, you would see something similar to the following:

```
*** PGP Signature Status: good
*** Signer: John Doe <johndoe@fakedomainname.com>
*** Signed: 2002/05/24 2:18:12 PM
*** Verified: 2002/05/24 4:13:21 PM
*** BEGIN PGP VERIFIED MESSAGE ***


Sing, sing a song ...



*** END PGP VERIFIED MESSAGE ***
```

You can read the actual message between the lines that state the beginning and end of the PGP verified message. If the message had been tampered with, or the signature couldn't be verified, then it would be indicated in the *Status* line of the message.

Importing a Personal Certificate File into Opera

Personal certificates can also be used in Opera, allowing you to be authenticated as a genuine user when using secure sites on the Internet. To install a personal certificate into Opera, you would use the Security section of the Preferences dialog box. This can be done by following these steps:

1. In Opera, click **File**, and then click **Preferences**.

2. When the dialog box shown in Figure 3.5 appears, click the item labeled **Security** in the right pane.

3. In the Certificates section, click the Personal button to bring up the Personal Certificates dialog box.

4. On the dialog box, click the **Import** button, and then specify the location of the personal certificate you'd like to import. Upon specifying this, click **Open** to return to the previous dialog box.

5. Click **OK** to confirm your settings.

Figure 3.5 Security Preferences in Opera

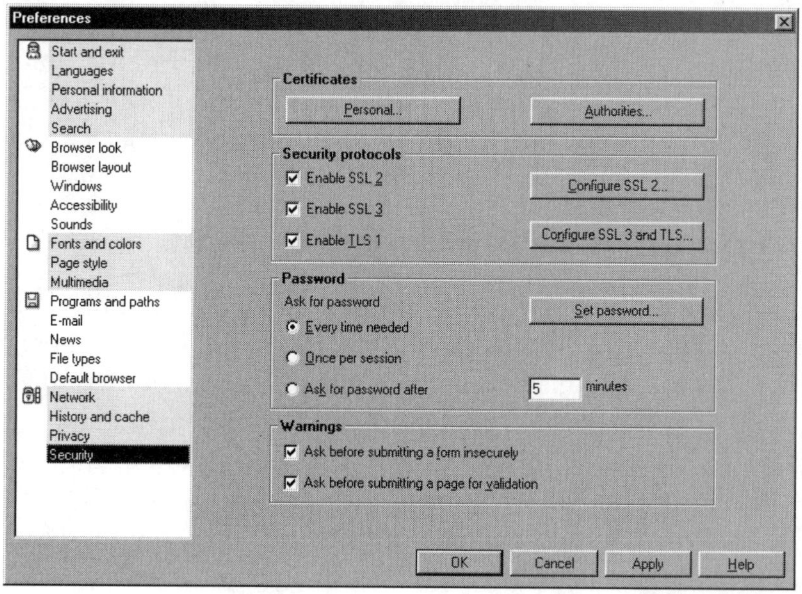

Choosing a Secure E-mail Provider

When you get an Internet connection, you are generally provided with an e-mail address as part of your package with the Internet Service Provider. You would hope that your e-mail through this provider is secure, but this isn't always the case. Some providers might only provide limited or almost nonexistent e-mail security for their customers, while others make your security dreams come true.

If secure e-mail is a concern, then you should see whether your e-mail provider supports Secure Sockets Layer (SSL) for sending and receiving e-mail. SSL is a protocol that was developed by Netscape for transmitting e-mail and attached documents securely over the Internet. SSL uses encryption to transfer documents, and it's commonly used by sites that require the transfer of confidential information.

Not every section of a Web site will use SSL, but, when it is used, an icon depicting a closed lock will appear in the lower-right corner of Internet Explorer and Netscape. Opera displays the icon on the left side of the browser. In Chapter 4, when we discuss using the Web safely, we discuss SSL in greater detail.

Other factors that might be important to you are whether e-mail encryption and anonymous re-mailing is provided through your e-mail provider. These topics are discussed in previous sections, but you should realize that the services provided by e-mail providers vary. It is important to carefully examine the services provided by a site before making a solid decision to use them.

If your ISP provides Web-based e-mail, you can read and send messages from any computer using a Web browser. This is particularly useful if you are traveling and might not always have access to your own computer. However, you might want to find a secure e-mail provider other than your ISP, if your ISP's Web-based mail does not provide encryption for your messages. Let's take a look at some options for encrypted Web-based e-mail providers.

Using Encrypted Web-based E-mail

When you choose to encrypt e-mail messages, you will need to realize that Web-based e-mail encryption is not the same as the encryption used with your e-mail client. When you use an e-mail client like Outlook, Opera, or Netscape Messenger, the e-mail message is encrypted on your computer and then transmitted to the mail server. With Web-based e-mail, encryption might not be supported or the encryption will occur on the server itself.

As described the "E-mail Encryption Made Simple" section of this chapter, e-mail can be encrypted in a variety of ways. Encryption available through Web servers is limited to what a site supports. For example, Web-based e-mail sites like Hotmail (www.hotmail.com) and Yahoo (www.yahoo.com) aren't S/MIME compatible, so they are unable to support digital certificates and encryption through S/MIME. Other Web-based e-mail sites that support encryption can support S/MIME but the encryption occurs on the server (not through your computer). Still others, like Hushmail and SecureNym use Open PGP for their accounts. Before choosing a Web-based e-mail site, you need to investigate what encryption method (if any) is offered.

As with anonymous e-mail, which we discussed earlier, a number of free and commercial encrypted e-mail services are available on the Web. Using these services, your e-mail becomes secure and can't be viewed by anyone other than the person it's meant for. Some encrypted e-mail services include:

- **Hushmail** Hushmail is a free Web-based e-mail service that allows you to send and receive encrypted messages and attachments. Encryption is automatic, requiring no effort on the part of the user. The encryption method used for this site is Open PGP. S/MIME isn't supported. To sign up for a Hushmail account, visit their site at www.hushmail.com.

- **SecureNym** SecureNym is a service that provides encrypted e-mail for a fee. It offers a choice of either Open PGP or S/MIME encryption methods. This is different from many other sites that only support Open PGP. To sign up for an account, visit their site at www.securenym.net.

- **Perfectly Private** Perfectly Private is a great encrypted e-mail provider that's free to use. To sign up for an account, visit their site at www.perfectlyprivate.com.

- **Privacy X** PrivacyX has a good reputation. But, while it provides free encrypted e-mail, it is only free for a 30-day trial period. After the trial period, you either need to pay for the services or find a new service elsewhere. Using the free e-mail service allows you to see what they offer before making a commitment. To sign up for their e-mail service, visit www.privacyx.com.

- **Pop3Now** Pop3Now provides secure e-mail services for a fee. It provides 128 bit SSL encryption, and its interface allows you to manage up to five e-mail accounts from one window. To find out more about Pop3Now, visit www.pop3now.com.

Summary

Individuals with access to your e-mail can view a considerable amount of information. E-mail can be accessed in a variety of ways. People who physically use your computer, access your computer remotely, or access any mail servers or other points used in transmitting e-mail to its destination might be able to view your data. For this reason, you should take care in what you include in your messages and/or use technologies that will make your data unreadable to those seeking to intercept and read it.

E-mail contains hidden information that is needed to direct a message across the Internet, but the information can also be used to reveal your identity. Conceivably, someone accessing your e-mail could track down the computer you were using, access your account information, and acquire personal facts about you. Such facts might include the credit card number used to pay for your Internet connection and/or e-mail. Other information, such as your e-mail address and name, could be used to impersonate you online.

Viruses are a major risk you face when using e-mail. You should install and regularly use antivirus software with up-to-date signature files to ensure that your data is safe. In addition, you have the option of using anonymous and encrypted e-mail; this shields people from knowing where an e-mail message originated and prevents those who might intercept the message from seeing its contents. Some of these services are free, while others cost a fee.

You should use encryption and digital signatures for any messages that reveal sensitive information about you or are of a vital nature. By using encryption and identification technologies, you can ensure that your messages are transmitted securely over the Internet and haven't been tampered with in transit. By taking an extra measure of security, you can protect yourself from cyber criminals seeking to steal your identity or harm you in other ways.

Solutions Fast Track

E-mail Privacy Is Not Just about Spam

☑ Check Web sites' privacy policies of to determine what they do with any information they acquire from you.

☑ If you receive spam, check the message to see if it provides a method to be removed from the mailing list. Look into software or services

provided by your Internet Service Provider to have e-mail flagged
and/or deleted before reaching your inbox.

☑ You should disable cookies to prevent information from being sent to
Web sites.

E-mail Attacks Are Not Just about Viruses

☑ Denial of Service attacks involve massive numbers of requests being sent
to servers, causing the servers to eventually crash or shut down. In
numerous cases, enormous numbers of e-mails have been sent to mail
servers. When this occurs, no one will be able to send or retrieve e-mail
from the mail server.

☑ The cost of losing data, repairing damages, and improving security after
an attack is generally passed onto customers or, in the case of
government sites, taxpayers.

☑ If you fail to close programs and logoff the network or Internet after
you finish reading your e-mail or browsing the Web, others who use the
computer can access your e-mail and browse the Internet posing as you.

Recognizing Mail Scams

☑ If you receive an offer that seems too good to be true, assume that it is.
Mail scams commonly promise items, services, or other offers that can't
be acquired through legitimate methods.

☑ If you're wary of an offer or it seems too incredible, don't respond to the
e-mail—just delete it. If you're the victim of a mail fraud, contact your
local police and/or the Federal Trade Commission.

☑ The Nigerian 419 scam is also called the Nigerian Letter Scam. This
is a popular scheme that has bilked people out of significant amounts
of money, and has even resulted in threats, violence, and the death of
victims.

Using Antivirus Protection for E-mail

☑ Viruses are commonly spread through files attached to e-mails. When
the file is opened, the virus can infect your system.

☑ Antivirus protection for e-mail will scan the attachments of new e-mails for viruses, and then deal with them accordingly.

☑ Some viruses, like the Melissa virus, will use your address book to distribute viruses to people whose addresses are in the book.

Hiding Your E-mail Identity

☑ SMTP information, or data contained in the header of your e-mail, can reveal a significant amount of information about a user.

☑ Businesses have the legal right to monitor Internet activity and view e-mail written on company computers.

☑ Anonymous remailers involves re-mailing e-mail to a different address as soon as it's received.

Avoiding E-mail Social Engineering

☑ Social engineering involves tactics that are designed to acquire information from you personally. Using social engineering, criminals have gotten people to provide their passwords, credit card numbers, and numerous other types of data.

☑ Social engineering might be used to trick people into opening viruses, by promising that a file attachment is something they need or desire.

☑ Social engineering can occur in chat rooms, by criminals slowly fishing information out of you.

E-mail Encryption Made Simple

☑ E-mail encryption is used to scramble messages so that they can't be viewed by anyone other than the recipient.

☑ Pretty Good Privacy allows you to encrypt, decrypt, and digitally sign messages sent through Outlook and Outlook Express.

☑ Encryption should always be used when sending sensitive data over the Internet.

Choosing a Secure E-mail Provider

- ☑ Even if your Internet connection includes an e-mail address, you might want to get a secure e-mail provider to send information securely.

- ☑ Free encrypted e-mail is available on the Internet. It can be acquired by visiting a provider's Web site and signing up for an account.

- ☑ Web-based encrypted e-mail providers allow you to send e-mail securely from any computer, using a Web browser.

Frequently Asked Questions

The following Frequently Asked Questions, answered by the authors of this book, are designed to both measure your understanding of the concepts presented in this chapter and to assist you with real-life implementation of these concepts. To have your questions about this chapter answered by the author, browse to **www.syngress.com/solutions** and click on the **"Ask the Author"** form.

Q: A company I'm unfamiliar with sent me an e-mail message asking me to participate in a survey. They offered the chance to win prizes. Should I participate?

A: If you're unfamiliar with the company, chances are you received spam. The e-mail might invite you to visit their site and enter personal information, but there is no guarantee as to what will be done with your information.

Q: I disabled cookies from being received on my computer, and now I can't shop online anymore. If cookies can be used to acquire information about me, what kind of information would such a site be gathering about me?

A: When you visit an online store, cookies might be used for shopping cart programs, which keep track of your purchases. If you're having trouble using a trustworthy site, turn on your cookies temporarily, or configure your browser to accept cookies from certain sites.

Q: I received an e-mail from a friend with a program attached to it. It says it's a game. Should I open it?

A: If you weren't expecting the file to be sent to you, confirm whether your friend actually sent the program to you before opening it. Many viruses will use the address book of an e-mail program to distribute the virus to other people, making it look like that person actually sent the file.

Q: I printed off some e-mail that verified a purchase I made online. Now that the purchase has arrived at my house, what should I do with the e-mail?

A: Shred it. The e-mail probably contains personal and credit card information about you. Rather than throwing it out and having someone take it from the garbage and use this information for identity theft, shred the document so no one can read it. If you don't have a shredder, you should buy one—they can be small and inexpensive and can certainly help you avoid the greater cost of data theft.

Q: I'm thinking about e-mailing a family recipe to a friend over the Internet. I have Pretty Good Privacy installed on my computer. Should I encrypt it?

A: Whether you should encrypt a message depends on whether you feel the information has any value, or contains data that could be used detrimentally. In the case of sending a recipe or a friendly message, encryption usually isn't necessary.

Chapter 4

Self Defense on the Web

Solutions in this chapter:

- **Understanding Risk on the Web**
- **Managing Risk on the Web**
- **Improving Browser Safety**
- **Covering Your Internet Footprints**

☑ **Summary**

☑ **Solutions Fast Track**

☑ **Frequently Asked Questions**

Introduction

So far in this book we've discussed measures you can take to prevent identity theft by changing the way you handle physical items linked to your identification, such as mail and credit cards, and the way you handle electronic items linked to your identification, such as e-mails or files stored on your computer. In this chapter, we examine the ways that private data can be exposed over the Web and suggest some ways you can help prevent that from happening.

Understanding Risk on the Web

Electronic commerce (e-commerce) transactions usually require credit card numbers, name, address, and telephone numbers. Each time you type one of these items into a form on a Web site, the data is transferred from your computer to the Web server. As we saw in Chapter 2, information may be either encrypted or in plain text as it traverses computers. If it is not encrypted, the data can be intercepted by anyone with access to the network between your computer and the Web server.

Electronic commerce sites aren't the only ones where you are asked to provide private, identifying information. Participation in online government programs may require you to enter Social Security numbers or other government ID numbers into a Web form. Financial management sites such as electronic banking or stock-trading sites might also ask for Social Security Numbers, tax ID numbers, or other business information. Even online medical services, entertainment sites, Internet service providers (ISPs), and other vendor sites may offer you the ability to use your checking account routing numbers or credit cards to obtain goods or services online. These are all private identifiers useful to an identity thief if the identifiers can be intercepted in transit or stolen directly from the computer on which they are stored.

In Chapter 1 (Figure 1.3), we looked at a Web site that asked you to enter your Social Security Number. That Web site looked pretty suspicious, didn't it? It didn't display any other information you'd expect to see for a company or organization that might have a legitimate reason to ask for this information. What kind of information would you expect to see on a Web site for a legitimate company? You'd be likely to see company logo, a variety of information about the company such as sales and contact information, help or support addresses and phone numbers, pictures of the company's product line, and perhaps an entire product catalog or service menu. The absence of these items should set off warning bells telling you something isn't quite right.

Even if the Web site had displayed appropriate company information, it doesn't mean the site is legitimate. What if the author of the bogus Web site had gone to a little more trouble and added a fake company logo and some fake product information? It would be a Trojan Web site asking for your private information, just not as suspicious-looking. *Trojan Web sites* are those that masquerade as providers of one service or function when in actuality they have a destructive or malicious purpose.

What if the Web site author had gone one step further and made the site look similar to one you deal with frequently? You could easily be tricked into thinking you're dealing with a site you trust. For example, you're probably familiar with the President's Web site, www.whitehouse.gov. But did you know that www.whitehouse.com not only doesn't belong to the government, it's actually a pornographic Web site? This sort of site naming is perfectly legitimate as long as no registered trademarks are infringed on.

Even if a Web site is not malicious, it could prompt you to input too much personal information unnecessarily. Some Web sites are specifically designed to draw you in with offers of coupons, games, or other trivial interests, only to ask you to enter your name, phone number, and e-mail address prior to proceeding to the offered product or service. These sites are doing good business, according to the sites themselves—they are in business to collect marketing information. They are not doing good business, according to you—they might be sharing your private information with others against your wishes.

By and large, companies and organizations offering online services do take adequate measures to protect your private information. However, accidents can happen that allow your private information to be exposed or stolen. Occasionally a criminal is able to break into a computer and steal credit card numbers. In the worst case, the criminal might even try to sell the credit card numbers to other criminals, as we saw with the Prudential case in Chapter 1. As we saw in Chapter 3, criminals occasionally try age-old con games using the new technology of the Internet to mask what might otherwise be a recognizable social engineering trick. We can mitigate these risks by becoming "street smart" on the Internet, staying observant and vigilant when we disclose information to Web sites and ensuring that we are taking adequate measures to use secure technology to interact with Web sites we encounter.

Learning to Be Street Smart on the Web

Before deciding to enter private information into any Web form or Web-based application, you need to actively make a decision about whether or not you will trust the site's owner with the information. You shouldn't assume that your private information will be used precisely the way you intend, since your own expectations of privacy might differ from those of the site owner. Even the most secure Web services can suffer accidents that expose private data. You need to know that the site can be trusted to protect your private information the way you want *before* you disclose that information.

What does it mean to trust a Web site? People make decisions about trust based on instinct in the face of evidence. Let's look at some evidence of trust on the Web. A trustworthy e-commerce Web site, for example, should do the following:

- Provide visible assurances to customers that their information is protected

- Voluntarily adopt ethical standards for conducting business on the Web

- Visibly partner with organizations in which the public maintains a high degree of trust, such as the Better Business Bureau

- Subject itself to periodic external reviews of security and privacy standards

- Visibly use and support the latest information security technologies available

One thing you can do is look for the symbols of organizations that indicate that the site has taken action to present itself as trustworthy, such as the TrustE or BBB*OnLine* seals shown in Figure 4.1. You can expect to find these seals displayed on a Web site that has partnered with TrustE (www.truste.com), a company that assures Web sites conduct business according to a defined privacy standard, or the Better Business Bureau (www.bbbonline.org). These organizations require that Web sites adopt certain ethical standards for doing business online, such as displaying privacy policies, before the sites may display the trust seals. These organizations take steps to ensure that it's impossible for Web sites to display these seals unless they meet the organizations' requirements. If you see these seals, you can be sure the site is not malicious and adheres to a reasonable set of privacy standards.

If a Web site doesn't display these seals, it doesn't necessarily mean the site is malicious or untrustworthy. The site owners could be in the process of meeting the requirements of these trust organizations, or they might feel their standards are high enough that participating in these programs isn't necessary. You need to trust your instincts when doing business with such Web sites. Remember, you always have the option of doing business with another Web site or placing an old-fashioned order by phone or mail.

Figure 4.1 Recognizable Seals of Trust on the Web

NOTE

If you get the feeling something isn't quite right at a Web site, it probably isn't. Follow your instincts and be suspicious of it. Find out more about the site before you pass any private information to it. Look up the Web site at the Better Business Bureau's online search tool (www.bbbonline.org). If a Web site doesn't live up to its own privacy policy, you should feel free to report it to the Better Business Bureau.

Another sign of trust you can look for is whether or not the Web site employs Secure Sockets Layer (SSL) and other visible security measures to protect your data. Basically, SSL is a mechanism for doing two things: confirming the Web server is authentic and encrypting private data as it traverses between your browser and the Web server. SSL should always be used when private, sensitive information (such as in a financial transaction) needs to be sent to a Web server, but it is typically not used when you're simply browsing or sending nonsensitive information. Use of such measures demonstrates a site's commitment to protecting your data using the latest security technologies. By and large, though, the most effective tool for evaluating risk while doing business with a Web site is the site's *privacy policy*, which we examine next.

Understanding the Privacy Policy

A reputable organization that asks for private information from you will provide *something* on its Web site to indicate the site's intent for securing your interactions with it. Some sites may combine their security and privacy policies into one document, or they might label it *security policy* or *privacy notice*. Usually, you'll find a link to the privacy policy somewhere on the Web site's main page.

A good privacy policy answers the following questions:

- What information is gathered involuntarily about customers as they interact with the Web site?

- What options do customers have if they don't want to voluntarily disclose requested private information?

- What information is gathered about customers as they use the company's products?

- What information is gathered about customers' computers and software?

- How does the Web site distinguish private from nonprivate information?

- How does the Web site protect private information?

- Who has access to customers' private information?

- What use does the site make of cookies?

- Does the site owner share or sell information collected about its customers?

- How does the Web site's protections differ for private and public information?

- Does the site require customers to opt in or opt out of information gathering?

- Do customers have the ability to access information that is gathered about them?

- What procedures must customers follow if they want to opt out of information gathering or have their private information removed from the company's systems?

- How does the site ensure its privacy policy is enforced?

- Who can customers contact for help with privacy concerns not addressed in the policy?

Before deciding to trust or do business with any Web site, locate and read its privacy policy. In most cases, the privacy policy will provide reassurance that your data is being treated as safely as it can be. In rare cases, you might be surprised to find that the site quite plainly spells out that it will collect all kinds of information about you and then sell it. If the site is honest, you can at least make an informed decision to accept the risk or go elsewhere.

As a practical example of how you might use a privacy policy, let's consider a situation in which you are considering buying something from one of three online shopping services, all of which require you to fill in the field that asks for your e-mail address as you set up your account (ostensibly to allow them to communicate with you about your order).

On the first site, the sign-up page provides a check box that says, "Yes, send me announcements of new products and updates," thereby giving you the option of deciding whether or not you want to receive future correspondence from that company. The button is said to allow you to opt in to be added to their regular customer mailing list. You'd like more information before deciding, so you click the link to the site's security policy, which is displayed elsewhere on the Web site. The security policy states that the Web site will never sell customer information, stores it securely, and uses it only for the purpose of communicating news about new products to customers. If you are happy with this use of your information, you proceed to enter your data.

But what if the privacy policy had said that customer data is shared with third-party advertisers, for whom the Web site owner cannot be held responsible? Most likely, those advertisers are going to display banner advertisements in your browser or other software or pop-up advertisements on your desktop. Such advertisers often correlate your customer data with other purchasing data stored in ad cookies that are set by the very Web site you are considering doing business with. In such cases, you risk divulging a lot of personal data to those advertisers if you enter it into the Web site's form. Thankfully, you were given the ability to understand this situation because the Web site publicly discloses its policies.

The second Web site does not provide a button that allows you to either opt in or out, but it does have a link to its privacy policy. In this case, you really don't know whether or not you will be added to a mailing list if you provide the requested information, so you again read the privacy policy. It's a good thing you did, too. It says that the Web site will automatically add you to their mailing list when you enter your e-mail address on their site. Had you not read the policy, you would have started automatically receiving unsolicited commercial e-mail from the company shortly after you create your account, never knowing why or how to stop it. This type of site is said to require you to *opt out* of being added to their mailing lists. By default, if you provide your information to their site, you are added to their mailing list whether you want to be or not.

The third Web site that you're considering using provides you with neither control over being added to the company's mailing list (no check boxes) nor a privacy policy instructing customers how they can opt out once they've been added. This is not a very reputable way to do business on the Internet. You should avoid handing out your e-mail address to sites such as this one since there's no way to know what the site owner intends to do with your information. *Caveat emptor*—buyer beware!

What You Can't See Can Hurt You

Cookies

There's that word again: *cookie*. You've heard it a hundred times, but what is a cookie, really? A cookie is simply a text file that contains a small piece of information. The file is transferred to your computer from a Web site. When a Web site "sets a cookie," it sends this small piece of information to your Web browser to be stored on your computer.

Why do Web sites set cookies? If a Web site happens to be an online shopping catalog, it could "set a cookie" to identify your session at a later time, in case you decide to quit and come back later. The cookie enables the shopping site to display items in your shopping cart when you return, as though you never left. Sites might set a cookie to allow seamless redirection from one server to another within their site, to smooth out your experience as a browsing customer. In such cases, the Web site might not work at all if cookies were disabled. Some Web advertising software sets cookies as a record of having visited the site. These cookies might then be used to determine your interests so that advertising can be tailored to your specific interests.

Cookies are stored together in a file somewhere on your hard drive, usually in the same directory tree where the browser software is installed. It's named cookies.dat for Opera, cookies.txt for Netscape. You'll find cookies for Internet Explorer by viewing your Windows/cookies directory. You might be surprised at what you find inside a cookie file. As we'll see later, you can view the contents of Netscape cookies directly within Netscape. If you open a cookie with Notepad, you might find your name and address, phone number, login information, or just about anything else that might be used during a Web session. If someone else can copy your cookie file from your hard drive, that person can view the same information about you.

Some cookies contain only a unique number to identify you or your computer while you visit the site, some contain encrypted information about your session, and some are constructed in a way that would allow a third party to replay or re-establish your Web session. This means that if someone could obtain your cookie file that contained

Continued

session information for a Web site where your credit card number is displayed prior to committing to a purchase, that person could possibly re-establish your session and read your credit card number. This is a particular problem if you use a Web kiosk, such as a public Web terminal inside a department store, to make a purchase. There's no assurance who will use the terminal next or what that person might do with the information you just deposited onto it as part of your purchase transaction.

We discuss how to delete cookies and temporary files from browser directories later in this chapter. In addition, Chapter 8 contains a full discussion of how to disable, block, or manage cookies.

Managing Risk on the Web

Once you decide to trust a Web site, you still need to minimize exposure to situations in which private information can be intercepted during transit by managing the risk you've accepted. Managing risk on the Web means taking the necessary steps to assure your private information is protected as you interact with Web servers. To do this, you'll need to understand using SSL for secure transactions, using SSL certificates, managing passwords, payment options, and being able to surf anonymously, which we examine in this section in detail.

Protecting Yourself With SSL Certificates

As we mentioned earlier, your Web browser helps determine server authenticity by using a protocol called Secure Sockets Layer (SSL) for secure transactions. When your browser connects to a Web server using SSL, it validates the identity of the Web server on your behalf. It asks a certificate authority (CA) to validate the Web server, which is known to the CA because the Web server owner has purchased an *SSL certificate* from the CA. The CA compares the Web site's certificate to information it has on file and verifies that the two are identical. Unless the authority can't validate the server, a secure SSL connection is then established between your browser and the Web server.

You'll know when you're connected using SSL because the browser tells you. It displays a small, closed padlock icon as an indicator. In Internet Explorer, look for a small yellow closed padlock in the lower-right corner of the window. Netscape 6 displays a closed padlock in the same spot for pages that are encrypted with SSL and an open padlock for pages that aren't. Opera displays a closed padlock on the left side of the address bar. Always check for these icons to confirm you have a secure connection before entering a credit card number,

Social Security Number, or other private information into a Web form. If the icon isn't present or is in the unlocked position, SSL is not being used and you should not enter private information at that Web site.

In rare instances, a Web site could prompt you for private information without using SSL but not represent any real danger. For instance, the Web site could have a recently expired certificate that was accidentally allowed to lapse by the Web site maintenance staff. It's sloppy management, but it can happen. If the site is large and generally well trusted and you've done business with it many times in the past, you are probably safe in trusting your instincts to proceed. Still, you should make sure the Web address has not changed from the one you originally entered, check the site to make sure it visually looks as it normally does, or look for a customer message that explains the outage to satisfy yourself that it's okay to continue.

You should also read the site's SSL certificate to make sure all other information about the Web site is as it should be, except for the expiration date. Your browser software provides the ability to do this. Internet Explorer displays the server certificate if you click the **Certificates** button from the **File | Properties** menu. Your own browser's help instructions should tell you how to do this if you aren't using IE6. Figure 4.2 shows a valid SSL certificate viewed during an SSL connection to Amazon.com (www.amazon.com) using Internet Explorer 6. The Issued to: line confirms that the user is connected to Amazon.com, which is comforting unless the user thinks she is connected a different site.

Figure 4.2 Viewing Web Server SSL Certificates Using Internet Explorer 6

Digging Deeper...

Personal SSL Certificates

A personal SSL certificate is a piece of identification, just like a driver's license or Social Security card. The main differences are that you carry an SSL certificate on your PC, not in your wallet, and it typically has an expiration date. Also, unlike a driver's license or Social Security card, there is more than one organization where you can obtain an SSL certificate.

A personal SSL certificate demonstrates your identity to Web servers. When you obtain the certificate, you must first prove your identity to the issuer, known as a CA, by presenting other identification such as a driver's license or Social Security card. The CA then gives you a unique digital file, or *certificate*, that you import into your Web browser, using the browser's menu functions provided for this purpose. Afterward, as you surf the Web, your browser asserts your identity to Web-based applications using the certificate. When a Web server asks for your personal certificate, it queries the CA that issued it, which sends a validation message back to the Web server vouching that you are who you claim to be.

Personal digital certificates are often required in order to use a Web-based e-mail service supporting S/MIME directly from your PC, as discussed in Chapter 3. If you use a Web-based e-mail service that supports digital signatures, you'll probably need a certificate for the mail server to create your digital signature. Over the course of time, many other types of Web services such as online banking or stock trading will increasingly require you to have a personal certificate in order to access their services. This is good for you. It helps deter others from accessing your online accounts, since they won't possess your certificate. Other computers can't be used to make changes to your account, because your computer is the only one that possesses the certificate. This gives you better physical control over your identity online.

Personal SSL certificates can also be used to validate your identity when you're digitally signing or encrypting e-mail using software that is not Web based or signing onto certain types of applications. Most certificate authorities offer personal certificates for free so you can learn how to use them. If you'd like to learn more about obtaining a personal certificate, a good place to begin is by visiting a CA Web site and reading about the services they offer. Several authorities are listed here as a starting point:

Continued

www.syngress.com

- **VeriSign** (www.verisign.com)
- **Thawte** (www.thawte.com) Go to the Personal Certificates section.
- **Baltimore** (www.baltimore.com/cert)

Once you obtain a certificate, consult the CA and your browser manufacturer's instructions for installing it in your browser.

Avoiding Malicious Applets

Some Web sites want to enrich your browsing experience by using flashy plug-ins, animation, music, or other features to make their online service or advertising presence more attractive or more functional. To accomplish this, they might ask you to download a small program, or *applet*, to enhance your browser and enable their Web site to be viewed the way they intended. In the vast majority of cases, accepting the download causes no harm.

However, in a few cases, intruders have been known to compromise a Web site and substitute an applet that contains malicious code for the real one. Or they could create a Trojan Web site and write their own malicious applet. Visitors to the site unwittingly download the altered applet, which then infects their system with a Trojan that sends private data back to the owner of the site or performs other destructive acts. How can you be certain that the software you are being asked to download can be trusted?

There are actually two issues involved in this question. One involves determining if known trusted programs are still trustworthy after some period of time has elapsed. The other involves determining if programs are trustworthy in the first place. Digital signatures can solve the first problem; antivirus software can solve the second.

In Chapter 3, we examined the concept of a digital signature as a method of validating a message or message attachment to ensure that the sender is who he says he is and that the message or attachment hasn't been tampered with during transit across the Internet. This same concept works with any type of software, not just a message attachment. Software such as applets can also be digitally signed. The digital signature acts as an assurance that the software has not been altered prior to the time you download or use it.

Many trustworthy Web sites provide you a digital signature when it's necessary to install an applet or plug-in in order to view the site. You can view the digital certificate for the signed applet in the same way you view a Web server site certificate, using the features of your browser provided for this purpose. A code-signing certificate describes the name of the company, dates for which the certificate is valid, and so on. Refer to your browser's instructions for how to view the digital certificate using your individual browser.

If the Web site is one with which you're familiar and is for a well-known company or organization, and if you've taken the steps described in the rest of this book to secure your browser and computer software, it's much less risky to download an unsigned applet. However, it's always best to do business with companies that provide this element of assurance, and always use antivirus software as a safety net. Make sure that interacting with the site by downloading the applet is worth the remote possibility of undesired consequences, such as a system crash or an attempt to steal valuable information. Just as you would avoid opening an executable program e-mailed to you by a stranger, it's always better not to allow any Web pages to install software on your computer.

What You Can't See Can Hurt You

Web Redirection

When you type a Web address into your favorite Web browser and a Web page is displayed, what exactly are you looking at? You are expected to believe that the owner of the address has provided this page for you to see. Especially if the domain name suggests a very trustworthy organization or a topic that doesn't seem likely to be the realm of a hacker, you might lower your guard when making decisions about handing out information to the site.

However, most organizations with which you choose to conduct business online do not maintain every single possible Web address containing their business name. For instance, Widgets.*com* might be the famous place that sells widgets, but Widgets.*org* might be a site that posts comics or something else totally unrelated to widgets, or it might not be used by anyone at all. Some companies do try to maintain Web servers in every possible top-level domain, however, such as www.microsoft.ca for users living in Canada or www.microsoft.it for users in Italy. This is an easy way to provide language-appropriate content for the users that are most likely to need it.

Continued

Unused domains, though, can sometimes be used to trick customers and *redirect* their legitimate Web traffic to an unrelated, possibly malicious Web site. If a company named Fake Domain Inc. purchased the Internet domain fakedomain.com but forgot to purchase fakedomain.ca, anyone could come along and register fakedomain.ca if they so chose. People who visited Web servers in that domain would likely think they were doing business with Fake Domain Inc. when in actuality the site might be owned by another company or, worse, someone with malicious intent.

Another type of redirection happens when a legitimate Web site has been maliciously hacked to redirect traffic to a malicious server. The malicious page might look similar to the legitimate one, prompting you to type in your account number or other personal information. But when you type in your login information, the malicious page might save it and then redirect your traffic once again to the correct Web site, which displays the login screen a second time. Your tip-off that something is wrong is that uneasy feeling of "Hey, didn't I just type in my login information already? Why is it asking me to do it again?"

This is a type of information theft using social engineering in combination with a Trojan Web site designed to specifically to steal your information. The social engineering happens when you are tricked into believing that the Trojan Web site is legitimate. These kinds of Web sites might be up for only a few hours at a time, to prevent discovery. You can avoid falling prey to this kind of scam by always looking at the Web address in your browser after the page is displayed, to verify that the address hasn't changed from what you originally typed in. If SSL is used, view the certificate in your browser to confirm what site you're dealing with. Finally, understand the risks of doing business with any online site that asks for your SSN or other sensitive information.

Managing Passwords

If you're like most people who make frequent use of the Web, you've got a couple dozen Web accounts scattered around the Internet. It's very common for people to use the same account name and password for each Web site they visit, to make it simpler to remember how to log in the next time. If you have used different account names and passwords, you might be tempted to write them down somewhere, such as a notebook, a file on the hard drive, or a sticky note attached to your computer's monitor for easy reference. You might be tempted to use the "Remember this Password" buttons that appear on many login screens and software applications. But those are all good ways to give others access to your passwords when you aren't around.

In Chapter 2 we discussed how to create a strong password that appears random to an intruder but is easy for you to remember. How does this habit help you remember a couple dozen passwords, one for each Web site where you have an account? How can you remember which password goes with which Web site? As discussed in Chapter 2, you could write them down using a form of encoding and hope that nobody discovers how the encoding works or where you've written them down. For some people, that might be sufficient. For others, an electronic form of password management might be a better idea.

Ideally, however, you should never write down your passwords. You should also use a unique account name and password pair for each Web site so that if one password is stolen, it doesn't grant access to other Web accounts you might have. Sound impossible? It isn't. In this section, we examine a couple of tools you can use to accomplish this goal.

Using Microsoft's Passport

Microsoft has developed its Passport .NET technology as its answer to users having too many Web passwords to remember. To obtain a Passport, you create an account using an e-mail address and password. When you use the Microsoft Passport, you effectively allow Microsoft to disclose this private data on your behalf, using Microsoft's security measures, to Web servers that accept this form of login. You don't have to remember a password for each Web site, because you use the same one at all Web sites that accept Microsoft Passport. Microsoft assures in its security policy that your password will be stored safely and transported securely to Web sites using their Passport .NET technology.

Before you can use Microsoft Passport, you must sign up for it at www.passport.com. Web sites that support this service allow you to log into their service using your Passport password and e-mail address instead of requiring a unique account name and password that would otherwise be required.

With Passport, you rely on Microsoft to securely store your private data on their servers, instead of relying on a software package to store them on your local hard drive. Microsoft's servers are not subject to the same insecurities as your desktop PC, are not as easily stolen, and are maintained by people who focus on topics of security. Of course, Microsoft is still storing your password, which means it's less secure than a password that's never stored. In addition, using only one password for all Web sites means that if your Passport password is stolen, the thief can use it at all Passport-enabled Web sites. Remembering your own passwords is best, but if you can't do that, this product might be what you're looking for.

Protecting Your Purchasing Power

We observed earlier that one way to protect passwords is to use a service that stores them for you, preventing the need for you to type the password each time you use a particular service. Services such as Passport store your password and private data remotely, on servers managed by the company that provides the service.

Assuming that the service stores and transports your password securely, you no longer need to depend on your own knowledge of security for storing and sending the password securely. This benefits you by ensuring that the service, not you, is responsible for storing and transferring your private data securely.

Passwords aren't the only type of private information that can be protected in this fashion. You can also protect information you routinely use to make online purchases in the same fashion by using alternative payment services. In this section we examine several popular and trusted services: PayPal, CyberCash, American Express, and Microsoft Wallet.

PayPal and CyberCash

PayPal (www.paypal.com) and CyberCash (www.cybercash.com) are two electronic payment services that can help protect your financial information when you make purchases on the Internet. These services are payment systems that augment and build on the ways in which existing credit card or bank payment systems work.

When you create accounts with these services, you provide your private information, including checking account number or credit card number, only once. You don't have to send in any payments or deposit any money with the service ahead of time, so there is no risk that you will lose deposited money—there isn't any deposited money.

When you are ready to make an online purchase, you tell the vendor you will pay using PayPal or CyberCash by selecting this form of payment on the vendor Web site. The Web site must be set up to accept this form of payment. Once you commit to the purchase, the Web site requests PayPal or CyberCash to pay for the value of your purchase. The payment service, in turn, charges your credit card or deducts the purchase price from your checking account. Thus, you are saved from having to disclose your actual credit card number to the online vendor from which you are buying, reducing the chances that the number will be stolen during a break-in or accident. This transfers the risk of securing your credit card information from yourself and the online vendor to PayPal or CyberCash.

Electronic payment systems in general had a rocky start, due in part to some e-cash services such as Beenz and Flooz that went bankrupt. Beenz and Flooz, however, were entirely different creatures from PayPal and CyberCash. They were an entirely new form of electronic currency, not a payment system designed to transfer existing U.S. currency between buyers and sellers. With the extinct services, buyers would purchase units of e-currency called Beenz or Flooz using real currency and then use these units to make purchases at merchants who accepted the e-version. Paying with Beenz or Flooz was actually more like paying with a gift certificate than paying with cash or a credit card. Its value had to be prepaid, making these services less desirable than a payment system that used existing deposits of real currency.

American Express Private Payments

American Express offers a variant of the PayPal and CyberCash service using its own credit card authorization and payment systems. Instead of typing your American Express credit card number each time you want to make a purchase online, you instead type a Private Payment number that you obtain directly from the American Express Web site. The Private Payment number is valid for only a few minutes, is encrypted, and is transferred to the merchant using a secure network transaction, making the risk of theft much lower than using a credit card number that could remain stored on the merchant's Web server for a very long time. American Express then arranges for payment from your American Express account as identified using the Private Payment number. This system works something like a short-lived IOU. This service works only with Web sites that accept American Express, but any site that accepts American Express should be able to accept a Private Payment in lieu of an actual credit card number. To sign up for this service, visit www.americanexpress.com/privatepayments/info_page.jsp.s

Microsoft Wallet

Microsoft Wallet is a feature of the Microsoft .NET Passport. Web sites that accept transactions made via a .NET Passport Wallet obtain purchasing information from your Passport account rather than requiring you to type it in at the time you make a purchase. When you use this feature, you are transferring the risk of typing in credit card information to the Passport service, away from whatever security mechanisms you and your computer can provide, similar to using PayPal. To learn more about setting up a Microsoft Passport for use with this service, visit the Microsoft Web site at www.microsoft.com.

Anonymous Web Surfing

When you surf the Web, it seems like a fairly anonymous act. Until you actually type something that you recognize as identifying information about yourself, it might feel like you're hiding behind the keyboard, emboldened to act in a way that you might not if the connection to you were more obvious. This is one of the hazards of Web surfing, because users are lulled into a level of confidence about their actions that they probably shouldn't have.

Digging Deeper...

Anonymous Proxies

For more technically adept readers, one way you can increase your level of anonymity while surfing the Web is to use special services for that purpose, such as Anonymizer.com (www.anonymizer.com). When you type a Web address into the Anonymizer.com address bar, Anonymizer.com retrieves the page you requested and displays it. Your computer's IP address isn't logged; the server's address is.

Another way to increase anonymity is to configure your browser to use an anonymous proxy. An *anonymous proxy* is a Web server that retrieves Web pages on your behalf but doesn't offer a pretty address bar the way Anonymizer.com does. To configure an anonymous proxy, add the address of your favorite anonymous proxy server to your browser's network configuration. Consult your browser's instructions or help facility for details on how to use a proxy server.

This way your browser doesn't actually connect to any Web servers, so there's nothing to log about you, except the connection to the anonymous proxy. Therein lies the rub. The connection to the anonymous proxy is still logged. The degree of anonymity is increased, but it's not complete. To learn more about anonymous proxies, click the **Directory** menu for Google (www.google.com) and select **Computers | Internet | Proxies | Free**.

However, there's a lot of information about you that can be gathered without your knowledge. When your browser connects to a Web server, for instance, information about your connection is typically logged at that time. The information contained in the log might include your computer's address, its operating system type, the type of application you're using to connect, and what you view as you visit the site.

If you use a Web connection to participate in a chat room, messaging service, or other discussion forum, you might hide behind a screen name during the discussion, but your computer can't. The anonymous screen name provides only a *degree* of anonymity. It's a good idea to use services that increase your anonymity, such as Anonymizer (see the "Digging Deeper" sidebar), but do have a healthy mistrust for the degree of anonymity they actually provide you.

There's also no reason you have to give out real information every time you want to follow up on an interesting advertisement or Web page that wants to know everything about you, including your shoe size. You don't have to provide a real name until you actually make a purchase, and even then, only if the method of payment requires disclosing your real name. You have to provide a real address only for shipping a product or service you order, so if a physical product isn't involved, perhaps you can avoid disclosing your address, too. Using contrived information until real information is absolutely needed is certainly one strategy for maximizing anonymity.

Improving Browser Safety

New computers with Windows software already installed on them typically come pre-installed with Internet Explorer browser software. Some people prefer to use different browser software, such as Netscape or Opera. Whether you use the copy of IE that came pre-installed on your Windows computer or install a fresh copy of another browser, it's important to take some additional steps to properly secure the browser software before you use it, to repair any bugs or security exploits to which it might be vulnerable. If a fair bit of time has lapsed since the software was first released, several bugs have probably been discovered, some of which could be used for malicious purposes. This section examines how to update your browser software to make it as safe as it can be before you use it.

Updating Your Browser Software

If your computer came with a utility that automatically updates and patches your software, be sure to run it before using the computer for the first time. If it doesn't, you should perform an update manually prior to using your browser to surf the Web.

Internet Explorer

If your browser software is Internet Explorer, the first step is to make sure that you're using the latest and greatest version. To find out what version you're using, start the IE software, click the **Help** menu, and choose **About Internet Explorer**. Then go to www.microsoft.com and see if there's a more current version available. If so, follow the instructions for downloading and installing the newer version. After you've upgraded your IE software, you'll still need to apply any security patches or updates that might not be included in the upgrade you just installed.

Microsoft makes it simple to locate security patches for your Windows IE software at its Windows update Web site, located at http://windowsupdate .microsoft.com. This Web site suggests important updates based on the versions of software currently installed on your Windows system (which is why you should upgrade to the latest version first). The first step in updating your browser is to follow the instructions for downloading and installing each one of these suggested updates. This process could involve rebooting your computer several times, so be sure to allow enough time to finish.

Netscape

If your browser of choice is Netscape, you'll also need to make sure you have downloaded and installed the latest version from http://browsers.netscape.com. The latest version includes repairs for any security issues that have arisen since the previous release, so even one or two versions can make a big difference when it comes to security.

Opera

Opera is a fairly new browser to hit the market. You can download the latest version of Opera from its support Web site at www.opera.com. Opera doesn't offer any security patches, so you need to make sure you have the latest version to ensure you've got the most recent bug fixes and, therefore, the most secure version available.

Putting Browser Security Features to Work

Once you've installed and updated your browser's software, you need to do one more thing to ensure you are surfing the Web as safely as you can: configure the security settings. Your browser's settings should reflect your requirements for managing cookies, storing passwords, and managing private data stored on disk.

Internet Explorer

The default settings for Internet Explorer 6, for instance, provide you a medium level of security and do not disable cookies. Higher security settings provide you increased security, although they might also cause certain Web sites that rely on those less secure features to not display properly. We provide a basic tutorial on security features of Internet Explorer in Chapter 8, so you can decide your own security comfort level. You should make sure your own browser's settings are set to the default settings, at a minimum.

Netscape

The default installation for Netscape 6 leaves cookies turned on and stores Web passwords on your behalf. Both are features you probably should turn off for safety. If you must use cookies for certain Web sites, Netscape allows you to manage each one individually. Consult Chapter 8 for details on how to change the security configuration for Netscape.

Opera

Opera provides many security features not found in other Web browsers. These features give you control over pop-up advertising, redirection, information disclosed by the browser, and managing cookies, among other things. We've included a few suggested configuration changes for Opera 6 in Chapter 8.

Covering Your Internet Footprints

So far in this chapter we've talked about installing patches, improving security settings, and preventing cookies as measures to protect yourself from people who are looking to collect information about you. If you are just now making these changes to your browser settings, however, chances are you've already left a lot of footprints on your computer that track where you've been in recent history. In this section, we talk about how to get rid of those footprints. You should take the steps described in this section on your own system a few times per week. If this proves too time consuming for you, many free utilities are available on the Internet to handle this task automatically, each time you start your computer. CNET (www.cnet.com) is a reputable place to download this type of utility.

Deleting Hidden Information About You

Each time you visit a Web page, images and text are downloaded from the Web server and stored locally on your computer before being displayed in your browser. Your travels on the Web are also recorded in a History file designed to track the pages you've visited in recent weeks, painting a fairly complete picture of your Web journeys. As we've already observed, you'll also have cookies that are set by Web sites you visit. All these tracks are files that could contain private data about you, so they should be removed from your computer as often as possible.

To delete private data in Internet Explorer 6, click the **Tools | Internet Options** menu and select the **General** tab. Click the **Delete Cookies** button shown in Figure 4.3 to remove all cookies. Click the **Delete Files** button to delete temporary files stored by Internet Explorer. Note that this action will not delete cookies or temporary files stored by a different browser. You'll need to delete those separately. Finally, click the **Clear History** button to clear the record of sites you've visited using this browser.

Figure 4.3 Deleting Private Data Using Internet Explorer 6

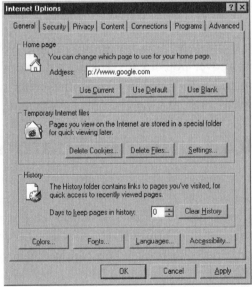

NOTE

If you have an earlier version of Internet Explorer, you might not have one or more of these delete buttons. You can still delete cookies manually by removing them from your Windows/Cookies directory just as you would delete an ordinary file. History files are likewise stored in the Windows/History directory and can be manually removed. Temporary Internet files are stored in the Windows/Temporary Internet Files directory; you can manually remove those, too.

Figure 4.4 demonstrates how to delete cookies using Netscape 6.2. Bring up this menu by clicking **Edit | Preferences**, choosing the **Privacy and Security** category, selecting the **Cookies** menu item, and then clicking the **View Stored Cookies** button. Select the cookie you want to remove from the scroll box, and click **Remove**. To remove all cookies Netscape has stored, click the **Remove All Cookies** button.

Figure 4.4 Deleting Cookies Using Netscape 6.2

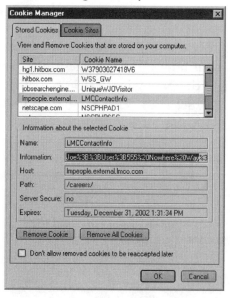

Figure 4.5 demonstrates a sample history file using Netscape. You can bring up the same window by clicking **Tasks | Tools | History** in your own copy of Netscape 6.2. Most users don't expect that anyone else will ever view their

browsing history, and so they ignore their history files. However, a thief could use your history to discern which Web pages you often visit. There's also the chance that a snoop at work or elsewhere could infer information about you, such as medical history, marital status, or mental health, based on the sites you frequently visit. Deleting this information stops a thief from readily accessing it, although it can still be retrieved from the hard disk using specialized software designed for this purpose. This software typically costs too much for the average person to have on hand and so is typically used only by law enforcement and forensics specialists trained to retrieve deleted evidence from computer disks.

Figure 4.5 Viewing Netscape Browser History

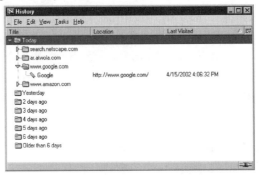

Netscape temporary files and history files are not deleted in the same menu as Netscape cookies. To clear browser history files using Netscape, click **Edit | Preferences** and highlight the **Navigator** category, which brings up the menu screen shown in Figure 4.6. Select the **History** option under Navigator and click the **Clear History** button before clicking **OK**.

Figure 4.6 Deleting History Files Using Netscape 6.2

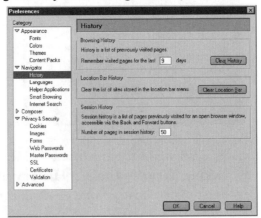

To delete files stored on disk or memory, click **Edit | Preferences**, and click the **Advanced** category. This brings up the menu screen shown in Figure 4.7. Highlight the **Cache** menu item and click the button for **Clear Disk Cache**. Click the **Clear Memory Cache** button to clear files stored in memory. Click **OK**.

Figure 4.7 Deleting Cached Files Using Netscape 6.2

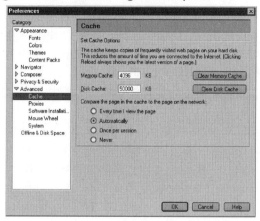

Opera 6 makes the task of deleting private data a bit easier than Netscape does. All the options for deleting private data are included on a single menu screen. To delete private data using Opera 6, click **File | Delete Private Data** to bring up the menu screen shown in Figure 4.8. Check the boxes shown in Figure 4.8, and click **OK**.

Figure 4.8 Deleting Private Data Using Opera 6

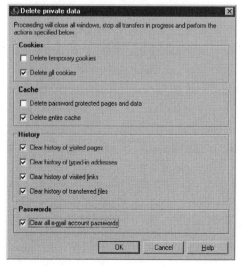

Opting Out of Ad-ware Cookies

Along with the popularity of the World Wide Web has grown advertisers' desire to find ways to harness the Web to sell their products. Believe it or not, there was a day (not very long ago) when banner ads didn't appear on any Web pages and cookies were never used. Now all the people surfing the Web are ripe for receiving advertising, or so the thinking goes. However, it's harder to advertise on the Internet than in other print and media, since there's less certainty as to where and for how long the audience will direct their attention. If you don't want to view an advertisement on a Web page, you can simply minimize the page, press the Back button, or follow a different link.

To compensate for these ways of circumventing ads, advertisers have tried to deliver their messages using Web technologies in new and creative ways—for instance, banner ads that appear at the top or side of your browser as you visit every page of a given Web site, or those small windows that pop up an advertisement when you move from one Web page to another. These advertisements are sometimes even targeted to your specific purchasing habits through the use of a technique called *advertising cookies*. As you visit Web sites that set these cookies, your surfing habits are effectively tracked by examining the data stored in the cookies, such as the name of the Web site or the pages you viewed while you were there. Advertisers can collect the information stored in these cookies and select an advertisement to display on your screen that you are more likely to appreciate and respond to.

For most people, it's common sense not to disclose your name and address to a stranger met on the street. It's less obvious that the risks are similar when you give out a name and address to a Web page. It is even less obvious when information about you is collected without your being aware of it. One of the ways you can reduce the amount of data that's being collected about you and your surfing or purchasing habits is to tell advertisers that you don't want Web sites to set any advertising cookies on your system and not to use any that might already be set.

In this section we examine three of the more ubiquitous providers of advertising content, discuss their particular policies for collecting information, and give you some control over how that information is collected or used. Unfortunately, this is not a complete list of advertising content providers. The privacy site WebVeil (www.webveil.com) has a more comprehensive list of about 10 sites offering opt-out procedures. It's prudent to periodically check any site known to collect and aggregate data about you and opt out from having it distributed to others, if that service is offered.

Abacus: A Division of DoubleClick

DoubleClick is a company that helps other companies spend their electronic advertising dollars more wisely by targeting that electronic advertising to the people who really want to see it. Cookies are set on your system as you browse the Web to indicate that you have visited the site. Software that works in tandem with these cookies tells the advertiser your preferences, so an appropriate advertisement can be sent to your desktop as a pop-up or displayed in a banner ad.

DoubleClick makes it clear in its privacy policy (www.doubleclick.com) that "DoubleClick does not use your name, address, e-mail address, or phone number to deliver Internet ads," but they stop short of saying they won't use, say, cookies set by Web sites you surf that might contain personal information about you. To ensure that advertising cookies aren't used to determine your surfing habits when displaying advertising for you, you'll need to opt out of this service with DoubleClick.

Figure 4.9 is a screenshot of the DoubleClick Web page where you can download its opt-out cookie. Interestingly, the way its opt-out program works requires you to download a cookie that flags your browser as one that doesn't want any future cookies to be used. As long as your browser is configured to allow cookies, the DoubleClick opt-out cookie will prevent further DoubleClick cookies for 30 days. Unless you really need cookies to interact with a particular Web site, you are always better turning them off entirely, although you'll lose the opt-out cookie as well. You can disable cookies in your browser altogether using methods we discuss in Chapter 8 or using third-party software that does the same thing. The opt-out cookie at least provides a way to control how much information about you is gathered when you can't turn cookies off entirely.

Figure 4.9 The DoubleClick Opt-Out Policy

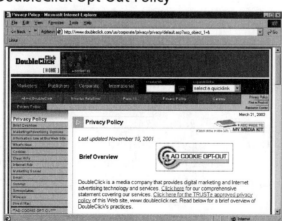

Opting out of DoubleClick ad cookies won't stop pop-up ads altogether, but it will stop you from getting future cookies that track your surfing habits, as long as you always use the same browser used to obtain the opt-out cookie. The advertisements will not be targeted to your preferences, but they will still be displayed. The opt-out cookie will still be read; you just won't be subject to having correlations made between your computer and your surfing habits. To prevent those pop-up ads altogether, you need a browser that provides this feature.

If you do decide to use the opt-out service, you need to get an opt-out cookie for each browser you use, since different browsers store cookies in different places. If you ever turn off cookies in a given browser, you'll turn off the opt-out cookie as well and will start being tracked again. You need to check every 30 days to make sure your opt-out cookie is still intact for each browser you use.

Buying something from a mail order catalog is likely to land your name and address information in a database maintained by a company named Abacus. Abacus compiles your information and resells it to other mail-order companies that might send you copies of their own catalogs based on your demographic information and purchasing history. DoubleClick helps build that demographic information through its cookie-based Web programs designed to track your online surfing habits.

Fortunately, Abacus also maintains an opt-out program. Its policy regarding opting out of its services is shown in Figure 4.10. Simply phone Abacus at 1-800-518-4453 and provide your name and address to be removed from its mailing list. It can take up to three months to notice a reduction in the number of catalogs and other junk mail you receive. Abacus can also be contacted by mail at:

Abacus: A Division of DoubleClick
P.O. Box 1478
Broomfield, CO 80038

ValueClick

ValueClick (www.valueclick.com) is another advertising content provider for Web sites. When you respond to an advertisement provided by ValueClick, personal information might be collected about you, such as name, address, e-mail address, gender, and birth date. You give permission for ValueClick to make this information available to the advertiser as part of the process. That advertiser is then free to sell your information as part of a bulk mailing list, if it chooses, without first notifying you.

Figure 4.10 The Abacus Opt-Out Policy Web Site

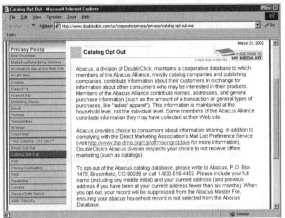

ValueClick merges your information with other sources of data in order to create targeted advertising relevant to your interests. Even if you never provide private information, ValueClick might record technical information about you, such as your IP address, browser type, and operating system type. This technical information is used to correlate with information from other sources in an attempt to, again, create targeted advertising relevant to your interests.

ValueClick's privacy statement, available at www.valueclick.com/privacy.html, regards the technical information collected about you as nonpersonally identifying information that can't be used for profiling. ValueClick retains the information indefinitely and claims to keep it secure and safe. The fact that ValueClick provides a privacy statement with instructions for how to opt out of its service is laudable and shows good intentions to protect privacy. ValueClick allows you to opt out of some, but not all, of the cookies set by its software. You can reach the opt-out page shown in Figure 4.11 from the ValueClick privacy page (www.valueclick.com/privacy.html).

Advertising.com

Advertising.com (www.advertising.com) also delivers advertising to people surfing the Web but with a variation on the theme. What makes this advertising company different is that it also maintains several Web sites that appear to have nothing to do with advertising but that directly ask for personal information that is used to correlate with information gathered through the use of cookies. Advertising.com states in its privacy policy that this information is used to correlate with other nonpersonally identifiable information collected as you surf the

Web, for the purpose of tailoring advertising toward your interests. The Web sites prompt you to enter private information such as your name, address, e-mail address, gender, and birth date, if you want to participate in the service they provide. This information is matched up with your IP address, browser type, and other nonprivate information gathered while you surf. The Advertising.com privacy policy (available at www.advertising.com/privacy/privacy2.html) provides lots of information about what kind of information it collects and how it is used.

Figure 4.11 The ValueClick Opt-Out Cookie Site

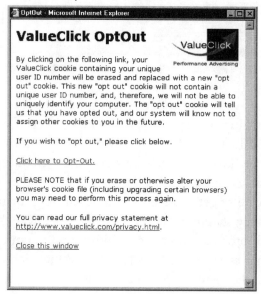

Advertising.com provides a list of all the Web sites it maintains at www.advertising.com/privacy/privacy3.html. You can view the information Advertising.com has collected about you, ask that it not be shared with others, or ask to have it deleted entirely by sending e-mail to support@advertising.com.

Summary

In this chapter we concerned ourselves with understanding how we can better protect our private information from theft on the Web. By understanding how to identify and avoid risks on the Web, we stand a much better chance of averting identity theft before it happens.

Our most effective tool for evaluating what a Web site will do with our private information is the site's privacy policy. A trustworthy Web site will provide a privacy policy that states the kinds of information the Web site will collect and how that information will be used. We can learn to identify trustworthy Web sites by looking for symbols of trust, such as the TrustE and BBB*OnLine* symbols displayed prominently on the Web site.

Managing risk on the Web involves learning to identify and avoid suspicious Web sites that are more likely to have malicious intent for our private information. We need to be careful how we manage our account and password information to minimize its exposure. We can protect credit card and other purchasing information using several services that help manage this information on our behalf more securely than we can. We can also make changes to the way we surf the Web, employing as many tactics as possible to increase our level of anonymity.

One factor in protecting our private information as we surf the Web is to keep our browser software current to the latest available security patches. We also need to make modifications to the security configurations, since browsers don't enable all security features by default.

Once we have begun surfing the Web, browsers store lots of information about our activities in the form of history files, temporary files, and cookies. We need to be cognizant of the information about us that these files contain, so the files can be properly secured or periodically deleted. We examined ways to delete these files for three of the more popular browsers. In the event we need to enable cookies for selected Web sites, we could find ourselves with advertising cookies set on our computers. We also looked at several sites that offer opt-out programs to give us better control over what is done with information gathered about us by advertising cookies.

Solutions Fast Track

Understanding Risk on the Web

☑ Evaluating the trustworthiness of a Web site means examining it for evidence of features in which we are willing to deposit our trust.

☑ E-commerce sites and sites that request personal information generally show they're trustworthy by providing visible evidence of security assurances for customers. They voluntarily adopt ethical online business standards, partner with other trustworthy organizations or companies, subject themselves to periodic review to ensure standards are being met, and visibly use the latest security technologies.

☑ Web sites communicate their intentions for gathering and using private information in their privacy policies. A good privacy policy informs the customer what information will be gathered, how it will be used, and what a customer can do if there are concerns about privacy. Always locate and read the privacy policy for Web sites before handing over private information to the site so that you understand your rights.

Managing Risk on the Web

☑ In order to protect our private information, we need to become street smart about how we interact with Web sites. We need to be able to spot suspicious Web sites that can't be trusted with our private information. Several organizations help Web sites build privacy policies and display labels of trust that we can use as evidence of trustworthiness.

☑ SSL is a method that protects our private information as it traverses between our computers and remote Web servers. We need to learn how to make sure SSL is actually being used before typing private, sensitive information into a Web form. Evidence of SSL can be observed in the lock icons displayed by our browser. We also can view the server's SSL certificate using browser features provided for this purpose.

☑ Downloading software from remote Web sites is always risky business because we have no way of knowing what's actually inside the software being downloaded. Some Web sites ask us to download Java applets in order to enhance our viewing of their sites. We should maintain a healthy mistrust of these applets, but avoiding them entirely isn't necessary if we are familiar with the site, take steps to secure our computer and browser, and take appropriate steps to confirm that the author of the software is legitimate.

☑ Using a unique, secure password along with a unique account name for each Web service with which we interact is the safest way to manage passwords. Password and account information should never be written down. Using software that stores passwords on our own hard drive is usually a bad idea because the software's main purpose might not actually be to protect passwords, making its security suspect. One way to create passwords we can remember is to use a visual cue from the Web site to create a pass phrase about the site, and then use the first letter of each word of that phrase as one letter in the password or account name. Another way to secure passwords on the Web is to use a service that stores our passwords remotely and transports them securely to Web servers, as they are needed. Microsoft's .NET Passport service is one such example.

☑ Services that protect our credit card information for online purchases are important tools for protecting our private information. PayPal, CyberCash, American Express Private Payments, and Microsoft .NET Passport Wallet are examples of services that allow us to store credit card and other private information one time and never type it in again as we make purchases online. These services send our private information securely to the remote server at the time we make a purchase, transferring the security risk from our desktop to the service itself.

☑ Surfing anonymously helps maintain our privacy online, but it isn't a complete answer to protecting our private information. Sometimes information is gathered about our online activities without our being aware of it. Use anonymity software but understand that it can't entirely hide your activities from others.

Improving Browser Safety

☑ It's not enough to simply install browser software and then immediately begin using it to surf the Web. The software needs to be updated to the latest version available to avoid known exploits that could expose our private information. Most browser vendors provide security patches for their software almost before the latest version is released. It's important to obtain and install all updates and patches before using the browser for the first time.

☑ Once browser software has been installed and updated, it's still not necessarily as secure as it can be. We need to implement security features provided with the software, which might not be active when the software is first installed. Step-by-step procedures for several popular browsers are included in Chapter 8.

Covering Your Internet Footprints

☑ As we surf the Web, information about our activities is stored on our computers behind the scenes, in the form of cookies, temporary files, and history files. These files can contain private information without our knowledge. Unless we periodically take appropriate steps to protect or delete these files, there is a risk they could expose information about us to others.

☑ We should periodically manually delete private data collected by browser software running on our system. Each browser has a slightly different method for doing this and stores the files in different locations.

☑ We should try to discourage Web sites from setting cookies on our computers. We can do this by disabling cookies using settings within our browser software. Different browsers allow us to manage cookies in different ways. In some cases we might enable cookies for some sites and not others. We can also employ opt-out services for advertisers that set cookies if we leave cookies enabled in our browser software.

Frequently Asked Questions

The following Frequently Asked Questions, answered by the authors of this book, are designed to both measure your understanding of the concepts presented in this chapter and to assist you with real-life implementation of these concepts. To have your questions about this chapter answered by the author, browse to **www.syngress.com/solutions** and click on the **"Ask the Author"** form.

Q: Does TrustE tell Web sites what their level of privacy should be?

A: No. TrustE enables Web site owners to decide for themselves what their level of privacy should be. What TrustE does is ensure that Web sites inform customers about the level of privacy being used, if these sites wants to display the TrustE symbol.

Q: Why don't browser manufacturers turn on all their security features by default?

A: Rather than risk making their browsers look bad, the default configuration leans toward allowing customers to view flashy Web sites rather than providing the most secure browsing environment. Many Web sites have come to rely on flashy technologies such as ActiveX and Java to improve the way their sites look. Unfortunately, some of these flashier technologies bring with them security vulnerabilities that wouldn't exist if the features weren't in use. Browser manufacturers let you turn them off if you're concerned about security but leave them on by default to make their browsers look good.

Q: I'm terrible at remembering passwords—Passport sounds great! Is there any reason that I shouldn't have Passport remember all my passwords for me?

A: Microsoft's .NET Passport technology is fairly new, so theoretically the software could have vulnerabilities that haven't been discovered yet. Passport is also not in wide use at the current time, so you might find that some of your favorite Web sites aren't yet Passport enabled.

Q: Why might I want to report a Web site to the Better Business Bureau?

A: You'd want to make a report if the Web site doesn't treat your private information the way you expect it should, after you've read its privacy policy. This would indicate that the Web site owner isn't following through with its stated information protections.

Q: Which is better, PayPal or CyberCash?

A: PayPal is probably more widely used, but CyberCash was acquired fairly recently by VeriSign, a company with quite a history of providing Internet-enabled security services. Either will protect your credit card information using VeriSign certificates.

Q: It seems odd that I need to turn on cookies in order to opt out of advertising cookies. What's up with that?

A: Remember, opting out of advertising cookies is necessary only if you decide to leave cookies turned on in the first place or don't manage them properly once they are turned on. There is no need to opt out of advertising cookies if you don't allow cookies to be set in the first place and you delete any existing cookies from your system. The opt-out features are useful if you find that you must leave cookies turned on for one or two sites and later discover that this has resulted in having some advertising cookies set on your computer.

Chapter 5

Connecting to the Internet Safely

Solutions in this chapter:

- **Different Connections, Different Risks**
- **Taking Precautions**
- **Firewalls for the Home**

☑ **Summary**

☑ **Solutions Fast Track**

☑ **Frequently Asked Questions**

Introduction

Up to this point in the book, we've talked about your computer and some of the software that can expose your personal information to others. What we haven't talked about yet is what happens to that information while it's in transit from one computer to another. Many people don't realize that every time they connect their PC to the rest of the world, they are connecting the rest of the world to their PC. In other words, just as a computer can be used as a tool to break into servers sitting on the Internet, servers sitting on the Internet can be used as tools to break into your home PC. Either situation can result in stolen information useful to an identity thief, unless steps are taken to protect that information from theft.

In this chapter, you'll learn what a network is, how it can be used in identity theft, and how to avoid common mistakes that make it easy for a thief to do his work. As you examine the risks of various types of network connections, we demonstrate a few surprisingly simple ways to access another computer using a network. These demonstrations are intended only for educational purposes—to show you the kinds of information other computers on your network can see. Using the described methods to install programs or view files on someone else's computer without the owner's permission is illegal.

Just as a determined thief will break into your home no matter how good your security system, a determined attacker will intrude into your computer and privacy, no matter what online precautions you take. The suggestions in this chapter are common sense approaches to making a thief's work more difficult, similar to keeping your doors and windows locked.

For a start, you need *firewall* software installed on your computer. Firewall software inspects network traffic as it comes into a PC from a modem and filters out connections that can be harmful. It can also limit outgoing connections you don't want to be seen by other computers on the Internet. For instance, firewalls can be used to limit the times of day certain actions can be performed on your PC, such as sending e-mail or surfing the Web. They can also be used to prevent certain kinds of actions altogether, such as file downloads or the automatic broadcasting of network data by the Windows operating system to computers outside your home.

You might expect that some or most of the networking information in this chapter will be too deep or technical and be tempted to skim over it—but if you jump right in instead, you might be surprised by this chapter's straightforwardness and how you'll be able to apply the information to your system. The network details we examine will help you figure out what your network looks like, which is essential in order to determine what kind of firewall you need to install.

Different Connections, Different Risks

Before you can implement privacy protections for your computer's Internet connection, you need to understand what it is you're trying to protect. You will need to implement protections differently for a single computer using a dial-up connection than for a small home office with several computers. If you have multiple computers sharing a DSL or cable modem Internet connection, buying a single external firewall device that protects all of your computers will be more economical and efficient than buying firewall software for each of the computers individually. If you use your home computer for a small business or to store important financial data, your firewall needs to include the added protection of features that can detect unauthorized connections or data theft.

In this section, we take a look at several types of Internet connections and the risks each one poses to your private data. The goals in doing this are twofold. First, you'll need to identify your computer's connection type in order to decide which type of firewall (external device or internal software) is best suited for your needs. We discuss firewall types in detail later in this chapter. Second, if you are considering moving from one connection type to another someday, you should understand the risks involved so you can purchase appropriate security protections at the same time.

Understanding Network Terminology

You can think of the network that connects your PC to the Internet very much like the street running in front of your house or apartment—it takes you to where you want to go, but it also brings others to you, if they know how to get there. If you don't keep your doors and windows locked when you aren't there, you could be asking for trouble. In order to understand how to use your home network to protect your private information, you need to understand which types of network connections you might be using. Each type has its own level of risk and needs to be protected somewhat differently.

A network connection is what enables one computer to share information with another. A simple way to visualize the Internet is to see it as a huge collection of different kinds of computers that are all interconnected, or *internetworked*, using copper wires, fiber-optic cabling, or specialized radio transmitters. Your computer connects to the rest of the Internet through your Internet Service Provider (ISP), which provides your network connection.

Your ISP provides service to your computer using one of a variety of *media types*. By media type, we mean the cable or receiver that sits between your computer and your ISP's service, whatever it looks like. Different media types look and work slightly differently. A regular telephone line has two wires and is used with a modem in order to connect to your ISP. An Ethernet cable has eight wires and is used with a network interface card (NIC), instead of a modem. A cable modem, on the other hand, connects to a round coaxial cable that looks similar to a cable used for cable TV. Each type of media has unique specifications for the type of equipment the ISP needs to provide in order to establish service.

Your PC's Internet wiring might be a telephone line, a coaxial cable, a USB cable from a satellite dish, twisted 4-pair Ethernet from a hub, or a radio signal from a wireless transmitter, but the purpose is still the same—to pass network traffic from your computer to wherever the traffic needs to go. Your ISP is in turn connected to other ISPs over very high capacity networks known as *backbones*. Companies that maintain Web servers or perform other online services for their customers connect to each other (and to you) through their own high-speed ISP networks. Thus, while your computer is online, it's as much a part of the Internet as the servers that run the Google and Yahoo! search engines or Amazon.com.

In order for one computer to transfer data to another, the computer must know the other computer's IP address, which serves a similar purpose to your home's street address. Unlike your home, however, there are over 65,000 doors through which the data can enter a computer. These doors also need identifiers, which are known as *port numbers* in the TCP/IP protocol suite. TCP/IP is the *network protocol* used by all computers connected to the Internet. You can think of a network protocol like rules of the road—drive on the left or drive on the right, stop on a red light or go on green, and so forth. The rules themselves are rather arbitrary but everybody needs to agree on the rules or chaos will ensue. Thus, computers need to agree on the network protocol they'll use to pass data among themselves.

Dial-up Connections

If you are like the majority of home PC users, you surf the Web by first dialing into an ISP, using a modem connected to an ordinary telephone line. Some modems are external to the PC, while others are cards that sit inside the computer; both types use a standard 1-pair telephone wire. When you sign up for new Internet service, your ISP provides you with a telephone number to dial, which you then configure your modem to use. America Online (AOL) does this for you, behind the scenes.

Figure 5.1 is a simplified diagram of how a modem connection works. In this diagram, the modem is installed inside your computer. After two modems have connected to each other, the computers on each end of the connection can "converse" as if they were connected physically in the same room. Your ISP actually is capable of handling hundreds of simultaneous modem connections, but there's only one shown in the drawing. The Internet is shown as a cloud to indicate thousands of interconnections that look like the one shown in the illustration. (A corporate network also connects to its own ISP using high-speed connections instead of the slower 56K modems most home computers use. We omitted this from the drawing for simplicity.)

Your PC can send information to a Web server, and the Web server can send information back to your PC, forming a connection with two ends—one *local* (your PC) and one *remote* (the Web server). For instance, if you want to view a Web page, your PC sends the Web server a request for its main starting page and the server sends the contents of that page in response. If you need to log into the service provided by the Web page, you'll type your login name and password into your browser software, which the PC then sends to the remote Web server. The Web server sends information back, either authorizing your login for access or denying it for whatever reason.

The remote service doesn't have to be a Web server. It might be a music file server, news server, e-mail server, or another home user's PC, but the idea is essentially the same. In the case of electronic mail, when you start up your favorite e-mail program, your PC might send a request to your ISP's mail server asking to download any e-mail that's waiting for you. The PC sends to the remote e-mail server the login name and password you enter into the mail application. The e-mail server then responds with the mail, if the name and password you entered are correct.

The important point to notice in Figure 5.1 is that an unprotected PC (one that is not protected by a firewall) is entirely exposed to your ISP (and thus to all the other computers on the Internet) while it is connected. Someone at *your* ISP can read your unencrypted network traffic, if they choose to do so. And someone at the *Web server's* ISP can read your unencrypted network traffic, if they choose to do so. Other computers on the Internet can send any kind of malicious traffic they want to your PC, unless your ISP performs some type of filtering or unless you install your filtering software directly onto your computer. Bear in mind, the less time you spend connected to the Internet, the less time the Internet can be used to gather information from your PC.

Figure 5.1 A Simple Dial-up Network

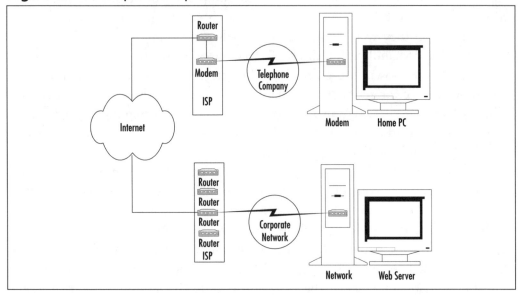

If you share one computer with other members of your household, files might have been shared or downloaded in your absence. Perhaps someone shared a file with others that you wanted to keep private, or someone inadvertently downloaded or installed virus-infected software. As discussed in Chapter 2, antivirus software will help tremendously with these problems, but it can't catch everything. The same is true for encrypting your files to make them unreadable to others. These measures won't prevent someone from connecting to your shared drives to install malicious software. They won't prevent your PC from contracting or spreading a virus that has never been seen before. For these functions, you need firewall software. We examine firewalls in much greater detail later in this chapter but, for now, just understand that the best firewall setup for a single computer that dials into the Internet would be personal firewall software installed directly on the PC, as opposed to an external firewall device of some kind.

America Online

By and large, America Online (AOL) is the most widely used Internet Service Provider for dial-up services, accounting for about one-third of at-home and at-work logins in the U.S. as of March 2001 (www.newsbytes.com/news/01/

166403.html). One point that must be made about AOL, they've made it simple for anyone to connect to the Internet, even children.

When you use AOL to dial up the Internet, AOL is acting as your ISP. After you are connected, the AOL software acts as a Web browser, chat program, and e-mail program all in one. AOL has built several features into its software to give parents more control over their children's activities online. However, these features can be bypassed simply by using a different browser, different chat program, or different e-mail program.

As an example, let's look at a typical AOL dial-up connection. When you first launch the AOL software, it proceeds to dial the modem and make an Internet connection. After this is accomplished, the AOL browser window displays, along with utilities such as the buddy list.

At this point, the AOL browser can be minimized and not even used, but your PC will still remain connected to the Internet. You could launch Internet Explorer, for example, and a non-AOL e-mail program, and they will work just fine. AOL parental controls that filter undesirable Web sites using the AOL browser don't have any effect on non-AOL software. We can understand why by considering that AOL is actually three products rolled into one:

- AOL the ISP provides modems for dialing into the Internet. AOL the ISP does not provide a firewall that blocks connections to your PC from the Internet.

- AOL the browser/e-mail/chat program works essentially like any other browser/e-mail/chat program.

- AOL the parental-control feature allows you to restrict connection times and Web content.

Parental controls alone don't affect how your computer appears to others on the Internet, only how the Internet appears to your computer. AOL's browser security functions also don't protect your PC from network-based attacks that don't rely on the browser software to operate. For instance, even if you are using the AOL browser software, the parental controls by themselves don't prevent you or your child from downloading and using different browser software that doesn't include any parental controls, or from accidentally downloading and installing malicious software that, say, records keystrokes as you shop online or reports the contents of your hard drive to someone else. AOL security features also don't prevent you from accidentally exposing private information on a shared drive. Those activities are independent of the AOL browser and can still pose a threat to your private information despite any parental controls you have configured.

What does all this mean for you? It means that, while AOL provides some nice security features, those features don't match the power of a firewall for keeping your private computer files out of the view of outsiders. You can and should use a firewall with AOL or any other dial-up service provider. If you have installed and properly configured firewall software on your computer, it will protect you from network attacks regardless of whether the AOL browser or a different browser is being used. Using firewall software augments, and doesn't interfere with, your choice to use or not use AOL parental controls or any other type of content or time restriction software.

Employer-Provided Internet Access

Some employers provide dial-up services to employees for the purpose of reading corporate e-mail or conducting other business while traveling or working from home. Using an employer-provided laptop or desktop PC at home to access your company's network poses a new set of risks to your personal information. Figure 5.2 demonstrates how all traffic to and from the Internet passes through your employer-provided dial-up account when you use it to connect to the Internet.

Figure 5.2 Dialing into an Employer-Provided Network

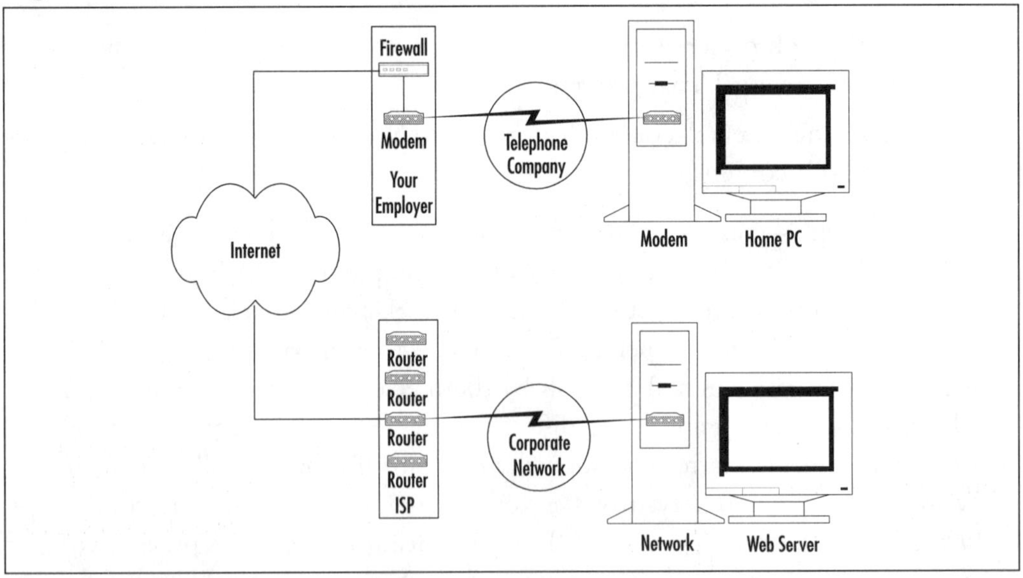

The primary threat in this otherwise convenient setup is the temptation to use your employer-provided computer and/or Internet connection to send personal e-mails or conduct other personal business online. Your company might monitor or capture information from the computer while you are connected, because the computer and Internet connection belong to the employer. Because the computer and dial-up account are provided to the employee solely for business purposes, any data on the computer therefore belongs to the company, even personal e-mails, tax returns, or other private data. You have no control over how that information is monitored or used by the employer. It should be noted that the same is true for Internet access provided to your desktop workstation. Any private data you store on it belongs to your employer and can be viewed or retrieved at the employer's discretion.

According to the FBI, the vast majority of corporate information theft occurs by employees taking advantage of access to information they probably shouldn't have, as in the Prudential example in Chapter 1. Companies have every right to protect their own information assets by monitoring how those assets are being used. They need to ensure that employees that dial in from a remote location do not bring viruses into corporate computers, use the corporate network for viewing pornography or other nonbusiness use, or possibly attempt to break into the human resources database.

Now, consider that files you might store on your PC to share with your friends might be entirely inappropriate for viewing at work. You might be sending or receiving private e-mail correspondence you wouldn't want coworkers or your boss to read. Your Web surfing or other online activities while connected to the company's network might be recorded in your employer's firewall logs.

These are reasons why it's important to separate your personal online activities from business activities. It might be tempting to use your company's free dial-up connection for online shopping or other personal activities during lunch or after business hours, but you are exposing information that might not only affect your credit but also your ability to earn a living. Always maintain a personal ISP and private e-mail account for nonbusiness purposes, using a computer that solely belongs to you.

If you can't avoid connecting to an employer network with your personal computer, encrypt your entire disk as we discuss in Chapter 2, so files can't be viewed by anyone but you. Never tell others how to access your employer's dial-up accounts. Lastly, always be cognizant of what files your computer is storing and what those files might say about you.

Digging Deeper...

There's Data in Those Blinking Modem Lights

In March 2002, the Boston Globe reported a story about a security vulnerability whereby activities on your modem lights can be used to monitor your network traffic (http://digitalmass.boston.com/news/2002/03/12/data_leak.html). A programmer at Lockheed Martin and a computer science professor at Auburn University wrote a paper detailing how your modem lights allow someone else to read your network traffic, by observing the blinks. When the modem is sending a bit of data, the light blinks on and then goes off. It happens so fast, it might be imperceptible to the human eye, but not to a hardware device.

How many of us have our computers or modems sitting on a desk in front of a window? While it's certainly not a widespread problem, we found this story intriguing because it shows how low-tech solutions combat high-tech problems: You can counter the blinking-light threat by simply putting a piece of tape over the lights. Or, you can move your modem away from the window.

Always-on Broadband

The newest trend in home computing is the always-on connection, known as *broadband*. With broadband, there's no need to dial up an ISP to connect to the Internet. A broadband connection is ready to handle network traffic from the moment your computer is plugged in and powered on. Each time you turn on your computer, the network connection is automatically established and waiting for your computer to use it.

Broadband is very attractive because it eliminates the time spent dialing up, getting busy signals, and configuring phone numbers in dial-up software. Broadband connections are also faster than those that dial-up modems can provide, making broadband more suitable for homes where the connection speed is important or a home with several computers. Moreover, this type of service is typically capable of handling data and voice calls simultaneously, unlike regular telephone lines.

However, the always-on connection exposes you to greater risk, and, when several computers share the connection, information contained on one PC might not only be exposed to the Internet but also to other computers on the local network. In this section, we look at some of the issues surrounding protecting your PC when it has an always-on connection.

DSL, ISDN, and Cable Modem

Every other television commercial these days seems to be touting the benefits of faster connection speeds you can get by switching to a *digital subscriber line* (DSL). A DSL connection looks essentially like the dial-up configuration shown earlier in Figure 5.1, but it's always on and much faster. It also might use a modem card inside your PC, connected to a specialized telephone line, in which case the issues for protecting this type of network connection are the same as those for a regular dial-up modem discussed earlier. Because your computer is connected to the Internet the entire time it is on, the risk is higher that someone will use the Internet to break into your computer and steal private data.

If you have an external DSL modem, your connection looks more like Figure 5.3. External DSL modems typically have one connector for the telephone line (shown on the left) and one or more connectors for plugging in computers (shown on the right). The telephone line connector might be labeled wide area network (WAN), and the computer connectors might be labeled local area network (LAN). You can think of the LAN as being local to your home, where your computers are (even if there is only one), and the WAN as being the Internet connection from the ISP. The DSL modem acts as the main route to the Internet for your PC and is known as the PC's *primary gateway*.

The cabling between an external DSL modem and a computer is typically *Category 5 twisted-pair Ethernet*, which is just a different kind of telephone cabling with four pairs of wires instead of one. In this type of network, your personal computer uses a network interface card (with the 4-pair Ethernet cable) instead of a modem (with a 1-pair telephone cable). You can tell the difference by looking at the end of cable, and counting the number of gold metal pins on the end of it. If there are two or four, it's a telephone cable. If there are eight, it's Ethernet.

Some ISPs claim to provide DSL modems with firewalls already included in them. If so, you should discuss its features with your ISP. You should look for the following firewall components, which we discuss in greater detail later in this chapter: Network Address Translation (NAT), outbound port filtering, content filtering, and intrusion detection. Sometimes, the DSL modem will provide only NAT but will be advertised as a full-featured firewall. If your DSL modem doesn't include all the mentioned firewall features and your modem is external as shown in Figure 5.3, you can install a network-based firewall device between your PC and the DSL modem to add the additional features. We discuss how to do that later in this chapter. If your DSL modem is internal to your PC, you'll want to use personal firewall software installed directly on the PC to add the firewall features your DSL modem doesn't provide.

Figure 5.3 A Simple Network with an External DSL Modem

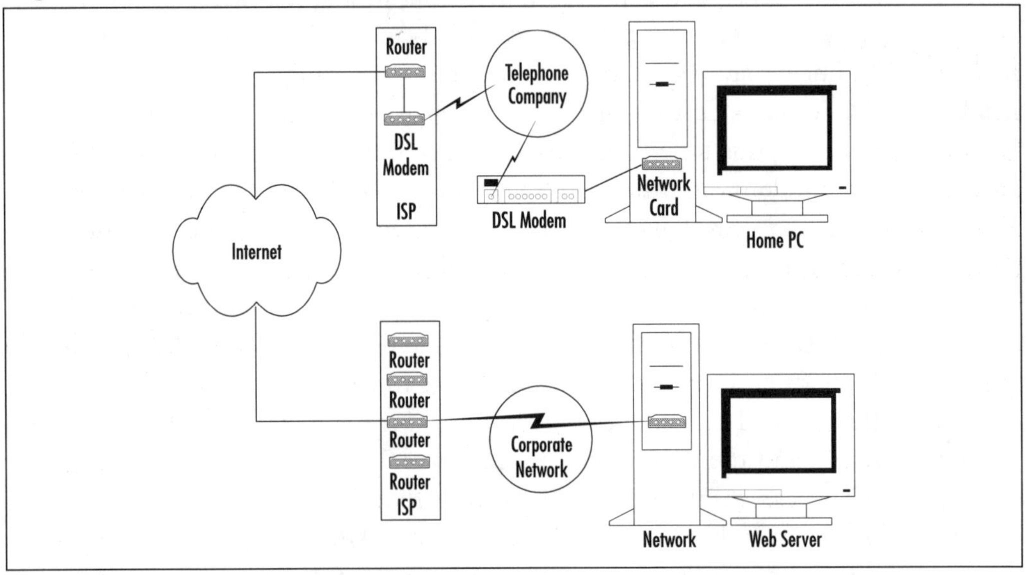

Cable Modem

A cable modem connects to your PC in a similar manner to DSL, except the speed is somewhere between a regular modem and DSL speeds, plus the cable coming into your external modem will be round coaxial cable from a cable TV company instead of a telephone line. Like DSL, your cable modem can be a card inside your PC or it can be an external box that sits between your PC and the cable from the cable company. Protecting your PC with a cable modem Internet connection is similar to protecting a computer that uses DSL, as described in the preceding section. If the cable modem is external and doesn't already include any firewall features, you can install a network-based firewall between your PC and the cable modem. If it's internal, you'll want to use personal firewall software installed on the PC.

The main difference between cable and DSL lies in the fact that several residences being serviced by cable modem might share a single connection with the cable company, whereas the connection between a residence serviced by DSL modem and the telephone company is not shared with another residence. The effect is similar to that of party lines in earlier days of telephone service. Because listening in on another conversation isn't as simple as picking up a telephone receiver, it's not obvious that the connection is shared. Cable modems are designed not to listen in on data that's not intended for them, but it's possible for a knowledgeable intruder to bypass those safeguards and intercept data for other residences that are sharing the same connection to the cable company.

ISDN Modem

An ISDN modem connects to your PC in a similar fashion as DSL, except ISDN has a fixed maximum speed of either 64K or 128K and uses plain 1-pair telephone wire. The cable coming into the ISDN modem looks like a regular telephone wire, but you won't get a dial tone if you plug it into a regular telephone. ISDN lines can provide data service and telephone service on a single 1-pair wire, whereas regular telephone lines can only do one or the other at a time. Like a regular telephone line, ISDN lines can be used to make local or long distance calls, so you'll probably have a long distance provider associated with an ISDN line just like your regular telephone service.

As with DSL and cable modem, if your ISDN modem is external and doesn't include any firewall features, you can install a network-based firewall device between your PC and the ISDN modem to add this functionality. If the modem is internal to your PC, you'll want to use personal firewall software installed directly on the PC.

Wireless

Wireless Internet access is the latest service offering for most ISPs (you might not be able to find a wireless ISP in your area yet). Some are available everywhere, broadcasting from a satellite directly to a dish installed near your home or on your roof, provided you subscribe to an ISP that offers this service. Some ISPs broadcast from a nearby radio tower to a different kind of satellite dish. In both cases, the dish is then wired to a card inside your PC using a USB cable. Figure 5.4 shows both types of wireless connections.

Both of these types of wireless Internet bring unique security problems for your personal information, because you are essentially broadcasting information to the entire neighborhood. A couple years back after a security convention in San Francisco, well-known security researcher Peter Shipley demonstrated that it was possible to drive around town with a radio receiver attached to his laptop, picking up network signals from the wireless networks for several area businesses.

His intention was to shed light on something most people didn't realize was possible, so they can prevent their networks from being broken into.

The same advice works for home-based wireless devices. You have no idea who's driving around listening to your online conversations. Wireless devices made for this purpose are readily available on the Internet, and there are no restrictions on who can purchase one. Many wireless services tout security options as the solution to this, yet wireless security hasn't been proven to be reliable. Unless you live in an area where high-speed Internet connections are not available, you might want to think twice about wireless Internet as your best option. The newest technologies are always the most easily exploited. You might want to let this one mature awhile before diving into it.

Figure 5.4 Satellite Internet Connection Diagram

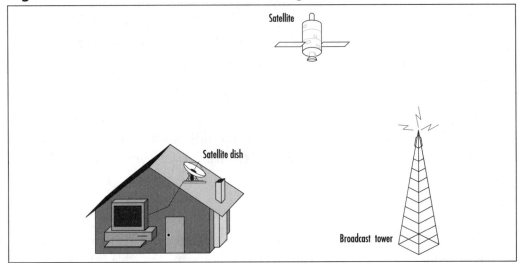

Understanding Data Interception

Before we examine some ways to protect your data using your home network, you should understand how data can be intercepted using the network. In this section, we present three ways someone might gather information about you by using basic tools, available to anyone, to inspect data from your computer without actually having to sit in front of it. If your Internet connection is via cable modem, for example, someone who is sharing your connection to the cable company could use one of the following methods or many other methods to learn more about you by inspecting your computer.

Snooping on a Network with a Sniffer

You can listen to a conversation between any two computers connected by a network (whether wired or wireless). This is done using a third computer running special software, plugged into the same network. When properly configured and connected, the computer and software are collectively called a *sniffer*, because the setup sniffs, or takes in, data directly from the network on which it's listening.

Normally, computers connected by a network are designed to ignore data that is not intended for them. A sniffer simply bypasses this function and listens to all data on the network, including that intended only for other computers. It then presents that data in a form readable by the person sitting in front of the computer running the sniffer.

Figure 5.5 shows how someone might use a sniffer. In the diagram, two computers are sharing the same Internet connection using the same DSL/cable modem. In this diagram, the home PC is conversing with a server on the Internet. During the conversation, data is passed from the home PC to the DSL/cable modem, which forwards it to the Internet (WAN) connection.

Figure 5.5 Using a Sniffer

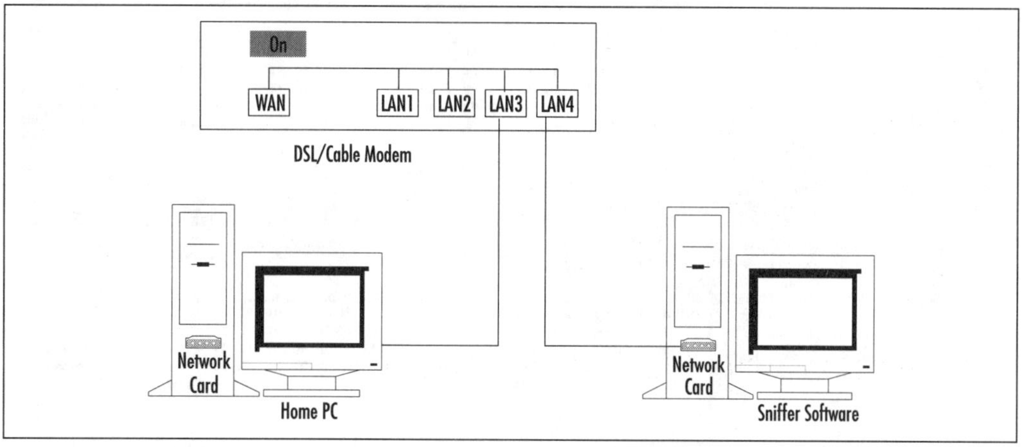

The wiring inside this particular modem copies network traffic from one LAN connection to the others. In the diagram, data that is sent to the Internet from LAN3 is also copied to LAN4. Normally, any other computer plugged into one of the LAN connections, such as LAN4, would ignore the traffic between the home PC and the Internet server. However, in this case, the computer plugged into LAN4 is running sniffer software, which listens to and records the conversation between the home PC and the Internet server.

When the user sitting in front of the home PC types in his Web password, it is copied to LAN4 at the same time it is sent to the Internet server and recorded by the sniffer program. When the user downloads his mail, the mail password is sent to the mail server and copied to the other LAN ports too. As the mail is sent to the home PC from the Internet mail server, the sniffer can record that too.

Figure 5.6 shows the type of information a sniffer setup like this can pick up. This example was made using software called Analyzer, available for free at http://netgroup-serv.polito.it/analyzer. This is a capture of Joe User's mail session. The two most interesting lines captured from the network are displayed. The first clearly shows Joe's account name "joe_user" in the data (far right). The second clearly shows his password "mypassword" (far right).

Figure 5.6 Sample Sniffer Capture

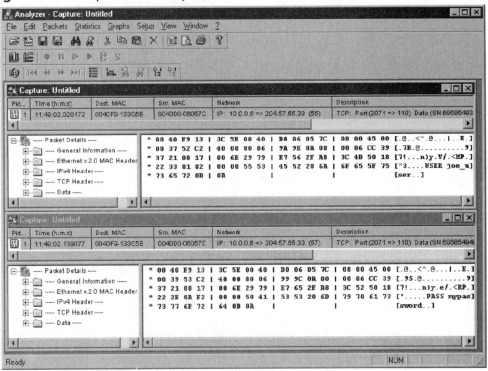

At this point, the person capturing the data knows Joe User's e-mail server (204.57.55.33, also known as hotpop.com), e-mail address (joe_user@hotpop.com), e-mail password (mypassword), and can read and reply to Joe's mail from here on out if he so chooses. Firewalls don't protect against this type of activity, because, for example, your mail password has to pass outside, through the firewall, in order to obtain the desired mail service. Of course, as discussed in Chapter 4, you should always make sure SSL is being used when you surf the Web, so that your passwords and data are encrypted. We also discuss encrypting individual messages and using secure SSL mail in Chapter 3. Anonymity software is also useful as a protection from network sniffing, because your real identity isn't associated with a captured password or login name. Figure 5.6 demonstrates what can happen if you don't use any of these protections.

Snooping on Your Network with Network Neighborhood/My Network Places

Microsoft Windows is notorious for broadcasting network information about itself for displaying in tools that show what the network looks like. One such tool displays all the computers on the network, including their shared drives, printers, and so on. This tool was called *Network Neighborhood* in older versions of Windows and is called *My Network Places* in Windows Me, XP, and other newer versions. We use the label *My Network Places* here to mean either tool.

Someone might be able to see shared files and hardware on other computers just by looking in My Network Places, shown in Figure 5.7. In this case, there are three shared drives and a CD writer. Because the drives are shared with everyone without limitation, someone can simply click one to view its contents. The tool doesn't say that the drives are shared without limitation, but it's easy enough for someone to find out just by clicking it.

Figure 5.7 Permissive My Network Places

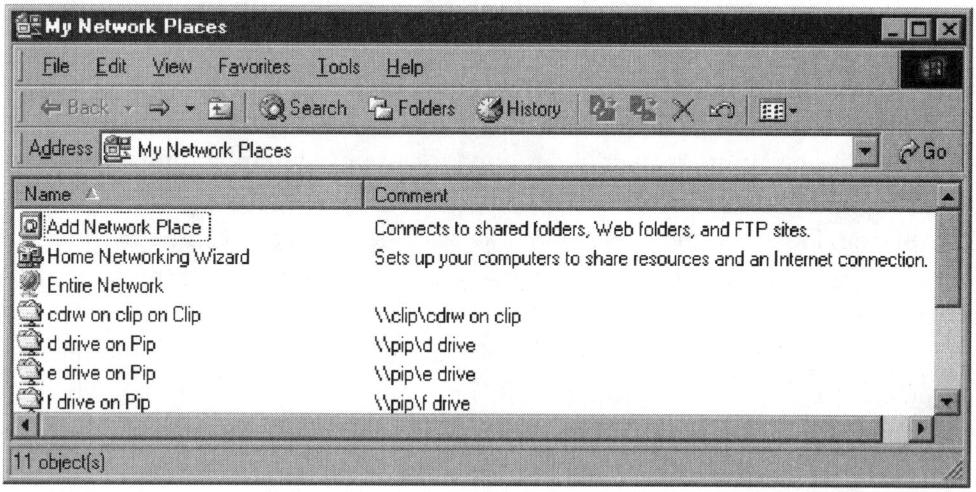

Don't forget, the whole reason we're looking at data on a network is to see what protections need to be installed. A firewall does offer protection against this type of snooping by preventing your PC from sending out information about shared resources. You can also configure your PC to stop sharing those resources, which we discuss how to do later in the section "Taking Precautions."

Snooping on Your Network with nbtstat

Connections to shared drives as shown in Figure 5.7 are possible because of a Microsoft Windows feature known as *Windows Networking*. Windows Networking is based on *NETBIOS*, a network service that Windows embeds into TCP/IP to add additional features that the TCP/IP protocol alone doesn't provide. Because it's embedded inside the protocol your PC uses to connect to the Internet, there's a potential that services provided as part of Windows Networking can be viewed by other computers you didn't intend to see those services.

In order for two computers to share files or printers across the Internet, both must be properly configured for TCP/IP, Windows Networking, and File or Printer Sharing. Additionally, both computers must either be on the same local network or there must be provisions made by the ISP to forward NETBIOS data between the networks on which the two computers sit. Generally, this only happens inside larger companies with multiple networks so multiple computers can share expensive resources, like laser printers or common file depositories. However, it's also possible that two computers sharing a DSL, ISDN, or cable modem connection can connect to each other using Windows Networking, if the networking equipment that separates the two computers isn't configured to block the NETBIOS network service. If you can see a computer in the Network Neighborhood or My Network Places, then Windows Networking is enabled between your PC and the other computer.

Windows provides a diagnostic utility called *nbtstat* as part of Windows Networking. This utility is mainly designed for use by system administrators to confirm if a connection between two computers is possible using Windows Networking. However, the command also has a side effect. It can be used to see who is logged onto a particular Windows computer that's sharing the same network connection.

Figure 5.8 shows the output of the nbtstat command directed at the remote computer named JOESPC. Note the last line under the *Name* column, which indicates that Joe User is logged on. Windows Networking has reported this information about JOESPC, including the security domain of which JOESPC is a member, along with who is currently logged onto the computer on which the nbtstat command was run. A knowledgeable computer user connecting to shared files on JOESPC using the information obtained in the previous section can view those files and also now knows that Joe User is a potential owner of those files. Hence, it's not possible to share files anonymously using Windows Networking. If a shared file contained, say, a credit card number but no name, it's not a far leap to match up that credit card number to the name Joe User.

Figure 5.8 Using nbtstat

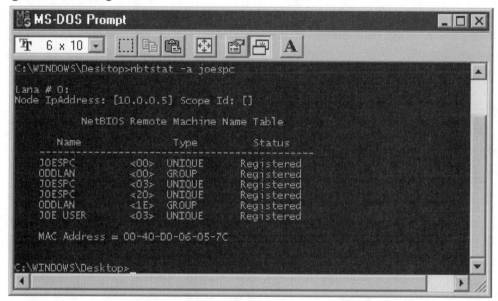

A firewall protects your home PC from this type of snooping by preventing outsiders from requesting this type of information from your computer. Another tactic you can take is to use a screen name to log into your computer instead of your real name. If you must use your real name because, say, your employer provides it, you need to be aware that the computer might be giving up this type of information any time it's plugged into an untrusted network, such as when you attend a conference and plug your laptop into the conference's mail network to read your e-mail.

While the likelihood of someone using nbtstat to see if you're logged onto your home computer is extremely small, try to understand Figure 5.8 as an illustration of one of the things computer criminals do best—taking disparate pieces of information (which might seem innocuous and unrelated to you) and piecing them together to get a whole picture of useful information. Cyber criminals understand how to use obscure tools to gather this information and might be listening at any time your computer is accessible.

Why is this kind of information useful to an identity thief? Because now she can configure her computer so it appears that she's actually sitting in front of JOESPC instead of her own computer. This is a form of attack known as *spoofing*. An identity thief can do this because she knows what login name and security domain to configure on her own computer. It's also useful from a social engineering standpoint. People are creatures of habit. A login name that is observed in one location has a high probability of working in another. Perhaps the thief already has guessed your online banking password but doesn't know what login name to use.

What You Can't See Can Hurt You

Scanners, Sniffers, and Worms, Oh My!

As mentioned in Chapter 2, a virus is a self-spreading program that can carry a malicious payload. It might delete files, destroy hard drives, or forward private information from one computer to another. Trojan software is similar to a virus in that it can carry a malicious payload, but its purpose is usually to provide a backdoor for later use by a computer criminal. A Trojan typically runs in the background, hiding from view, until it is needed. Some Trojans might be triggered to begin their malicious work remotely, days or months after initial infection. Others might just quietly send data back to a remote computer, capturing passwords and other data as you type.

What makes Trojans or worms tough to combat is their ability to spread themselves quickly combined with their ability to operate invisibly. But attack tools that don't spread themselves are still very useful for gaining information about you. A network scanner is a tool that attempts to find out what software you are running. If an intruder knows what services are running on your computer, perhaps he can find a bug published on the Web that will allow him to gain control of your computer.

Another tool often used by computer criminals is the network sniffer, which you are typically tricked into installing without realizing. You might be sent an e-mail asking you to click a link that installs the sniffer software and sets it to start automatically next time you reboot. As the sniffer runs, it might record keystrokes you send across

Continued

the network, including passwords, login names, and credit card numbers. The data might be stored in a file or quietly sent back to the data thief by e-mail.

The newcomer on the block is an insidious piece of software known as a network worm. Worms have been around for a number of years, but the newest ones can transfer between computers either by e-mail or by infecting a shared drive on the same network as the infected computer. Recent versions can spread two ways typically—by e-mail or by copying itself to shared drives on your network. If someone sends you a worm as an e-mail attachment and you click it, it will infect your system, send itself to everyone in your Outlook address book, and then copy itself to any shared drives on your network to which your PC can write. One computer on your home network is all it takes to infect all of them. Unfortunately, firewalls don't protect against this one, but e-mail filtering can. Use a mail program that's not vulnerable, and learn how to detect a suspicious attachment. One resource is Syngress Publishing's *E-mail Virus Protection Handbook* (ISBN: 1-928994-23-7).

Taking Precautions

Now that we've examined some things that can go wrong with a network, you should be in a panic about how much information is invisibly given away about you whenever you use a computer, right? No; that's not quite right. The purpose of this chapter isn't to cause fear, uncertainty, and doubt about your network activities. It's to show you, specifically, why you need to take network measures to protect your online identity, which we're now going to discuss. Not to worry, there are lots of actions you can take.

Unfortunately, configuring your PC to stop sending out resource availability information is impossible if you want to use standard Windows features, like file sharing. However, if you use a firewall, you can limit who is able to see the resource information. The solution is to place a firewall somewhere between your PC and the Internet, preventing remote computers from connecting to yours using Windows Networking. If you're running more than one PC in your home office, you can install a single external firewall device that all the computers can share. If you only have one PC, you can run firewall software directly on your computer.

If you live in a single-family residence with a DSL modem all to yourself, you might feel a sense of safety because you trust all the computers that are sharing the network connection. Perhaps you're a parent with one computer and a kid with his own. Or, perhaps you like one kind of PC and your roommate likes another, but you can only afford one Internet connection between you. You might feel safe but if someone targets one computer on your home network for a break in, you can be sure the rest of the computers on the network will be compromised shortly thereafter. One external firewall can protect them all against a directed attack aimed at any of them. We'll talk about firewalls in greater detail a little later, but first, let's take a look at some other simple tasks that you can do to prevent outsiders from accessing private data on home computers.

Setting Permissions for Shared Drives and Files

The first item on the agenda, regardless of your type of Internet connection, is to find folders you voluntarily share with other computers, check the share permissions, and stop sharing them, if possible. Windows XP makes this simple by providing a shared documents folder, but, under Windows 95/98/Me, you need to search for them either by looking in Network Neighborhood (My Network Places for Windows Me), or in each individual folder. If you're running XP, you'll need to log onto the administrator account to perform the tasks in this section. This is not required if you're running Windows 95/98/Me.

A shared folder possibly might be hidden, in which case it won't show up in Network Neighborhood or My Network Places. However, you can still find hidden shared folders. Before you begin your search, make sure you're able to view hidden files and folders on your computer. To do this using Windows Me, follow these steps:

1. Double-click the **My Computer** icon on your desktop, and select the **Tools | Folder Options** menu item.

2. Click the **View** tab, and click the **Show hidden files and folders** option.

3. Click **OK**.

To display hidden files in Windows 98, follow these steps:

1. Double-click the **My Computer** icon, and select the **View | Folder Options** menu.

2. Click the **View** tab.

3. Click the **Show All files** option, and click **OK**.

In either case, after you're finished, go back and uncheck the same setting so you no longer have to view hidden files and folders, to help protect any hidden system files from accidentally being deleted or changed.

In Figure 5.9, notice a hand displays under the School Projects folder. The hand indicates that the School Projects folder is shared. In contrast, you can see that the music folder isn't shared. Maybe you didn't intend the School Projects file to be shared, but someone in your household shared it once two years ago and it doesn't need to be shared any more (it's also possible that a virus might have affected permissions). You need to look at the permissions and clean them up.

Figure 5.9 Viewing Shared Folders

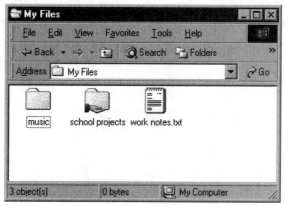

Figure 5.10 shows the permissions dialog box that pops up when you right-click a shared folder and select **Sharing** in the menu. If you don't have File and Print Sharing enabled on your PC, you won't see the **Sharing** menu item, and you can't have any shared folders. If this is the case, you can skip ahead to the next section.

In the School Projects case, the folder is set up as the SCHOOL share. There are three possible access types: **Read-Only**, **Full**, and **Depends on Password**. If the access type is set to **Read-Only**, then others can view files stored in the shared folder but can not change or delete those files. If you want only select others to be able to view the files, you need to also configure a **Read-Only Password** and provide it only to the users you authorize to view them.

If the permissions setting **Depends on Password** is checked, three possible password configurations are available: **none** (no passwords are used), **Read-Only Password**, and **Full Access Password**. The idea behind this password scheme is to allow you to give out the read-only password to others with whom you choose to share the folder, using the full access password yourself. This way, only you can make changes or delete files stored in the shared folder. If both password fields are left blank, no password would be required to either read or edit files contained in the shared folder.

If the access type is set to **Full** and no **Full Access Password** is required, files stored in the folder could be changed or deleted by anyone who can connect to the computer. Remember looking at the Network Neighborhood and My Network Places for open shares earlier? This is how those shares get configured. You really should never share files with full permissions and no password, so set one. Better, use a read-only password, and make your edits only on your computer. Better still, don't share the folder at all. If a few select people must be able to change or delete files in the folder, set the access type to **Full**, and enter a **Full Access Password**. Then, check the files that are stored in the shared folder to ensure that they don't contain any private data you wouldn't want others to be able to change or delete.

Figure 5.10 Setting Shared Folder Permissions

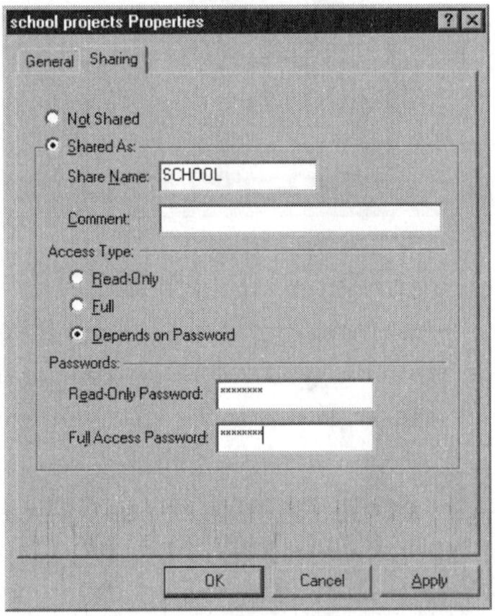

You can avert shared folder accidents by following a few simple rules when setting up shared folders:

■ Never, under any circumstances, share your entire C: drive or the directory where your Windows software is installed, because this can lead to being infected by viruses very easily.

- Examine each folder to ensure whether it really must be shared, and repeat this process at least monthly.

- Don't share folders unless absolutely necessary, and then use read-only access if possible.

- Never put important financial files—like tax returns, social security records, work vouchers, expense reports, or any other files containing sensitive information—into shared folders that others can access.

- Never install a personal Web server in a shared folder. This presents a security risk by allowing others to easily change or replace Web pages.

- If your employer provides special software called virtual private network (VPN) for your use in accessing the employer's network from home, you need to ensure that the VPN software is handling all shared resources. Otherwise, the data you intend to share with the employer via the VPN software could be accidentally viewable to the entire Internet. The VPN software might have a setting that allows some data to be shared with the Internet while the VPN is in use, versus requiring that all data use the VPN. The latter setting should be used, to prevent accidents. Discuss this possibility with your employer's system administrator if you need to share files and use VPN software at the same time.

Registering Your Domain.com

Have you registered your name as a domain yet? Or, do you own a small business for which you manage the Internet domain yourself? If so, you should make sure you haven't given out personal information in the process.

Domain registration reserves a certain Internet name for your use, such as joeluser.com. Many people like to use their name as the domain name, with their first name for their e-mail account, so their e-mail address becomes, say, joe@joeluser.com. Very easy for your friends to remember, but in the process, the owner might have published his name, address, and phone number in a world-wide database that anyone can view. This information can be harvested for phone numbers, e-mail addresses, and physical addresses for junk mail.

Figure 5.11 shows the result of a **Whois** query at a domain registrar on the Web. The domain joeluser.com is fictitious, but the figure shows the same information available for domains by other names. A better choice for Joe might be to ask his Internet Service Provider to manage the domain name on his behalf. The

ISP would then register the domain with its own address, phone number, and contact information instead of Joe's, while having no affect at all on the availability of Joe's new domain. If you subscribe to an e-mail service that provides your last name as your domain name, you should go to www.register.com and search for your domain name. If your personal information is shown, make arrangements to have it removed.

Figure 5.11 Viewing a Domain Name Owner Using Whois

```
Registrant:
Joeluser (JOELUSER-DOM)
    555 Nowhere Drive
    Yourtown, SC 29999
    US


    Domain Name: JOELUSER.COM


    Administrative Contact, Technical Contact, Billing Contact:
        User, Joe L. joe@joeluser.com
        555 Nowhere Drive
        Yourtown, SC 29999
        555-555-5555


    Record last updated on 30-Jun-2000.
    Record expires on 02-Jun-2002.
    Record created on 01-Jun-1996.
    Database last updated on 30-Mar-2002 04:35:00 EST.
```

Turning Off Unneeded Services

Every software program you run on your computer brings with it all sorts of bugs, some of which can be used to break into your computer to steal information. It makes sense, then, to minimize the amount of software running on your PC at any given time. This is particularly true with regard to network protocols. A network protocol defines the way information is passed from one computer to another. Running a protocol that's not needed holds the potential for sharing files or data without intending to.

Accessing the Internet means using the TCP/IP network protocol, but PCs might require other protocols for accessing a local area network, such as NetWare, IPX, Banyan Vines, LocalTalk, or ATM LAN Emulation. If the computer isn't part of a network (that is, there's only one computer in the home) and only needs access to the Internet, then TCP/IP should be the only protocol installed on it. If your employer provides the computer, be sure to consult with your system administrator to learn what protocols should be running, prior to removing anything. If it's your personal Windows PC, you can obtain help removing unneeded protocols from the Microsoft support Web site (http://support.microsoft.com). You can always reinstall a protocol later if you delete one by mistake. As always, if you're not 100 percent comfortable with what you're doing, consult a professional.

Figure 5.12 shows the pop-up dialog box depicting the kinds of network protocols that are running on a Windows Me system. To access this dialog box, click **Start | Settings | Control Panel | Network**. The figure shows that the TCP/IP protocol is installed and running over a Realtek RTL8139(A) network interface card (fourth line in the installed components box). If IPX were being used instead, the label "TCP/IP" would display as "IPX." Your network interface card will obviously be a different model than Realtek RTL8139(A). You might even have more than one, such as might occur if you've upgraded your home PC from a 10BT NIC to a 100BT NIC.

NOTE

If you have more than one NIC in your computer, you should take the time to physically remove any you don't actively use. Leaving unused network interface cards installed in your PC can cause conflicts with other devices on your computer. It also presents a security risk from multiple connections to your computer coming from different locations. It's not sufficient to remove an adapter using the Network icon in Control Panel, because Windows will attempt to reinstall the physical device the next time the computer is rebooted.

What you're looking for is two different protocols running over the same model NIC. If protocols other than TCP/IP are running and you're certain that you don't need the other protocols for connecting to a LAN, select the unneeded protocol, and click the **Remove** button. Don't remove any lines with TCP/IP in

them, and don't remove the network adapter itself, or you won't be able to connect to the Internet.

Figure 5.12 Turning off Unneeded Network Protocols

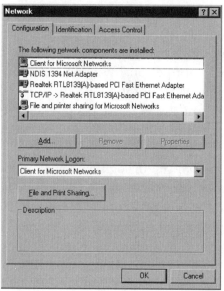

The **Primary Network Logon** shown in the figure—**Client for
Microsoft Networks**—is required to logon to Windows NT or Windows 2000
domains, which are commonly used by companies to provide access to specific
resources (shared drives, printers, and so forth) on their networks. If the computer
is provided by your employer, changing or removing this service could discon-
nect you from your employer's Windows NT or Windows 2000 domain, preventing you from accessing printers or shared resources at work. You should
consult your system administrator for advice if this is the case.

However, consider changing the Primary Network Logon setting to
Windows Logon if the computer is a personal home PC; you never use it to
dial into your employer's network; and you don't need to share a printer, CD-
ROM, or hard drive with other computers. This prevents your PC from broadcasting sensitive user data to the network. This is desirable, to prevent other
computers on the network from learning what drives might be shared or who is
logged on at the moment. As always, if the service is on and you aren't 100 percent certain if you need it, then you should consult with a professional before
turning it off. If it's already set to **Windows Logon**, then great—you're done!

File and printer sharing is needed if you need to share a hard drive, directory, CD-ROM, or printer from your PC to another; if not, or if there's only one computer in the home, then this can be turned off by clicking the **File and Print Sharing** button, clearing the check boxes, and clicking **OK**.

Your TCP/IP connection has a setting for using WINS, which is software that registers your PC with a Windows *name server*. A WINS name server provides a *mapping* between a computer's name, such as JOESPC, and its IP address, such as 10.0.0.5. If one computer needs to connect to a computer named JOESPC, the computer needs a name server to tell it what IP address to send the connection to, just like the U.S. Postmaster needs to know your home address in order to deliver your mail. Other types of software also provide this name service, such as Domain Name Service (DNS). DNS is the primary name service used on the Internet. WINS is used primarily within companies that use Windows NT or Windows 2000 security domains. If your computer isn't part of a domain and is not used to connect to your employer's network, you probably don't need WINS to be turned on. It's desirable to leave it off, to prevent your computer from broadcasting information unnecessarily to its network connection. Most people won't need this feature and should turn it off.

If you are using a dial-up adapter only, configure your modem so that it never accepts incoming calls. If your modem accepts incoming calls, others can dial into your computer and remove data when you aren't around. Consult your modem or PC's documentation for complete instructions for disabling this feature.

Securing Your Personal Web Server

Running a personal Web server is a popular way to advertise a home business or learn how to do Web programming. If you run your own Web server, you should secure it. Chapter 2 discusses the need to perform security updates for your software. Your personal Web server software is no exception. Before you allow others on the Internet to access your server for the first time, make sure you have downloaded and installed all the available patches for your software version. One of the more common ways to break into a computer is through buggy Web server software.

After you have patched your Web server software, you need to make sure it is properly configured. A common mistake is to install Web server software on a shared drive to enable others to post files to your Web server—instead, this enables them to install any file they want! Use the more secure features of a Web-publishing package instead.

Lastly, the contents of your Web pages might give away information you don't intend, especially if you use software to create the pages for you. If you open a Web page in a browser that supports viewing of the source code, you can sometimes view extra information placed in the document by your Web publishing software. Perhaps you create the pages manually using a plain text editor and wanted to take credit for writing it. Unfortunately, this provides more information than the general public really needs to know about you.

Figure 5.13 is an excerpt from a Web page we found on the Internet, viewed using Internet Explorer's source code viewing feature. I've replaced the name of the real author with a fictitious one here, but you can see the page advertises a login name (JoeUser) and an e-mail address (JoeUser@joeluser.org) unnecessarily. If you want to provide Web page readers your contact information, use generic information instead of a real person's name. The contact's e-mail address should be something like "info@" instead of "Mary.Whoever@." The first doesn't give any clues as to a human's real name, but the second does. You can give readers a P.O. box instead of a home address too, to obscure personal information.

Figure 5.13 Viewing Personal Information in a Web Page

```
<meta name="revisit-after" content="31">

<meta name="reply-to" content="JoeUser@joeluser.org">

<meta name="Rating" content="General">

<meta name="Language" content="en">

<meta name="Generator" content="ColdFusion">

<meta name="distribution" content="Global">

<meta name="Copyright" content="©2002 Consumer Sprocket Industry
Association">

<meta name="Classification" content="Business and Economy">

<meta name="Author" content="Joe User">
```

Firewalls for the Home

So far in this chapter, we've shown that dial-up, DSL, cable modem, and wireless Internet Service Providers might not provide privacy features essential to protecting your identity; you need a firewall to help with this. But, what is a firewall, how does it work, and how is it configured?

A firewall, in its simplest form, is any device that blocks incoming connections to your computer from an outside source. It can be software running directly on the computer, or it can be an external device that sits between your computer and its connection to the Internet. It can use one of several methods to perform its task. One method is NAT, which hides your computer's IP address by translating it to a different address seen by the Internet. Alternatively, it can use rules to filter out undesirable connections while still allowing your computer's real IP address to be used.

It can additionally provide the ability to filter outbound connections from your computer to the Internet, or set limitations on the times of day certain services will be passed out through the firewall to the Internet. It can provide content filtering, as a protection against viruses or as a protection from children viewing undesirable Web content. The firewall can also provide alerts when someone on the Internet is attempting to connect to your home PC inappropriately, a feature known as intrusion detection. In some form or another, all of these features should be present in order to properly protect any network from intrusion.

Any or all of these features might already be built into your DSL, ISDN, or cable modem. If you use wireless, your access point device might also provide these features. Or, none of the firewall features might be present. You will need to be familiar with your particular modem's capabilities in order to know what features you need to add. You can add them in the form of software running on your PC or in the form of external devices that perform the same task.

The decision regarding which firewall to buy depends on your network setup and some performance tradeoffs. If you are a dial-up user, you won't be able to use an external firewall device. If you are a DSL, ISDN, or cable modem user, the decision might depend on how many computers you own. If you have several computers, you might find that using a single external network-based firewall to protect them all is the cheapest and most efficient resolution. Or, you can choose to install firewall software on each computer independently. Generally, software on the PC is easier to upgrade than an external device, but, like any software, it might interfere with other software running on the PC. External devices don't place any additional load on your computer, and they are relatively simple to install. But, external devices are usually more difficult to upgrade. External devices also require you to have a network interface card installed on your computer, which you won't have if you are a dial-up Internet user.

For home use, essentially two types of firewalls are available—personal and network-based. The first we examine is in the form of software you install on your PC. We refer to this as a *personal firewall*, because it will protect only one computer at a time. Examples of personal firewall software include:

- Sygate Personal Firewall Pro (http://soho.sygate.com)

- Zone Alarm Pro (www.zonelabs.com)

- BlackIce PC Protection (www.iss.net)

The other type we call a *network-based firewall*. It's an external device you connect to your PC using Ethernet network cabling, with your computer's Ethernet connection going in one side of the firewall device and your home's Internet connection going out the other. Actually, both types of firewalls protect the network and could be called network-based, but we use this label as a reminder that your PC is connected to it using network cabling. Examples of a few external, network-based firewall devices include:

- Netgear External Security Router Model RO318 (www.netgear.com)

- Siemens DSL External DSL router model SS2602 (www.speedstream.com/products.html)

- Linksys EtherFast Cable/DSL Security Router Model BEFSR41 (www.linksys.com)

Before we dive into the unique features of network-based firewalls versus personal firewall software, let's examine a few features that firewalls share in general. First, all firewalls block incoming connections by inspecting data as it comes into the firewall. As such, they can be viewed as a wall between the *outside,* or untrusted Internet, and the *inside*, or the network where the computers being protected by the firewall are connected.

A firewall examines incoming connections, decides whether connections should be allowed, and then either lets the connection through or blocks them. To make this decision, it uses a set of internal rules to determine which connections should be blocked. These rules might not be configurable by you, the end user. Usually, a firewall provides some mechanism for logging connections it blocks, for later inspection.

The main differences in firewalls lie in how these functions are performed and what additional services are added to augment the firewall's primary function. For instance, some firewalls might provide Web content filtering in addition to blocking incoming connections. Others might provide e-mail content filtering. Still others might provide the ability to restrict the times of day when specified computers on the inside are allowed to access certain services on the outside.

Personal Firewalls for Home Office Use

Personal firewall software is installed directly onto your computer, as compared with network-based firewalls, which are external systems that connect separately to a network. If you have only one computer and use dial-up to access the Internet, then personal firewall software is for you. If you have one or more computers using a broadband Internet connection, then you can either install personal firewall software directly on the computer(s) or install an external network-based firewall device; it's your choice. If you only own one computer but share a network connection with roommates or have another arrangement, such as a dormitory where responsibility for a shared Internet connection is distributed among several individuals, then using personal firewall software on your computer will be much easier than requiring one person to manage a network-based firewall for the entire network. Personal firewalls are also particularly well-suited for single PCs that are used for both personal and business use, especially when business use involves a VPN connection to your corporate network.

Figure 5.14 is a conceptual drawing of how your PC is protected with personal firewall software installed. Connection requests from computers on the Internet are passed from your computer's modem to the firewall software through mechanisms provided by the operating system. The firewall software checks its rules to see if the connection should be allowed. If so, the connection is completed; otherwise, it is blocked. If the connection is allowed, data can then flow between the computer on the Internet and yours. If the firewall were not in place, the connection request from the Internet would automatically be completed and allowed. With it in place, the incoming connection is automatically denied unless you have set up rules in advance specifically allowing it.

Figure 5.14 Personal Firewall Software

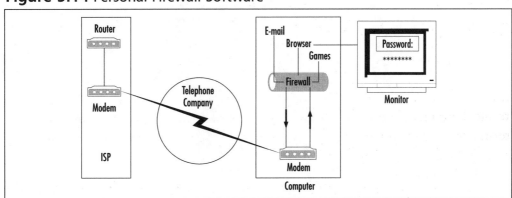

Outbound connections from your computer to the Internet work in a similar fashion. Software applications—such as e-mail software, Web browsers, or games running on your computer—pass data out to Internet servers through the firewall software. The firewall checks the Internet destination, type of service, and so on against its filtering rules. As you can see later in this chapter, most firewalls are configured by default to allow all outbound connections, but perhaps you've configured yours to disallow certain traffic to be passed to the Internet at certain times of the day. If the traffic should be allowed, the connection is completed; otherwise, it is blocked.

Figure 5.15 is a simplified diagram of how firewall processing works inside your computer. First, a firewall examines network traffic as it comes into the system on which it's running. It compares the type of service and possibly the source and/or destination of the traffic to a set of rules that are preconfigured into the firewall's software. It then allows or disallows traffic to be passed on to its destination, depending on the rules. The primary difference between all firewalls lies in how the rules are processed, and how well or how fast decisions are made about allowing and disallowing traffic.

Figure 5.15 Firewall Processing Conceptual Diagram

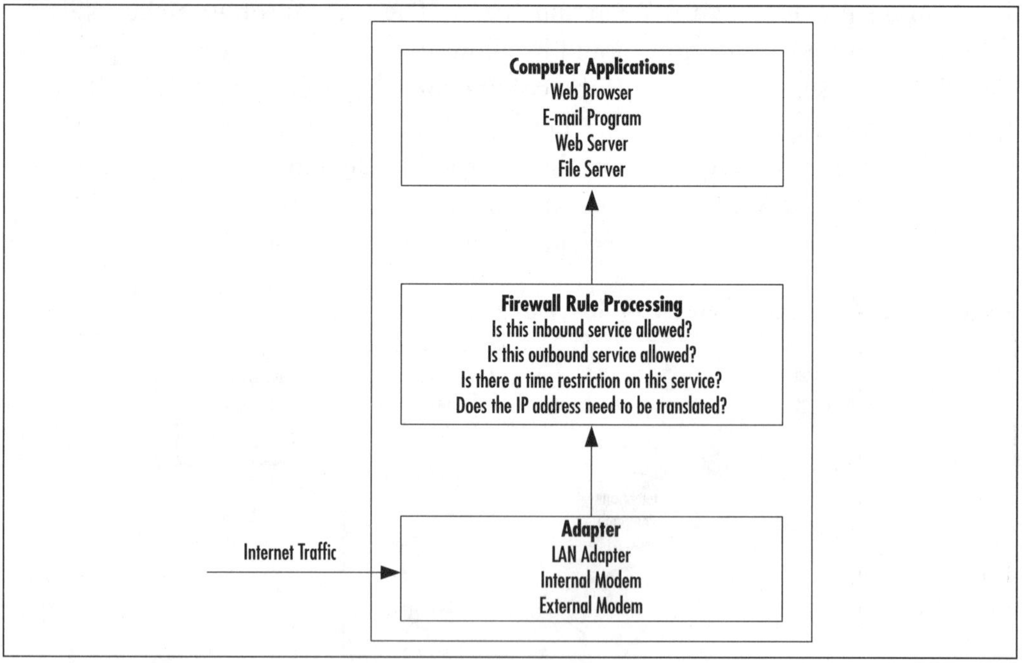

A poorly designed firewall might have a lot of false-positives, meaning it blocks desirable traffic unnecessarily. Or, it might have a lot of false-negatives, meaning it allows traffic in that shouldn't be allowed. The latter case is particularly bad, because a good hacker can exploit this type of design flaw to his advantage in gaining access through a firewall. Generally, as is true with most electronic products, popular manufacturers are popular for a reason. Their products are reliable or the value is good. Firewall software recommended by consumer review magazines, such as *PC Magazine* (www.pcmag.com) or *ZDNet* (www.zdnet.com), are probably good choices.

Network Firewalls for Home Office Use

If you have several computers on a home network that share an external DSL, ISDN, or cable modem, you can use a network-based firewall placed between the modem and the computers. These are often also called *DSL/cable routers* or *DSL/cable security routers*. They are external devices, about the size of a cable TV set-top box. These firewalls are very easy to install and configure, if you are lucky enough to have a DSL, ISDN, or cable modem with Ethernet as your computer's primary connection. The network-based firewall devices we discuss here are not for you if your Internet connection is a satellite dish connected to your computer using a USB cable or other non-Ethernet cable, such as might be required for Internet service via DirecTV or StarBand dishes. Some satellite Internet services, such as StarBand, require you to install special software called a *proxy server* on your PC. This software acts as your PC's firewall, so you won't need an external device in this case.

Figure 5.16 shows how a network-based firewall is connected to your DSL, ISDN, or cable modem and computer. The box labeled *DSL/Cable Modem* in the diagram could be a DSL, ISDN, or cable modem—we label it *DSL/cable modem* for brevity throughout the rest of this discussion. Because all three types of external modems typically have one Internet connection coming in and one or more Ethernet connections coming out to your computer(s), security issues revolving around them are similar (regardless of the kind of cable coming into the modem).

Your DSL/cable modem is typically leased from your ISP as part of your Internet package. The telephone or cable connection from your ISP plugs into a DSL/cable modem as part of your initial Internet setup. If you decide to install a network-based firewall, you'll connect an Ethernet cable from one of the LAN connectors on the DSL/cable modem to the WAN port of the network-based firewall using 4–pair Ethernet cable that typically comes with the firewall. You then connect the network-based firewall to all the computers that are to be protected by the firewall device using the same type of Ethernet cable. After this is done, you're ready to begin configuring the options available for your firewall, as discussed in the following section.

Figure 5.16 Installing a Network-Based Firewall

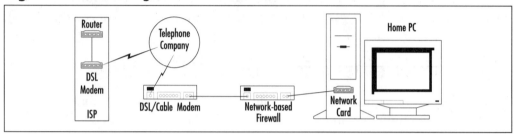

How a firewall makes decisions about traffic is a distinguishing feature that can affect its functionality and its price. Less expensive firewalls are capable of filtering traffic only based on the type of service, not necessarily where it came from or where it's going. These are known as *port filtering firewalls*. If you have this type of firewall, a service is typically either completely allowed or it isn't. This probably won't present a problem for most home users, and it's the least expensive product to buy. However, if you have several computers in a home office, maintain a Web server, or manage a shared network for several individuals, you might want to restrict connections to different computers in different ways.

For instance, you might want your Web server to be accessible to Internet users, but you don't want your child's personal computer to be available to Internet users. If your firewall only allows you to turn inbound Web service either **ON** or **OFF**, you won't be able to specify that incoming connections are okay for one computer but not another. Therefore, you would have to ensure that the firewall provides the proper functionality for your setup before you buy it.

Obviously, port filtering alone doesn't provide you any ability to allow or disallow services based on Web or e-mail content, either. However, your firewall might include an add-on product that provides this functionality, which we examine later in this chapter. Chapter 3 talks about a few add-on products for filtering malicious content from e-mail, in case your firewall doesn't provide it. Further, Chapter 6 discusses some other software-based approaches to Web content filtering, so it's not 100 percent essential that your firewall provides Web filtering.

The other type of network-based firewall relies on a different type of technology called *stateful packet inspection*. Instead of inspecting only the type of service, this kind of firewall also inspects where the traffic originated, where it's destined, and perhaps even some other details about the type of connection before deciding whether to allow it. This type of firewall can do a much better job of detecting common intrusion attempts because it analyzes more of the data as it passes through. You have much finer control over which computer can see precisely what traffic, but you also pay for it. Stateful packet filtering firewalls can run you twice the price of port filtering firewalls or more. The ones we found at a popular local retailer ran from $179 to $499. Compare that to the port filtering routers that ran from $79 to $149.

Using Common Firewall Configuration Features

Whichever firewall you decide to use, the options for configuring it will be very similar, though the settings might be presented in different ways, such as a Web page or a software interface that guides you through the process. This section is designed to explain the configuration options, point out the best settings, and describe how the settings help protect your computer from intrusion. See the Appendix for configuration specifics for several of the most popular internal and external firewalls.

Network Configuration

First, your firewall is going to need to know some information about how it is connected to the Internet. Internal firewall software will pick this up from your computer's network configuration, but you'll need to tell the software whether it is acting as the firewall for multiple computers on a home network or just the computer on which the firewall software is running. If it's protecting multiple computers, those computers will need to be configured to use the computer that's running the firewall software as their main route to the Internet, or *primary gateway*. External firewall devices might pick the network information up automatically from the DSL/cable modem, but it will provide a way for you to change the external connection (WAN) setting, if needed. Consult your firewall's installation instructions for complete details on configuring the network settings.

The network-based firewalls discussed in this book come preconfigured with the ability to assign IP addresses to all the computers on the network, which makes installation fairly simple. This automatic IP addressing service is called DHCP. You will typically just need to reboot your computers so they obtain a new network address that the firewall understands, and DHCP will handle the details. If your computers aren't configured to obtain their IP addresses automatically, you'll need to configure them to do so and then reboot.

If, for some reason, you don't want IP addresses automatically assigned, you can turn off DHCP on the firewall. It won't affect the operation of the firewall, provided that the computers the firewall is protecting send all their outgoing traffic to it. They will need to have IP addresses in the same numeric range as the firewall's internal (LAN) connection and be configured to use the firewall as their *default gateway*. Alternatively, it doesn't affect the performance of a firewall if some of the computers on your home network use IP addresses that are assigned by the firewall while others use static IP addresses you manually assign, as long as the addressing scheme is consistent for all the computers (including the firewall's internal LAN connection).

For example, let's say you have a home network with three computers on it sharing a cable modem connection. You decide to buy a Netgear RO318 external security router. You plug the Netgear WAN connector into the cable modem, and plug your three computers into three of the four Netgear LAN connectors. If the three computers are configured to obtain an IP address automatically, all you need to do at this point is turn on the Netgear security router and reboot the three computers. The Netgear will assign IP addresses automatically, by default, to all three computers using the numeric range 192.168.0.2, 192.168.0.3, 192.168.0.4, and so on, and the Netgear router itself will have the IP address of 192.168.0.1. If you want one of your computers to have a static IP address, you can configure that computer as, say, 192.168.0.50 without affecting the operation of the firewall. The computer's default gateway would need to be configured as 192.168.0.1 in this case. Or, you can turn off automatic addressing entirely on the Netgear, and give each of your three computers an IP address in this same range.

NOTE

The IP addresses given in the preceding example are specific to the Netgear RO318. Your firewall might use a different set of numbers by default. Consult your firewall's installation instructions for details about its default IP addressing scheme.

Next, you'll need to tell your firewall whether it should turn on network address translation to translate addresses. NAT is a mechanism for hiding what a network looks like on the inside. Figure 5.17 is a simplified diagram of how NAT works. The IP addresses on one side of the firewall are hidden from the Internet. The firewall translates the *inside* address to the *outside* address as the traffic passes through the firewall, and vice versa. This happens invisibly to you on the internal network, and it provides protection from attacks aimed at finding out what software you are running, among other precautions.

Figure 5.17 Network Address Translation (NAT)

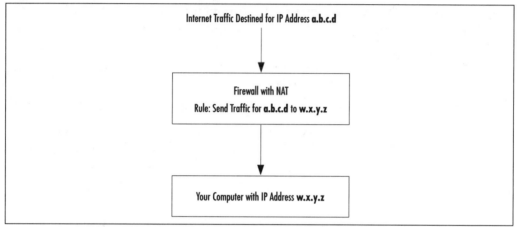

This might all sound pretty hard to configure, but some of the better firewall products come out of the box already configured with NAT enabled, ready for you to use, which is certainly recommended. The decision whether you need NAT is based on your network configuration. Your DSL, ISDN, or cable modem might already be performing NAT, in which case you don't need to enable it again on the firewall. It's still useful to install a firewall in this case, because the firewall will likely give you more security features than NAT alone on a modem would provide.

If you have several computers on a home network, you can install personal firewalls on each one, or you can use a single PC as the primary gateway to run the firewall software. The latter case particularly applies if you are using a satellite dish provider as your Internet connection, with a single PC as the proxy server, or are using Microsoft Internet Connection Sharing so that multiple computers can share a single broadband Internet connection. You probably need NAT if either of these is your situation, because your home network will not be in the same address range as the IP address provided by your ISP. The only computer that needs to be configured for NAT is the one acting as the primary gateway for the other computers on your home network.

The Siemens DSL router model SS2602 is an example of a network-based firewall that relies primarily on NAT to provide the firewall capability. It doesn't do stateful packet inspection, so it's not very good at detecting intrusions or logging any details about incoming connections. It also doesn't provide any Web or e-mail content filtering. However, it does provide the ability to limit the times of day certain services are available, and you can configure it to allow certain services in to only certain computers, as long as the number of computers and services is fairly small. It's also very cheap at $79, making it an inexpensive and suitable choice for homes with one or a few nonbusiness computers sharing a broadband connection. We included a sample configuration for this product in the Appendix, to get you started.

Setting Inbound Filtering

Your firewall software will provide the ability to disallow incoming connections based either on the type of service or some combination of types of service, time of day, destination, and/or source address. You can think of an inbound connection as a round-trip, originating from outside your home network and returning to the Internet with information from a visit to your system. Inbound connections originate on a computer you don't control and connect to a computer you do. Generally, all incoming connections from the Internet should be disallowed, unless you are running a service on behalf of Internet users, such as a Web server, music file server, or other service. Better firewalls are usually preconfigured to disallow all incoming traffic unless you specifically ask to allow something in.

Disallowing incoming traffic from the Internet doesn't affect your ability to view content on the Internet, because requests for content going from your computer to the Internet are outbound connections, not inbound connections. Inbound filtering is only concerned with allowing Internet users to see services you are providing to them, not the other way around. It specifies what connections are allowed *in* through the firewall. The point is that when you tell a firewall to allow an inbound service, such as Web service, you are opening a door enabling Internet users to connect to a service, such as a Web server, which you provide. If you don't provide a Web server, telling your firewall to allow inbound Web connections is unnecessary. Turning on any inbound service is commonly referred to as "poking a hole in the firewall," which should be done as seldom as is absolutely essential to prevent the firewall from becoming Swiss cheese.

When you are configuring any firewall option labeled *Virtual Server*, *Trusted Zone*, *Internet Zone*, *Protection Level*, or *Incoming Traffic*, you are affecting the kinds of connections that are allowed from the Internet into your home PC or network.

Most firewall manufacturers have tried to make the configuration simple for you by categorizing connections coming from the Internet as being labeled *High Risk*, *Untrusted Zone*, or *Paranoid* in the configuration, while connections going out from computers on your home network are categorized as *Low Risk*, *Trusted Zone*, *Cautious*, or *Trusting*. If you have only one computer, you won't have any trusted, low-risk connections, unless they come from your computer.

Firewalls that use stateful packet inspection will give you a finer level of control over inbound filtering. However, configuring this information into the firewall will be more involved. This type of firewall is probably not for beginners unless you understand TCP/IP fairly well and are comfortable with the concept of port numbers, so that you can make use of its more detailed features.

Setting Outbound Filtering

Outbound filtering refers to connections from your computer or home network outbound, to the Internet. Filtering outbound connections is the opposite of filtering inbound connections as described in the preceding section. It might seem odd to want to prevent your computer from connecting to information on the Internet, but it isn't really. For example, you might have a child in your home that you want to prevent using the computer at all during certain hours of the day. From a security perspective, the more ports (doors) you leave open on your computer for traffic to exit, the more ways a Trojan or virus has to spread to other computers on the Internet, if your computer were to become infected. Some services on your home PC might advertise information unnecessarily out to the Internet unless you take steps to block them. It makes sense to keep these opportunities to a minimum by filtering any ports (locking any doors) you don't plan to use.

Not all firewalls support the ability to perform outbound filtering, but better ones do. Most firewalls come preconfigured to allow all outbound traffic, perhaps with a few specific exceptions for risky outbound traffic most people don't need anyway. For this reason, it's safe to wait until the firewall is installed and protecting your PC from incoming connections before setting up any outbound filtering you want done. Outbound filtering should be a secondary concern.

For example, if you want to limit the time of day that certain operations, such as Web surfing, can be performed on your PC, you'll need to set up an outbound filter. Different types of firewalls label their menu settings differently. If you are configuring options labeled *High Security*, *Outbound Filter*, or *Client Filter*, or configuring outbound connections from the *Untrusted Zone* or to the *Internet Zone*, you are affecting outbound traffic to the Internet.

One type of network connection you should generally filter out is outbound DHCP and NETBIOS traffic. These are the services that Windows uses to advertise resources viewed earlier in this chapter with the *nbtstat* command. You will probably need to specify both the name of the service and its *port* (door) number in the configuration. Specifically, traffic destined both inbound and outbound to ports 67 and 135 through 139 should be disallowed. By doing this, you can continue to share printers and files to other computers inside your home while blocking the ability of outsiders to see them.

Some kinds of firewalls, such as Zone Alarm Pro, make setting up outbound filters fairly easy, by prompting you to set up a firewall rule each time you use a program that makes an outbound connection. You don't have to know specifics about protocols to be able to use this feature, which makes it particularly attractive to first-time firewall users. However, if you are sharing the computer with someone else, they might enable outbound traffic you don't want to be enabled. Your primary firewall gateway computer should be restricted to the firewall administrator only, for safety.

If you are comfortable with TCP/IP, you can also configure Zone Alarm firewall rules all at once, using the TCP/IP port numbers associated with each type of service. External firewall devices will typically provide a menu option for doing this from a Web page served by the device. Netgear's RO318 External Security Router and the Siemens SS2602 External DSL firewall both provide Web pages (www.netgear.com and www.siemens.com) from which you can configure outbound filtering, among other features, which are explained in greater detail in the Appendix.

The Appendix also includes a list of commonly used services and their respective TCP/IP port numbers. If you're not familiar with TCP/IP and you need to use an external firewall device that requires extensive understanding of port numbers, you should consider obtaining the help of a network professional in setting up your firewall for the first time. If your firewall allows outbound connections by default, some of the outbound services you should seriously consider blocking are those associated with peer-to-peer file sharing applications, such as Gnutella, Limewire, Bearshare, and so forth. We also recommend that you disallow IRC, the popular chat services, NetMeeting, and other video conferencing applications for reasons described earlier in this book.

Virtual Private Networks

Have you ever left your PC dialed into the Internet so you could move a large file off it after you get to work? Have you ever shared a drive from your home computer to everyone on the planet, just so you could deposit a file onto it from work later in the day? Then, you need the VPN features that certain firewalls can provide, to allow outsiders to access your computers securely. This is different than the VPN your employer might provide, which allows you to access the employer's computers securely. However, you should never run both at the same time or on the same home network, to prevent accidentally opening a door into your employer's network.

A virtual private network (VPN) allows remote access into your home network from other locations on the Internet, such as a corporate network, a Web kiosk, or a hotel-provided Internet connection. By using special security features to create an encrypted connection, your information is not exposed to anyone but yourself or people for whom you set up accounts. Because traffic across a VPN is encrypted, your passwords and personal information are protected from prying eyes while in transit across the Internet. Think of it as a tunnel through the firewall that nobody but you can use. As always, if you don't absolutely need this feature, then, by all means, leave it turned off. Use VPNs only with extreme care, because a VPN opens a door through a firewall.

Connection Alerts

When somebody attempts to connect to your PC from the Internet, do you want to know about it? If so, you should buy a firewall that provides a network security feature called an intrusion detection system (IDS). These firewalls, in addition to blocking traffic, can detect and report attempted break-ins. Better firewalls, with more complex intrusion detection systems, are able to recognize patterns of activity that indicate an outsider is attacking your computer, such as when a virus is knocking on the door or your computer is being examined for which services are running. The firewalls can store this alert information in log files for later review, or you can receive a pop-up notification immediately in some cases. You might also be able to have alerts sent to a single computer on your network, if you have several.

As an example of how different firewall products provide different alert logging features, let's look at four popular products to see how they differ with respect to alert logging:

- **Netgear** Netgear's security router model RO318, available for about $160, stores alerts in a log file until you're ready to view them, or it can mail the log file to you at periodic intervals. You can configure the timing of the mailings to be hourly, daily, or weekly, to suit your schedule, but there is no provision for updating what the router considers to be an attack. Over time, detection capability can become outdated as a result.

- **Zone Alarm Pro** Zone Alarm Pro has a main configuration menu that provides a tab for viewing the connection log and controlling the types of alerts you want to be stored, but this firewall won't e-mail the log files to you because the software runs on the same PC it's protecting. The types of attacks it can detect are also somewhat limited.

- **Siemens** The Siemens External DSL router model SS2602, popular for its low price of $75, doesn't provide any ability for IDS alert logging, adding or changing IDS signature definitions, or e-mailing log files.

- **Sygate Personal Firewall Pro v5** For under $50, the Sygate Personal Firewall Pro v5 has won *PC Magazine* and *ZDNet* Editor's Choice awards in part for its IDS functionality, automatic update capability, and comprehensive control over alert logging.

Any product that provides good IDS functionality will provide some mechanism for updating the database of signatures that comprise the known attack patterns, similar to the signature updates provided by antivirus software. The update mechanism can be manual or automatic, but shouldn't be missing altogether if the product is to remain current in protecting you from the latest attacks. Likewise, a good IDS product should provide you some ability to export or back up the log files, and it should provide information to guide you about the severity of the activities logged and the actions you should take as a result.

Configuring alert handling in any firewall should take into account how often you can review log files to see if corrections are needed to your inbound or outbound filtering configuration. If you don't periodically review the alerts, you might not know when you have a hole on your PC that outsiders are exploiting to grab information from your computer. It's a good idea to set up alerts so you see them and take action immediately.

Summary

In this chapter, we examined some of the ways your computer's network connection to the Internet can be used to gather data about you, about your computer, and about software your computer is running. We examined several kinds of network setups and made note of specific risks associated with each type. If you connect to the Internet using a dial-up modem, your computer is better protected than if your Internet connection is always on. Computers using dial-up Internet connections are less susceptible to intruders from the Internet, because they are only connected for short periods of time. Nonetheless, personal firewalls are necessary even with dial-up connections, to protect the computer while it is connected to the Internet. A firewall is important even if your dial-up service provider is AOL and you make use of AOL's parental controls features, because these features are not equivalent to the protections provided by firewall software.

Some employers provide dial-up Internet accounts for their employees to use. Employees are sometimes tempted to consider this a perk and use the service for personal online time. However, employers can and do extensively monitor how their network resources are used, and they are likely to intercept personal information from your computer as it traverse's the employer's network on its way to the Internet.

Don't use employer-provided dial-up accounts for personal online business, to ensure private data isn't intercepted by your employer. Likewise, never use an employer's computer to conduct personal business, such as online shopping or private e-mail, even on a lunch hour or after business hours. Personal data stored on the computer as such transactions are processed becomes the property of the employer. You have no control over how the employer stores or uses data. If possible, avoid using your personal computer for business purposes. If you must use your personal computer for business purposes, be sure to encrypt all the data on your disk using the methods discussed in Chapter 2. This will prevent your employer from accessing and copying data from personal disks that you don't want them to have.

If your computer is connected to the Internet using broadband services—such as DSL, ISDN, or cable modem—the connection is established automatically each time the computer is turned on. As long as an unprotected computer is powered on while plugged into its broadband connection, it is susceptible to intrusions from the Internet and needs the protection of a firewall.

Cable modem connections are similar to telephone "party lines," which existed in the early days of the telephone industry. The cable modem in each residence is designed to minimize the amount of snooping that can occur between residences sharing the same line, but these safeguards are not difficult to bypass. You can't be certain that other computers on the same connection aren't running a network sniffer or some other software designed to listen in on your computer's conversations. As a result, private data you send across a cable modem connection holds the potential for interception by others before the ISP receives it. This is why it's especially important to use encryption services as discussed throughout this book. Examples include Secure Pop as discussed in Chapter 3, and SSL for Web and e-commerce transactions as discussed in Chapter 4. Firewalls are especially important with cable modems to protect your computer against intrusion from the Internet as well as from other computers using the same cable modem line as you.

Identity thieves can make use of certain kinds of information about you and your computer accounts that is sometimes easily available from a network. We've examined several ways to view personal information using a network and several ways to block the visibility of this information. One way to view information on a network is to use special software known as a *sniffer*. Normally, computers only listen on the network for data that is intended for them and ignores traffic intended for a different computer. Sniffer software, however, is designed instead to listen to all traffic, even that not intended for the computer on which the sniffer software is running. This allows one computer to view the contents of transactions between two remote computers, including such sensitive data as account names, passwords, social security numbers, and so forth, as they are sent from one computer to another. Guarding against interception of data using a sniffer means making use of encrypted services whenever sensitive private data is sent across the network.

Another way to view private data on a network is by using the Network Neighborhood or My Network Places features of Microsoft Windows to connect to shared drives on a remote computer. Once connected, you can browse files stored on the remote system as if they were stored on your computer. If you share files or entire hard disks from your computer to another without requiring a password, this opens the door for anyone to connect to your PC and view the files that are stored on the shared disk. If possible, don't share drives or files. If you can't avoid sharing drives or files, be sure to share only the bare minimum of files necessary to accomplish the task at hand and require a read-only password. Disclose the password only to individuals who must connect to the shared files.

Don't share files with a full access if possible, because this gives others the ability to edit your files if they know the full access password.

Sometimes, mistakes in configuring a computer contribute to the availability of information you really don't want others to see. We examined a few of the more common mistakes people make when setting up a network, shared files, and Web services. When registering a personal domain name, be careful that your home address and phone number aren't disclosed in the DNS registry. (You can learn what information is reported about your domain using the *whois* service from your favorite domain registrar, such as www.nsi.net.) Another common mistake is running services that are not needed or allowing unused network interface cards or protocols to remain installed on the computer. Personal Web servers or Web authoring software holds the potential to disclose too much information about you. Be sure to examine Web pages you publish to ensure that they don't include your account name, e-mail address, or other personal identifiers.

Firewalls can help block connections coming into services enabled on your computers that you didn't realize were available or didn't realize could be readily exploited to gather information about you. The utility of a firewall comes from its ability to fill in security gaps inherent in your network configuration, thereby preventing some of the ways an identity thief might be able to access your private and personal information.

Firewalls come in two essential flavors. One form is software you install directly on your PC. The other is an external device that connects between your PC and the Internet connection provided by your ISP. The former is typically used for dial-up connections and when only one computer is using an always-on broadband connection. The latter is typically used to protect multiple PCs using Ethernet to share a single Internet connection, such as might occur in a small home business or when family members each have their own computers. Both types of firewalls generally provide default configurations that are sufficient for the average home PC user, but many also provide the ability to customize settings to suit your particular needs to perform Web content filtering, disallow certain outbound services, or restrict the times of day certain Internet services are allowed to be used.

Many less expensive firewalls can configure their own network connections when they are installed, but they also allow you to override the automatic settings if your ISP doesn't provide an automatically assigned IP address. Most will block all incoming traffic by default and allow all outbound traffic unless you ask for it to be blocked. If the firewall blocks incoming traffic you want to allow, you'll need to customize the settings for inbound filtering. These settings might use easy-to-understand labels such as *Virtual Server, Internet Zone, Wide Area Network, Outside, High Risk,* or *Paranoid* settings. If the firewall doesn't block an outbound connection that you want to be blocked, you'll need to customize the settings for outbound filtering. These settings might use easy-to-understand labels such as *Trusted Zone, Inside, Low Risk, Local Network, Trusting,* or *Cautious*. Firewalls might also allow you to customize settings for virtual private networks, to allow secure, encrypted access to files stored on a home PC. You also will probably want to configure how connection alerts are managed or logged, to meet your individual needs for periodically reviewing the connections your firewall blocks for you.

Don't forget, the reason we're taking a look at firewalls is to see how they can help you protect your private information, so you can connect more safely to the Internet. Firewall configurations should be periodically reviewed to make sure any inbound holes you have open are still essential, that outbound filtering is sufficient and appropriate, and that alerts are being properly logged and reviewed. Your particular firewall might even offer features to protect e-mail, which should be periodically reviewed to ensure they are still correct for your e-mail setup.

Solutions Fast Track

Different Connections, Different Risks

- ☑ Most people use dial-up connections to access the Internet. The ISP providing your connection doesn't typically provide virus protection or any filtering of network traffic coming into your computer. Other computers on the Internet can use commonly available tools to view personal information about you when your computer is connected to the Internet.

- ☑ Employer-provided dial-up accounts bring a special risk from snooping by employers. Privacy laws are murky when your personal computer is being used to connect to an employer network, so keeping business separate from personal Internet use is essential.

- ☑ Broadband connections can be shared between households, bringing additional risk from network snooping among neighbors sharing a single Internet connection. Sniffers and common Windows utilities can be used to learn information about other computers sharing the connection.

Taking Precautions

☑ Sharing files on a computer is an easy way to mistakenly give out private information you don't intend to be seen by others. You should examine any shared files or devices periodically to ensure the permissions are set correctly.

☑ You might be giving out address, telephone, and e-mail address information in your personal domain registration. You can use generic information, such as P.O. boxes or nondescriptive e-mail addresses, for contact information in Web pages or on domain registrations.

☑ In the process of setting up your network, you might have enabled services you don't need. Sometimes, programs you install turn on services for you, whether or not you want them to be on. Turning off unneeded services in Control Panel reduces the ways in which a thief can connect to your computer to gather information about you.

☑ Personal Web servers are a fun way to learn about programming or provide advertising for a home business, but they can also hand out too much information about you. Web authoring software might insert private information into Web pages without your realization, and Web server software might need specific security settings.

Firewalls for the Home

☑ The choice of a proper firewall for home use depends on your type of network, the services you need, and what you want to protect. Dial-up and satellite networks using a proxy server typically need a personal firewall installed on a gateway PC. Home networks sharing a single Internet connection typically need a network-based firewall device.

☑ NAT is network address translation, a feature supported by many firewalls. NAT enables you to hide the IP addresses on the inside network, so computers on the Internet can learn less information about the inside network.

☑ Firewalls prevent connections coming into or leaving the home network. Generally, disallowing all inbound connections and allowing only essential outgoing connections is a good idea. For finer granularity in setting up filtering rules, a stateful packet filtering firewall should be used, although it costs more.

Frequently Asked Questions

The following Frequently Asked Questions, answered by the authors of this book, are designed to both measure your understanding of the concepts presented in this chapter and to assist you with real-life implementation of these concepts. To have your questions about this chapter answered by the author, browse to **www.syngress.com/solutions** and click on the **"Ask the Author"** form.

Q: Does a firewall prevent hackers from breaking into my computer?

A: A determined hacker will get into your system regardless of the precautions you take, but a firewall greatly reduces the risk.

Q: I'm afraid that if I install a firewall, my e-mail will quit working, and I won't know how to fix it.

A: Don't be concerned about this. When you start an e-mail program on your computer, it connects outbound to your ISP's mail server to retrieve mail. Personal firewalls, such as Zone Alarm or Black Ice Defender, only block incoming connections by default (that is, incoming connections that start somewhere on the Internet and try to connect to your computer). Outbound connections starting on your PC are not affected unless you make a change to the default configuration. You can also contact the product's technical support division for assistance if a feature or program stops working.

Q: I installed a personal firewall and now FTP won't work anymore. What do I do?

A: FTP is an odd service, because it doesn't use the same port for inbound and outbound traffic. You open an outbound connection to an FTP server on one port, and then the server opens a data connection back to you on a different port. If your firewall understands the FTP protocol, it will account for this on its own. If not, another solution would be to get some FTP software that supports the PASV function. This makes the protocol two-way; so it works over your outbound port 21 connection in both directions, no firewall holes necessary.

Q: I have several computers on my home network. How does a firewall keep track of which one is connecting to which service at any given time?

A: When your computer connects to a particular service on a particular server, the firewall records the destination IP address and service type along with your computer's IP address. It can distinguish your connection from another's because they came from different IP addresses inside, even if the firewall translates them to a different IP address using NAT.

Q: Do firewalls protect against viruses, or do I still need antivirus software if I install a firewall?

A: If the firewall allows a connection between a virus-infected computer and your computer, then your computer can also become infected. You still need antivirus software.

Q: My ISP says my DSL router has NAT, so I don't need a firewall. Is this true?

A: No. Network address translation without a method for filtering malicious traffic isn't enough to protect your computer. You need both.

Chapter 6

Are Your Kids Putting You at Risk?

Solutions in this chapter:

- Raising Children in the Digital Age
- Identifying Risky Software and Risky Behavior
- Monitoring Online Activities

☑ Summary

☑ Solutions Fast Track

☑ Frequently Asked Questions

Introduction

It would be nice if we could create a visual profile for ourselves of what an identity thief looks like. If we could, it would be simpler to avoid them. However, it's
difficult to merge our mind's images of thieves and hackers into a portrait of a
cyber criminal, and rightfully so. It's as incorrect to profile a cyber criminal as a
young teenager as it is to apply that same generalization to car thieves. There
simply is no common psychological or physical profile of a cyber criminal,
because a cyber criminal is anyone who performs any crime by using the aid of a
computer.

Psychologist Marc Rogers attempted to categorize cyber criminals according
to a variety of computer skill levels and motivations in his 1999 paper entitled
Psychology of Hackers: Steps Toward a New Taxonomy (www.infowar.com). Toward
the extreme end of dangerous criminal activity, he observed several categories of
adults exploiting access to information through employers or other positions of
authority, some even acting as mercenaries of corporate espionage. An example of
an identity thief from this group might be a disgruntled employee seeking
revenge or an opportunity to make some money selling social security numbers
or credit card numbers illegally. Sexual predators seeking victims on the Internet
fall into this category as well. Young people are especially vulnerable to crime,
including identity theft, when encountering these people on the Internet. This
chapter will offer you some help in protecting younger family members in this
situation.

Toward a less dangerous extreme, Rogers observed several categories of young
people whose activities range from juvenile delinquency to first-time criminal
encounters. He labels these groups *Cyber Punks* and *Toolkit/Newbies*, and notes
their ages are typically 12 through 28. An example of an identity thief from this
group might be a young person learning about the inner workings of computers
or network security, discovering how to steal private data from Web sites in the
process. Or, it might be a young person with little financial means stealing
another person's credit card to buy a coveted piece of electronic equipment. This
young person might be your own child living at home or attending college. You,
as a parent, might still be able to influence the direction this young person's life
might take. This chapter will offer some real-life illustrations to help you recognize (and hopefully prevent) your child's potential for criminal activities, like
identity theft.

Raising Children in the Digital Age

Rogers observed that many people have a forgiving attitude toward the term *hacker* due to its early, ethical beginnings when "MIT hacker" meant a very bright young male who had a gift for using computers for creatively solving problems. Today, the term is commonly associated with anyone committing crimes using a computer, much to the dismay of those who still consider it an ethical moniker.

The result is a two-faced societal view of a hacker. Parents of computer literate children probably prefer the pride-worthy portrait of a tech-savvy college-bound genius with complete command of technologies outside the grasp of his or her parents' understanding. A less desirable but nonetheless common portrait is that of antisocial juvenile delinquent, using a computer to find acceptance into a peer group by performing illegal acts accepted by the peer group as lofty (sounds like gang behavior in the digital age, doesn't it?)

In reality, teens charged with computer crimes are very similar to teens charged with other types of crimes, like car theft. They have much time on their hands as the result of being nonworking students. They are often disenfranchised in their peer groups, and their activities are grossly unsupervised, Rogers notes.

Parents understandably want to provide their children with every possible advantage to further their education. Providing a family computer is an obvious way to accomplish this. According to the National Telecommunications and Information Administration (www.ntia.doc.gov), ninety percent of children in the Untied States 5 through 17 years of age (48 million) now use computers. Seventy-five percent of children ages 14 through 17 use the Internet. But kids are often handed this complex tool with virtually no instruction about unethical uses or the legal consequences of their actions.

Schools are beginning to teach kids the technical and safety aspects of computer use, but ethical and legal aspects are still not being taught in many cases. Only recently have programs like SafeKids (www.safekids.com) started to appear on the scene, to teach parents and children about using the Internet safely. These programs don't usually focus on safety risks posed to the parent by the child's Internet activities, because most are concerned with protecting children themselves from becoming victims of crime on the Internet.

Your task as a parent is made more difficult because you must educate yourself before you can educate your child about unethical and illegal uses of a computer. Many parents lack the ability to fully distinguish between legitimate learning versus illegal or unethical computer activities of a child. It's not surprising that parents should find themselves in this situation. The Internet sprang up in short order, without a "good parenting" instruction guide.

Nobody warned parents that they needed training on a computer before providing the tool for a child's education. It's also much easier to believe your kids are on the road to success than to learn the technical skills necessary to properly monitor their online activities. But every teen that has broken into a Web site, impersonated someone else, stolen credit card numbers, or used a computer to perform some other illegal activity is the child of someone who missed an opportunity to teach him or her that such behavior is wrong.

Without proper parental intervention, your own child might be "in training" as a victim or a perpetrator of a computer-related crime. With early parental involvement to educate kids about unethical and illegal uses of the computer, some of crimes of identity theft, (along with other computer-related crimes), can be prevented. Still more identity thefts can be prevented by teaching your kids as well as your self the same techniques presented in this book for reducing personal risk factors for identity theft.

In the process, though, it's important to give kids leeway to dissect the Internet to see how it works. Students using a computer shouldn't be discouraged from learning how to "hack," using the definition of "creatively solving problems," or "taking things apart to learn how they work." Learning how computers, networks, and software operate isn't wrong, unethical, or illegal. Prying open the lid on computer programs to see what's inside is a good way to learn how to use the programs in creative ways. It's how kids learn to be innovative.

What they should be discouraged from doing is using their technical computer skills to harm others or perform criminal or unethical activities, such as removing or copying data from a computer they don't own. They need to be taught how to be streetwise on the Internet and how to recognize risky behavior that can result in accidents that expose private information unnecessarily. They also need to be taught where the line of ethics and legality in using a computer is drawn and what the consequences of their actions can be.

We ran into this in the following true story of a father-son relationship:

The son is a big fan of online computer games, the kind that allows people across the globe play against one another using the Internet. When he was 12 or so, the father discovered that the son had a war, of sorts, going with one of the online players and had tricked the other fellow into disclosing his game password. The son logged on as the other player and caused the other player's game character to give some prized game items to the son's game character. Because it was a computer game, the boy considered it cheating, but he didn't consider it stealing or otherwise unethical. He did it, he said, because the other player had once stolen some valuable game items from his character in the past.

The boy pointed out that there were entire Web sites devoted to software and game cheats that made it easier to gain an advantage over other players of this particular game. If this activity were stealing, he argued, why would these cheat sites exist? The father learned that the son often frequented such Web sites and had downloaded programs and scripts designed to allow him to play in ways that weren't originally built into the particular online game. In other words, the boy was hacking the game so he could achieve a result—to be the best at it. He viewed this as making his play more enjoyable.

The father viewed it as the son learning how to use his computer to get something he shouldn't otherwise have had access to. Computer security experts often use the term *script kiddie* for kids who download software written by others in order to break into a computer or online account. Script kiddies don't know how to write their own software, so they "borrow" software from the Internet to solve their immediate problem—skirting or flying over the edge of legality in the process. The father pointed out to the boy that this is exactly what the boy had done, and that using other people's accounts and passwords is wrong, even if it's "only a game."

In this example, there are two worrisome aspects to consider. First, the boy didn't recognize his actions as theft. We've seen this attitude before. It's common among technically savvy young people to view information as something that should be freely available. Passwords, software code, or games—anything that can be found on the Internet—are viewed as just another piece of freely readable information, like words in a library book.

Kids pass around toys; kids pass around books. Kids also sometimes swear not to tell secrets and then do. Why should elements of a computer game be any different? The concept the son (in the preceding example) failed to grasp had more to do with the notion of information ownership and copyright than possession of something tangible. Adults haven't even quite worked these issues out for themselves yet; it's no wonder kids have trouble understanding what a password really means. The father had to explain it to the boy in terms he could understand. So, the father explained that there are certain kinds of information that are private, and must not be shared with others, regardless of the situation. Just as the father expected the boy not to give his name to a stranger who asks, the father also expected the boy not to share passwords or account information provided for his use. The other boy's parents expect the same of him. The father helped his son understand that using the Internet is a privilege that brings with it this responsibility and showed him how he had caused harm to the other boy by taking his private information through trickery. Finally, the father showed the boy how he had caused harm to himself, because this was no different than copying someone else's answers on a test.

The secondary concern was that the boy used the father's Internet account to perform his activities. The whole family shared a single computer and Internet account at that time. It would have been impossible for the father to prove that any illegal activity was the boys and not performed by the father or someone else in the family. It was time for the father to create some boundaries between the online identities of all his family members.

Keeping Clear Online Identities within Families

Many families are in a similar boat, sharing a single computer and a single ISP account among all household members for the following reasons:

- It makes economic sense.

- It's expensive to provide a computer to each family member.

- Each new computer needs its own telephone line to avoid competing for the one family line for dialing up the Internet.

These reasons are valid. However, sharing computers presents everyone using this same Internet account as the same identity to outsiders. The computer's IP address identifies the computer, not the person sitting at the keyboard. Software serial numbers, known as Global Unique Identifiers (GUID), are unique to a given computer, not the person who creates documents using the software.

Unlike a telephone conversation, an e-mail conversation doesn't give the out-sider the benefit of hearing a voice as an age clue. It's thus impossible for an out-sider to tell whether the person currently logged onto the computer is a child or a parent. As a result, access to your computer gives your child an unprecedented ability to take on your identity.

When you share a single ISP account and password with a child, the password is exposed not only by your own activities but that of the child as well. You would never share the password with a stranger, but are you certain your child would not? Kids don't always know the ramifications of sharing or stealing a password. Tell your child explicitly that passwords must not be shared, and stealing other peoples' passwords is wrong. If you can, protect your own private information by providing a separate online account and e-mail account for your child's use. (We discuss how to create multiple accounts in Chapter 2.)

Digging Deeper...

Global Unique Identifiers

GUIDs are numbers that are embedded in files and programs to indicate software versions or other information needed by the software or operating system. GUIDs embedded in Microsoft Office 97 or Office 2000 documents, such as Word documents or Excel spreadsheets, have been found to include the GUID of the computer's card, which is unique for each computer. This enables documents produced using the software to be traced back to the computer that was used to create them.

Some people are provided dial-up Internet access through their employers for business purposes, as we mentioned in Chapter 1. It's tempting to consider this a job perk and allow the entire family to use the account for homework or other personal activities. But each time a child logs onto your account, he is impersonating you, from the employer's perspective. The employer might monitor his activities and believe they are your own. You might not realize the child is engaging in behaviors you don't want your employer to see. Your child might be disclosing private data about you in the process. Your identity is indistinguishable from your child's when this happens.

We also know of a true-account story of this situation. An employer provided a man an always-on Internet connection for his home office, which he used with a personal computer. The man didn't realize that, after he went to bed at night, his child used the computer for personal activities that were recorded in the employer's firewall logs. The firewall administrator fortunately was a friend and gave the man some leeway to correct the problem. He could just as easily have been fired for personal use of business resources, even though the child's activities were not his own. The man's mistake was in not providing a separate, personal dial-up account and computer for his son's use, however remote he viewed the chance that the child would use it when the man wasn't around to monitor the child's activities.

Another family had a similar problem. The father recently bought a computer for his college-aged son. Because the father is only now learning how to use e-mail, the father and his son share the son's university-provided dial-up account. It's impossible for an outsider to know if the person sitting at the keyboard is the father or the son. If the son were to engage in an illegal activity using this computer, it would be technically impossible to distinguish who actually committed the crime, other than perhaps motive or some other nontechnical aspect of the crime. If the son were to disclose private data about himself, that data is automatically associated with the father because they both share the same computer.

This is a particularly bad situation for the father, because he's a federal agent. It's easy for the son to, say, download copyrighted music files or DVDs from the Internet, and not realize he's done anything wrong. (We work with computer security every day and find it nearly impossible to distinguish between copyrighted versus free music and movies on the Internet. How can we expect our kids to be any better at it?) What if the son downloaded a file that was infected with a password-stealing Trojan virus? Accidents can happen.

What You Can't See Can Hurt You

Finding You Is Easy

Another complicating factor in separating a parent's identity from a child's identity is the trend for schools to require an e-mail address for sending school notices and information to parents. Some parents provide their e-mail addresses for this purpose, which then become published in a school directory. It's not a good idea to use an employer-provided e-mail address for this purpose, because it belongs to the employer. Doing so blurs the distinction between your employer, you, and your child. If you need to provide an e-mail address to your child's school, provide one that doesn't imply your child's (or your) real name, to protect your child's identity in the event the e-mail address must be used by several of the school staff members. Also ask that the address not be published or publicly associated with your child's name.

Supervising Online Activities

In Chapter 1, we discuss some ways that you can be tricked into disclosing private information unnecessarily through the use of social engineering. The same risks exist for your child. Even if you provide your child with a separate e-mail account, the child might receive the same type of e-mail scams as we discuss in

Chapter 3. He might be tricked into disclosing his own private information or, worse, yours.

Children who are allowed to use your computer to download programs might accidentally install virus-infected software on your system, just as you might. Unless you monitor your child's downloads, he or she could inadvertently install Trojan virus software that steals the passwords you use for online trading accounts, online banking or other financial activities. You should keep an eye on everything your child does using a computer that stores private information you wouldn't want made public.

Sometimes accidents can happen even when you are watching. This happened to a friend just last year. Her son received a new digital music player for Christmas and needed to upgrade the software for it. There was a fee for the upgrade, so she gave him her credit card to enter onto the Web site prior to downloading the new software. She watched him enter the credit card number, but not closely enough. He forgot to check to make sure SSL was being used and didn't look at the site's certificate before completing the transaction. The mother hadn't done any research into the integrity of the Web site, so it was impossible for her to know if her son had disclosed the credit card number to the legitimate site or to an imposter site. Sometimes, noticing what your child is *not* doing is as important as watching what they *are* doing. The mother took the opportunity to teach her son the importance of checking for the SSL icon and verifying the site certificate before entering a credit card number.

Kids are also prone to sharing passwords among themselves. It's hard for a child to keep a secret, especially one like a password. Knowing the password makes a kid feel important, and sharing the password means getting to demonstrate that fact. If one child gets grounded from the Internet, he might borrow a friend's ISP account so they can play their favorite online game. You have no way of knowing if your child's friends use your computer or ISP account unless you routinely monitor its use using activity monitoring software, such as the ones we examine later in the section "Monitoring Online Activities."

Channeling a Child's Interest in Hacking

Computers are intriguing pieces of machinery to kids who love to learn how things work. Introducing computers to children as a platform for playing online games can teach them how to type, how to use a mouse, how to download files, how to dial up an ISP, and how computers work in general. Once children become absorbed in the computer, they tend to learn intricate ways to use the computer to solve problems. They share their discoveries with their friends.

Cyber criminals don't just wake up one morning and decide to break into a Web site. They learn over time, as script kiddies, solving problems like how to make computer games do what was never intended. As they learn, they might become quite sophisticated. For instance, consider the very young ages of some very sophisticated cyber criminals:

■ In January 2001, 18 year old Dennis Moran, calling himself Coolio, pled guilty to breaking into several military computers and a well-known security Web site. He used his personal Internet service and downloaded programs he used during the attacks, according to David Saver, special agent with the Army Criminal Investigative Command's Computer Crime Investigative Unit.

■ In September of 2000, a 16 year old Miami resident calling himself c0mrade pled guilty to cracking Department of Defense computers used by the Defense Threat Reduction Agency, the agency charged with protecting the U.S. from nuclear and biological weapons. He also accessed thirteen NASA computers and stole software used for the International Space Station.

■ On August 1, 2001, 20 year old Jason Allen Diekman pleaded guilty to breaking into Oregon State University computers and attempting to use stolen credit card numbers to wire money through Western Union. This was his second federal offense. The previous November he pled guilty to breaking into several NASA computers and using stolen credit card numbers to purchase $6,000 in electronic equipment.

These young people learn on their own as well as frequenting online locations where other tech-savvy kids hang out to exchange information. A few years ago, those locations would have been exclusively dial-up bulletin boards (BBS), which are something like Web sites but require a modem to access. Today, these forums are mostly IRC channels or Web sites, like the 2600 Magazine Web site (www.2600.com), although dial-up BBSs are still around. These sites generally do more good than harm, by teaching kids about technology and giving them an edge in obtaining high-tech jobs.

Another source of information is from their schools. As kids begin high school or college, they might learn programming skills necessary to advance to a higher level of criminal skill. Most of these kids use their newly honed technical abilities to enter the Information Technology field for valid pursuits.

All of these kids, as they learn, no matter what the source of their education in technology, are in contact with information and people who might encourage them to move on to more unethical or illegal pursuits. They might deliberately learn how to exploit security vulnerabilities to commit identity theft, motivated by the need for money to buy new equipment. Or, they might just want to project a "hacker" image to their friends. In some cases, they are motivated by a desire to right some wrong, such as showing Web site owners how badly their site needs to be upgraded or repaired. Rogers categorizes cyber criminals of this skill level as *cyber punks*. Their statistical profile shows they are typically age 12 through 28, Caucasian, middle class, loners, and might do poorly in school. Many are still in college, or are using university computers to learn what can be done with them. In the process, they learn of security vulnerabilities that exist throughout the Internet.

In each of the criminal cases presented earlier, the young person involved had unsupervised access to computers and enough time to use that access for an illegal activity. This unsupervised access had to have been available for a long period of time, in order for the person involved to obtain sufficient skill level to perform the crime.

To prevent your own child from engaging in unethical online activities, you need to monitor what they do with the computer, starting from an early age. If you have a computer in your home, don't place it in the child's room where you can't watch what they're doing. Keep it in a family room or common area where adults are usually present. Make frequent inquiries about what the child is doing. Ask questions about her online life. Find out what software she likes to use, what her favorite Web sites are, and so on. Get involved in her online interests, so it's easier to talk about issues that are important to her.

Your child might have a clear and exceptional talent for computer programming, Web site development, or network security, which will develop as he or she learns. Just as an exceptional music talent needs specialized education to properly develop, so does a child with exceptional computer abilities. Find him or her a specialized technical school that will channel that talent in a proper direction at an early age. Seek out an internship from a local company specializing in computer security. Alternatively, help your child find constructive work that uses their abilities, such as creating Web pages for a school, civic, or religious organization. You might be surprised at how many organizations will happily hire a capable 14-year old to create or maintain their Web site. Schools are also always on the hunt for volunteers to help keep educational computer networks in good working order.

As you become more involved in your child's online activities, you'll become aware of the software he uses and how he uses it. Some software poses more of a risk to the safety of his identity and yours. In the next section, we examine some of those risks and what can be done to avert them.

Identifying Risky Software and Risky Behavior

Several types of software present a higher risk than others for divulging private information, by putting you or your child in contact with strangers on the Internet. Software that allows interactions that mimic interpersonal conversation poses a higher risk than those that don't, simply because conversation is beneficial for social engineering. In this section, we look at the types of software that encourage communication with strangers and how each can be used to obtain private data about you while being used by your child.

Chat Programs

If you use AOL, you're probably familiar with the AOL Instant Messenger (AIM) program. The software allows you to type a message to a buddy and receive his or her response immediately, without the delays seen with e-mail. AIM is similar to another chat program called ICQ, which was acquired by AOL several years ago. MSN Messenger is Microsoft's version. They are all spin-offs of a concept originally called Internet Relay Chat (IRC). IRC was the original way for people in separate geographical locations to hang out together in "rooms" known as channels. Some of these channels have topics of conversation associated with them and are popular places to learn about a particular subject matter from others who have experience with it.

IRC software allows you to chat as well as transfer files from one location to another. For instance, a popular shareware IRC program called *mIRC* provides the ability to chat as well as allows files to be sent to or received from others using a utility that comes with it called *dcc*. Figure 6.1 shows an mIRC dcc window about to send an image file to the person with screen name *pfm*. Because the person sending the file is in complete control of it, the recipient (pfm) has no way of knowing if it has been renamed, infected with a virus, or corrupted in some fashion. The image file could just as easily be a tax return, Quicken file, or a Trojan password-stealing virus.

Figure 6.1 mIRC File Transfer Feature

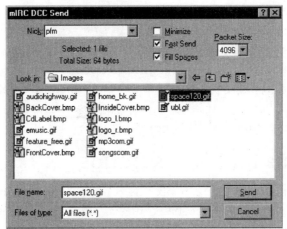

Using dcc, you or your child can be tricked into downloading files that actually install a Trojan IRC server on your system, giving others access to all your private files. As discussed in Chapter 4, those private files could be cookies or Temporary Internet Files that contain credit card numbers, addresses, or other private information you don't want to be made public. In Chapter 3, we note that unexpected attachments to e-mails should be deleted and never opened. Similarly, unexpected file transfers or those from distrusted individuals should be rejected.

Most IRC chat programs can be configured to disable file transfers entirely. If yours doesn't, consider moving to one that does. You should also educate your family members about the risks of downloading any files using it, in case they decide to reenable the feature. If your family makes use of this kind of software, you need to teach them the risks associated with it. Tell them to avoid downloading files using IRC software whenever possible, and make certain you've protected your computer with antivirus software and other measures described throughout the book. Maintaining anonymity through the use of nondescriptive screen names is also a good way to discourage others from contacting your family members.

Downloading files is not the only risky behavior related to IRC. Chat can be used as a way of social engineering. Conversations using chat programs tend to be short, because they can only last for the duration of time that both parties are sitting in front of the computer. Still, kids and adults alike can be tricked into disclosing private information during a chat conversation. Sexual predators often use this technique to learn the location of a potential victim, piecing together various seemingly unrelated pieces of information into a picture of the victim's whereabouts. Teach family members never to disclose any personal details when chatting online with friends, just in case the friend is really an imposter. Parental contracts, which we discuss later in the section "Monitoring Online Activities," can help in this regard.

Chat programs generally promote quick tricks or scams designed to produce an immediate result, like the download just described. "You have to check out this cool picture of j.Lo. Here, I'll send it to you." Software that promotes lengthy conversations lets others get to know you on a personal level, which is another type of social engineering described next.

Web Forums and Newsgroups

Before the Web came into being, people used newsgroups to share information in much the same way they use Web-based messaging forums today. To use a Web forum or newsgroup, you post a message, which is stored on a server and made available for anyone with Internet access to read. Web forums (also known as message boards) and newsgroups alike are often topical just like an IRC chat channel, so they tend to form followings and have a club-like atmosphere. This promotes ease between people who otherwise would be strangers.

Talking to others anonymously can be therapeutic in certain situations. It provides an outlet for feelings that might otherwise go unexpressed, encouraging people to let their guard down. Sometimes people will converse in this fashion for weeks or months, learning much about each other in the process. Some might even fall in love, disclose their identities, and eventually marry.

Long-term conversation with strangers can be risky though, because there is much time to gather information about a potential crime target. Data gathering can be covert, because it's difficult to remember what is said over a long period of time. Predators can discover who you are by piecing together several seemingly disparate pieces of information, even if you never disclose your name, address, or phone number.

For example, a young female student might frequent a sports-related Web forum, one day boasting about being assigned number 7 on her school's basketball team. Some weeks later, she mentions excitement over next Saturday's game against rival team "The Patriots." A party to the chat conversation could infer her school's name from the e-mail address she used to post the messages, research where that school's basketball game against the Patriots is being played next Saturday, and show up looking for number 7. All it takes then is following the girl to her car after the game, recording the license plate number, and doing a DMV search to learn a name and home address. In this case, her biggest mistake was in failing to provide enough anonymity in her e-mail address, although it required additional information provided on the message board in order to physically locate her.

Web forums and newsgroups can also be used to transfer files, just as e-mail can. The same precautions we examine in Chapter 3 regarding e-mail attachments apply to messages posted to newsgroups and message boards as well. Don't click Web URLs or follow instructions to download files that might be included on a message board or newsgroup unless you know and trust the person who originally posted the message. When posting or replying to messages, use an account name that doesn't imply your real name or location. Be on the lookout for scams and con games attempting to trick you into disclosing private data, such as a bank account number, e-mail address, or name.

Massive Multiplayer Online Games

Online computer gaming has become all the rage among young people in the past few years. Computer games have been around as long as computers have existed, but the Internet has made them available for play between people in separate geographical locations. A favorite among teens and adults alike is the *massive multiplayer online role-playing game* (MMORPG), in which a player creates an online persona and embarks on fantasy quests of various sorts. These games provide chat features so players can converse, thereby defining and reinforcing the personas they've created.

One popular example of a MMORPG is the game *Diablo*. Players create medieval-type characters that go on quests for prized weapons or armor, fight monsters, and gather treasure of various sorts. The players buy and sell weapons, armor, or magic items from each other, using the chat feature.

Because the game isn't moderated, anything can be said during a chat conversation with another player. This makes the game's chat feature open for pretexting, as discussed in Chapter 1; yet, kids playing the game are often less able to recognize it than adults. This doesn't mean kids shouldn't play the game, although parents will want to review whether any game is age-appropriate for their child. It does mean that parents need to recognize that games with chat features need to be treated the same as chat programs themselves when teaching kids safety precautions for passwords, downloads, personally identifying information, and so forth.

Diablo isn't the only online game that comes with a chat feature. Other titles include *Everquest, Half-Life, Dark Age of Camelot, Warcraft, Counter Strike*, and a host of others. Some of these games, such as *Everquest*, are moderated to ensure game chat features aren't abused, but that doesn't eliminate the risk entirely.

Because they might be asked to disclose private information during game play, kids should be taught never to disclose anything about themselves, no matter how trivial it might seem. Teach them how to be completely anonymous online, to never give out passwords, and to not say anything personal about themselves, their school, their family, or location as they play. If they need to use e-mail as part of their game play, provide your kids with an e-mail address that doesn't disclose their real names, to protect their identities and yours. Choose account names for game play that don't imply the child's (or your) real name.

Another common practice with these types of online games is character or account selling on eBay. Game players might spend a good deal of time developing a character or persona to a high ability level and then offer that character (or game items associated with it) for sale. Some games prohibit the practice; others don't. When a game character is sold, money changes hands between the seller and the buyer, making an association between an anonymous game persona and a real person's name, bank account, or credit card number. This provides a conduit for finding out the real identity of someone that a player has spent a long time getting to know within the original confines of the game.

Parents need to be involved in everything their kids do online, even playing games. So, learn to play them yourself. Play at the same times your kids do, and play with them online, on a second computer. This is useful as a way to stay involved in their lives, just as if they were playing soccer or baseball, and allows you to learn about any safety risks posed by the game. By doing so, you can take advantage of opportunities to teach your kids where lines of safety and legality are drawn. You might just have some fun in the process.

If you don't have a second computer, perhaps you can use one at a Cyber Café, which is the generic name for any establishment that provides computers for public use. Wizards of the Coast (www.wizards.com) is a game shop that also provides gaming terminals for an hourly fee. There are many other game shops that provide a similar service.

File-Sharing Software

Many software programs are popular among young people because they allow music and movies to be downloaded from a server or copied from a CD-ROM purchased at a music store. It's even possible to download software from the Internet to copy a DVD movie onto a computer hard drive or CD-ROM, although the producer's copyright may be violated by this process. Despite the fact that purchased music CD-ROMs also have copyright restrictions, young people often copy them and distribute the music files using these same file-sharing utilities. The practice is difficult to stop, due to the way the file-sharing programs, known as *peer-to-peer* (P2P) applications, work.

A P2P application is just a particular kind of software that lets two computers talk directly to each other without needing a server. Most parents don't realize that files being served up by these P2P applications are stored on a computer next door, down the street, or across town. Kids initially install these applications so they can easily download music, but it doesn't take long to discover they can download many other types of files, as well.

Unlike Napster (a service that provided a huge repository of music files via P2P networking), each person who uses peer-to-peer file-sharing software stores her own music (or other files) on his or her home computer's hard drive. The software advertises what music titles (or other file names) are stored on the computer. Special search utilities included with the software allow others to locate computers storing music they want to download. The software then copies it from the home computer where it resides. Each end of the file transfer could be anywhere in the world, so centralized control is impossible.

Figure 6.2 is a screenshot of Limewire after performing a search on the word *hack*. Note the resulting files displayed are music files (mp3), documents (doc) containing passwords for hacked pornography sites, a text (txt) file claiming to contain hacked Hotmail passwords, even a Macintosh archive file (.sit) claiming to contain hacked applets for Palm Pilots. Clicking any of these files starts the transfer onto the local computer where Limewire is running. Note that Limewire also provides a chat feature.

Figure 6.2 Limewire

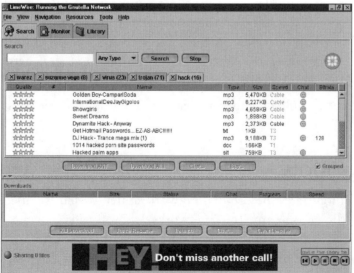

We discuss P2P applications here for several reasons. The following problems exist with these applications:

- They are widely used but difficult to control using firewall software. Gnutella (www.gnutellanews.com), for instance, is smart enough to choose a different outgoing port (door) if one is blocked by the firewall. Software variants that work on Gnutella networks include Bearshare and Limewire. Aimster and Morpheus are also similar. If you don't want your family to use one of these P2P applications, you're best course of action is to remove it from computers on which you find it running. This means you need to be familiar with what software is running on each computer your family uses.

- P2P software can transfer any kind of file, not just music or movies. This makes them vulnerable to transferring malicious Trojan files, viruses disguised with the names of music titles, or pornography. Antivirus programs, as discussed in Chapter 2, can help detect viruses and Trojans, but need to be kept up-to-date in order to catch the latest wave of infections that are spreading. Even then, new viruses can spread before antivirus software updates have been downloaded to detect and remove them.

- They advertise files stored in particular locations on your computer. If you aren't aware that the software is running, you might inadvertently place private files there that shouldn't be made publicly available, like a tax return or Quicken file. If a particular file-sharing software has a bug that allows outsiders to view files in directories other than the ones associated with the software, then no location on your computer's drive is safe from outside view. Keeping the software upgraded to the latest patch level is an important safeguard. Not running it at all is better still.

- They enable activities with dubious legal consequences. It's difficult to know when downloaded media have copyright restrictions attached to them.

Hacking Tools

Chapter 5 demonstrates the use of a network sniffer, which is a useful tool for prying open the lid on computers, networks, and software. Like any tool, it can be used correctly or it can be misused. The problem doesn't lie in the tool itself. It lies in whether the user engages in proper use of the tool.

However, if you found a set of lock picks, a crowbar, and a lock picking instruction manual in someone's car trunk, you'd probably wonder what that person's intentions are for using such an unusual set of tools. Perhaps the person is a locksmith. Perhaps the person is a thief. Possession of the tools doesn't make him a thief unless he uses them to steal something. But after the fact, possession of the tools can be seen as a warning sign leading up to a theft.

Likewise, it's unusual for the average person's computer to be running software tools commonly associated with breaking into computers. A network sniffer like Analyzer is one of those tools. Unless you have a specific need for this type of software, you won't find it on your computer unless someone else has installed it for you, possibly with the intent to use it for computer intrusion or data theft. Software that cracks passwords falls into the same category, as does software that scans other computers to determine what services are running.

All of these kinds of software have useful purposes but also hold a high potential for misuse. If you find one of these running on your computer and know you didn't install it, you should investigate how it got there. Perhaps an intruder installed it, or perhaps a family member installed it while learning how to break into computers. Antivirus software won't catch these types of applications because they are not viruses or Trojans per se. You'll need to become familiar with the software that should be running on your computer, in order to identify software that is installed without your being aware.

These tools in and of themselves don't pose a risk to your private data, but someone with malicious intent and an understanding of the tools' capabilities can easily use them to obtain your passwords or other private data. It's better not to leave them installed on your computer, as a general rule.

Monitoring Online Activities

An activity monitor is software that records the activities of family members when you aren't there to watch how they use the computer. This type of software typically records the user's activities while you are away, and stores the information in a file or Web page for you to view later. Different kinds of activity monitors record different aspects of a user's activities. For instance, application logger software records what's done with a particular application after it is started, but it won't help you understand how many applications were started and at what times while you were away. Web or browser monitors record what Web sites are visited using a browser, but won't help you understand what a child says during a chat session with a friend. That requires the services of a keystroke logger utility, which records each key as it is pressed on the keyboard. Keystroke logging software won't show you what the user viewed using an image viewer, however; for that, you need a monitor capable of screen imaging.

Using monitoring software to watch your child's online activities can accomplish several things to protect you and your family from identity theft. By understanding what your child does using the computer, you can evaluate the risk posed by the software programs he or she uses. Monitor software typically runs in the background, out of view of the person using the computer, reducing the possibility that the person being monitored will deliberately disable the recording function. If your computer is compromised while a monitor is running, the resulting log files might offer clues that can eventually result in apprehension of the intruder. If the intruder steals data that's used in committing an identity theft, those log files might become evidence for a conviction. They can also offer clues about the private data about you that was exposed in the process, allowing you to more quickly recover from any damage that is done.

The first thing you'll need to do if you decide to install any type of activity monitor software is to inform your family that you will be using it. Privacy is a concern to your children, too. A useful tool to break the ice with kids in this regard is to ask them to sign a parental contract, so they understand your expectations ahead of time. Give them a chance to ask questions about the kinds of activities you intend to monitor, and why. Stress that their safety is your primary concern, and that you are not trying to catch them doing anything wrong. In fact, emphasize that there will be *no punishments* resulting from activity monitoring, only guidance when it is deemed necessary. Then, follow through on that promise. Let them know that if they encounter a situation that isn't covered by the contract, they can always ask a parent or trusted adult for advice. With that in mind, let's take a look at a sample parental contract, followed by a comparison of some useful activity monitor software.

Parental Contracts

There are some very good Web sites on the Internet that advise parents about Internet safety. SafeKids (www.safekids.com) provides guidelines for parents and advice on what to teach kids to protect themselves online. Also provided at this Web site is a Kids Pledge, reproduced in Figure 6.3, for your children to read and sign as a tool to understand what is expected of them while they use the Internet.

Items one through six of Figure 6.3 are adapted from the brochure "Child Safety on the Information Highway" (www.safekids.com/child_safety.htm) by

Lawrence J. Magid. Copyright 1994 and 1998 by the National Center for Missing and Exploited Children (www.missingkids.com); printed copies are available free by calling 800 843-5678:

Figure 6.3 SafeKids Kid's Pledge

---

1. I will not give out personal information, such as my address, telephone number, parents' work address/telephone number, or the name and location of my school without my parents' permission.
2. I will tell my parents right away if I come across any information that makes me feel uncomfortable.
3. I will never agree to get together with someone I "meet" online without first checking with my parents. If my parents agree to the meeting, I will be sure that it is in a public place and bring my mother or father along.
4. I will never send a person my picture or anything else without first checking with my parents.
5. I will not respond to any messages that are mean or in any way make me feel uncomfortable. It is not my fault if I get a message like that. If I do, I will tell my parents right away so that they can contact the service provider.
6. I will talk with my parents so that we can set up rules for going online. We will decide upon the time of day that I can be online, the length of time I can be online, and appropriate areas for me to visit. I will not access other areas or break these rules without their permission.
7. I will not give out my Internet password to anyone (even my best friends) other than my parents.
8. I will be a good online citizen and not do anything that hurts other people or is against the law.

GetNetWise (www.getnetwise.org) is another Web site devoted to teaching kids how to stay safe on the Internet. This site provides several links for Internet usage contracts between parents and children as well as guides for online safety and software tools families can use to enforce online rules.

After you've taught your child what precautions to take to protect her identity (and yours) online, you'll need to remain vigilant in restricting and monitoring her online activities. In Chapter 5, we examine the notion of using a firewall, with its features for outbound filtering and setting time restrictions, to protect your home network. Likewise, those features make excellent tools for restricting when and how your child uses the Internet. Other software running on the home computer or network can also track which Web sites your child visits, what is viewed at each of those sites, and what text is sent or received using a chat program, e-mail, or message board.

Application Logging

Many applications that you probably already own offer logging features that track what's done while the application is running. For example, the history feature of a Web browser or the Recently Accessed Files features of Windows are simple logging features built into those applications. Some applications have even more complex logging features that you can enable, such as the saved mail feature of your favorite e-mail program.

Enabling logging features in your software is always a good idea if disk space and processing resources allow. For instance, if someone were to send a fax using your computer and telephone line, you could learn this fact from the fax software log. If a Trojan were using your fax software to send spyware data back to a central server, you might not discover its presence until viewing the fax server log.

Data collected from various applications is usually stored by default in a file or directory local to the application. This makes the log files difficult to locate, reducing the likelihood that you will ever view them. However, frequent log checking is important, because these log files can provide clues about software errors or bugs that could lead to a system compromise, unless you obtain a patch to repair the problem. Viewing application log files is simpler when they are stored in a single location. Backing up log files simplifies your efforts further, as we discuss in Chapter 2.

Windows XP, Windows NT, and Windows 2000 solve this problem by providing a feature called an *event log*. With event logging, applications send log data to a centralized database via the operating system. The event logs are viewable using an event viewer, which is capable of viewing event logs on remote computers sharing the same network. Three basic types of events are logged using this feature. Note that by default, the security log is turned off. You should enable it manually if your computer is running the Windows XP, Windows NT, or Windows 2000 operating systems. The three event logs are:

- **System Log** Logs information about the computer's hardware, operating system, and startup.

- **Application Log** Logs information reported by applications running on the system.

- **Security Log** Logs information about logins, authentication, and access control changes.

For older versions of Windows—such as Windows 95, Windows 98, or Windows Me—you will need to add third-party software, such as WinSyslog (www.winsyslog.com), to provide the same functionality as event logging. You might want to add third-party software to Windows XP, Windows NT, and Windows 2000, too, if event logs don't contain as much information as you'd like. This is probably the case if you want a complete record of Web sites visited, chat sessions, or e-mails sent to or from a computer. A good place to find this type of third-party software is at a Web site called PEP—short for Parents, Educators, and Publishers (www.microWeb.com/pepsite/Software/filters.html)—where you'll find a valuable comparison of monitoring software titles and the features offered by each one. Another good resource is the Monitoring Tools section at Hideaway.net (www.hideaway.net/PC_Security/pc_security.html), which offers shareware titles that are useful for business as well as family or home use. Next, we look at some of the basic features this type of logging software can provide.

Browser Activity Logging

Browser monitoring software comes in three basic varieties. The first is in the form of a special browser that must be used by the person being monitored. This type of software is most useful for people who can control what software is installed on the computer being monitored. To ensure that the browser captures a complete record of a user's Web surfing activities, all other browser software must be removed from the computer. Subsequently, the computer needs to be periodically checked to ensure that the person whose activities are being monitored has not downloaded and installed browser software that bypasses the monitoring feature.

Each time a Web address is requested using this type of browser software, the requested address is compared to a file or database that contains information about blocked sites. The decision whether to allow access to the site is usually based on some combination of keywords and Web addresses. Depending on the configuration, denied sites might be logged, but allowed Web connections are usually always logged.

Because the browser allows access to some sites and not others, it can be viewed as a *filter* that hides a certain portion of the Internet from view. Because filters aren't perfect, occasionally the filtering function will allow access to an undesirable site or will block access to a site that should be accessible. Another problem with this type of filtering is maintenance of the keyword list, to ensure it contains an adequate set of words to properly block the sites you want to be blocked. If the list is large, this can be quite a daunting task.

Instead of filtering, some browser monitors will block access to all sites unless the Web address is explicitly added as an allowed Web site. One example of software built this way is ChiBrow (www.chibrow.com). This particular software is geared for younger kids and serves up only family friendly Web sites individually added by a parent. If one of those sites allows a kid to download a different Web browser, though, he can use it to bypass both the security and logging features of the monitor.

A second type of Web monitoring software is in the form of an application, called a *proxy*, that sits between the Internet and the browser software being monitored. The proxy software can either run on the same computer or a different one on the same network. All browsers on the monitored computer(s) must be reconfigured so that they pass all Web site requests to the proxy, which in turn retrieves the requested Web pages and returns them to the browser. The proxy software also acts as a filter either by retrieving selected allowed Web sites and denying access to all others or by allowing all Web sites that don't contain certain keywords. As pages are processed, the proxy software logs the requests to a file for later viewing.

This type of software is especially suited for a centralized service that manages the keyword list on behalf of customers who subscribe to the service. An example is Bess, The Internet Retriever (www.n2h2.com), a subscription-based proxy service for schools and libraries.

The third and last type of software must run on the same computer that's being monitored, because it attaches itself between the browser and the networking features of the Windows operating system known as Winsock. This type of software is the stealthiest, running in the background outside the view of the computer user.

Cyber Snoop (www.cyber-snoop.com) is one such Winsock-based Web activity monitor. Figure 6.4 shows the Cyber Snoop configuration wizard, which allows you to choose the level of protection you want. Once the setting is chosen, it is password protected so that it cannot be changed by anyone but you. The software records Web pages visited, allowing you to click the recorded links to view the pages when you are reviewing log entries. This software also provides time restrictions, allowing you to block total access to the Internet during certain times of the day. Cyber Snoop records the text of e-mail, chat, and news messages, including the name of the person logged into the computer at the time and the Web sites visited. It also provides the ability to block access to specific sites on the Internet based on keywords.

Figure 6.4 Cyber Snoop Configuration Wizard for Internet Access

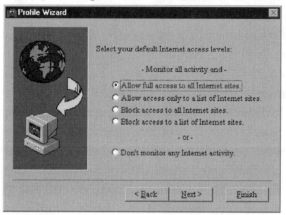

Figure 6.5 is a sample log file generated by Cyber Snoop. In the first line of this example, an e-mail was sent to joe_user@hotbox.com containing a keyword that is on the Cyber Snoop block list; so, Cyber Snoop recorded the e-mail. Clicking the line displays the entire text of the message. Next, a Yahoo! Web search was performed using the word *kinky*, also on the keyword block list. The last line shows an attempt to reach the www.allpasswords.com Web site using Internet Explorer. Cyber Snoop can be configured to use one of several browsers—you're not locked into this choice. The allpasswords.com Web site is on the site block list that comes with Cyber Snoop by default. You can download more comprehensive lists from the main Cyber Snoop support site or create your own. Any or all of these block lists can be edited to include or exclude any site or keyword you want.

Figure 6.5 Cyber Snoop Activity Monitor

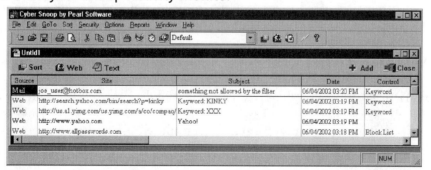

The downside to all three types of programs we've been discussing is that they don't typically display what the user sees, only a link to it. If the site becomes unavailable between the time the log is created and the time you view the log entry, you won't have the ability to see the same image. Likewise, unless the software is a package that includes other features, such as a keystroke logger, it won't record what is typed into a Web site after that site is visited. It also might only record the top-level page of a Web site, not all the pages visited at the site's main address.

To ease the burden of maintaining site or keyword block lists, several content-management standards have been developed that replace the keyword filtering system with a rating system. Web sites that voluntarily submit to these rating systems are filtered by the browser, based on the degree of protection offered by the rating system you choose. For example, Internet Explorer can be configured to use rating systems such as the Recreational Software Advisory Council (RASCi) or SafeSurf (www.classify.org/safesurf) rating systems. Web sites can embed rating system tags into their Web pages, allowing the browser software to block or allow access to the pages based on the particular rating system it is configured to use. The concept is wonderful, but unfortunately not all Web sites voluntarily rate themselves. Go ahead and enable this feature in your browser if you want but don't rely solely on it to block access content on the Internet.

Keystroke Logging

A keystroke log records each keyboard key as it is depressed. This is very useful for watching text that passes through software applications that don't involve a browser, such as chat programs or e-mail software like Outlook. Computer monitoring software often includes a keystroke logger as part of a software package. However, a keystroke logger alone won't record what's done using a mouse or trackball. If someone follows links instead of typing a URL into a browser, the link won't get recorded by a keystroke logger. If all you want to do is record chat sessions or other text-based messages sent from the computer, a keystroke logger might be sufficient.

Screen Imaging

Spector (www.spectorsoft.com) is a software program that will take a picture of the screen as well as perform all the functions discussed so far. It keeps copies of any e-mails that are sent, for later review, even if a Web-based mail program, such as Hotmail or Yahoo e-mail, is used to send it. This software also records both sides of chat room conversations for AOL Instant Messenger, AOL chat rooms, ICQ, Yahoo! Messenger, and MSN Messenger. It doesn't cover all IRC chat programs, though, but those conversations will be captured in the screen shots. Finally, it includes a keystroke logger that provides alerts on selected keywords. It will send you an e-mail when selected keywords are typed or detect in an e-mail, chat session, Web page, and so on.

Many kinds of shareware and commercial products have similar features. Some can also take periodic images from a camera attached to your computer, so you can know who's sitting in front of it at any given time. These are nice features to have but caution is necessary when using applications that take frequent images as a monitoring tool. The images produced by this kind of software can be large, and there are many of them. If you decide to configure the software to store the images on your hard drive, you'll need to make sure you have plenty of disk space available to store them until the next time you can view and delete them. You can always store them on CD-ROM or attach a VCR and store the images on video tape.

Avoiding Monitoring Pitfalls

A clever child or family member can easily disable monitoring software if they know what to look for, so don't tell them details about how you monitor their activities. Monitoring software that runs silently in the background with no icon displayed in the system tray is a good choice in this regard. However, even hidden software can be stopped if it's displayed in the Task Manager and if the user has administrator rights. Thus, proper account access controls, as discussed in Chapter 2, play an important role in your success in monitoring someone's computer activities. This is especially true to prevent outsiders from being able to disable the logging software prior to stealing private data.

However, none of the monitoring software discussed here is going to work for monitoring the activities of a tech-savvy teen capable of breaking into his own computer to give himself administrator access. She'll just disable the monitoring software or reconfigure the browser and that will be the end of that.

For situations such as this, you'll need to rely on activity logs produced by an external firewall she can't break into, such as one of the network-based firewalls discussed in Chapter 5. Figure 6.6 shows what a Web content log from a Netgear RO318 external router looks like. The IP address of the home computer is in the center (192.168.0.23) and the destination URL is on the left. In each case, the traffic was allowed (see the lines that end with "FORWARD").

Figure 6.6 Netgear RO318 Content Filter Log

#	Time	Source IP	Action
1	Tue May 7 23:34:36 2002 download.microsoft.com	192.168.0.23	FORWARD
2	Tue May 7 23:34:36 2002 www.microsoft.com	192.168.0.23	FORWARD
3	Tue May 7 23:26:05 2002 www.paypal.com	192.168.0.26	FORWARD

To protect the firewall box from physical tampering, it can be placed inside a locked metal box with holes for cabling or inside a locked closet. Of course, you child might be successful in bypassing the firewall through software means, or he might circumvent your monitoring attempts by using the services of a Cyber Café. If you have a family member whose talents fit this description, it's time to consider buying yourself a separate computer. The safety of your private data can't be assured as long as you share computing resources with him or her.

If you suspect someone is attempting to steal data from your computer or obtain information about you or your child using any of the methods described in this chapter, contact the authorities immediately. In the next chapter, we take a look at how to report a crime and recover from the damage when you find yourself a victim of identity theft.

Summary

This chapter reviews some of the challenges of preventing activities of family members from putting you at risk for identity theft. Families often share a single computer and Internet account, but this blurs distinctions between identities of family members. Tech-savvy children learning to push the boundaries of what computers can do might engage in activities that inadvertently or deliberately expose your private information. Protecting the identities of yourself and your children means educating yourself and your kids about how identity theft occurs, how it can be prevented, and how the children's activities can cross ethical and legal boundaries.

Certain types of software popular among young people pose a significant risk for exposing private information by encouraging conversation with strangers on the Internet. Chat programs, online role playing games, and message boards are examples of forums that allow information gathering by outsiders. Children need to be taught to use anonymity skills when using these types of applications.

Throughout the book we discuss ways in which you can accidentally expose private data. These accidents can also happen to family members sharing your computer. File-sharing software, such as dcc features of IRC chat programs or peer-to-peer applications like Gnutella, can be used to install Trojans or obtain data files from your computer. You'll need to take steps to ensure that family members understand risks associated with using these applications, or you'll need to restrict their use.

Understanding what your child does online is important in order for you to recognize opportunities to teach him or her where legal and ethical boundaries lay surrounding computer use. One way to accomplish this is to ask your child frequent questions about his or her online life. Another is to play games with your child online.

When you can't be with your child to monitor his activities, software can help you stay in touch with what he does online. Browser monitors, application logs, keystroke logging software, and other types of monitoring software can be useful tools in this regard.

Solutions Fast Track

Raising Children in the Digital Age

- ☑ Many parents lack the ability to recognize when a child is using a computer for illegal or unethical activities. Without parental intervention, a child might be "in training" for becoming a victim of identity theft or an unwitting participant in disclosing your private information.

- ☑ Kids need to learn how to use computers by taking them apart. However, some innocent-looking tools actually teach kids how to hack into games, software, or other people's computer accounts.

- ☑ Parents need to educate themselves about unethical and illegal uses of the computer and teach their kids not to cross these lines. Parents need to teach kids how not to become victims of identity theft as well as teach them anonymity skills to protect the identities of their parents.

Identifying Risky Software and Risky Behavior

- ☑ Certain kinds of software increase the risk of disclosing private information by parents and kids alike, but they are particularly risky to allow kids to use. Chat programs encourage conversations with strangers and can be a forum for tricking family members into downloading malicious programs that can expose private data.

- ☑ Message boards and online games also encourage conversations with strangers. Games additionally offer opportunities for kids to disclose passwords or account information.

- ☑ Music and movie file-sharing software popular among teens can easily be used to distribute virus-infected files or can be exploited to expose your private data. Peer-to-peer file-sharing applications are especially difficult to control, so consider removing them from computers in your home. If you decide to allow their use, be sure that antivirus software is running and that family members are taught about the risks associated with its use.

Monitoring Online Activities

☑ Monitoring and logging software are important tools for understanding how family members use a shared computer. Log files produced by activity monitoring software are also useful as evidence if an intruder steals private data from your computer.

☑ Applications sometimes provide logging capabilities that can be enabled from within the application. Windows NT, Windows XP, and Windows 2000 provide event logging as part of the operating system. Third-party products need to be added to Windows 9x and Windows Me systems to provide the same functionality.

☑ Browser monitors track visited Web sites and come in three basic flavors—proxy servers, logging-capable browsers, and software that monitors the Winsock function of the Windows operating system. Browser monitors can be configured as filters, which block or allow access to sites based on keywords, or they can be configured to deny access to all sites except those explicitly defined as allowed within the monitor software.

☑ Keystroke loggers and screen imaging software are browser monitor add-ons that are useful for collecting text from chat sessions or viewed images that can't otherwise be captured by an activity monitor. Clever family members might be able to bypass monitoring software, so buy one that hides in the background out of view.

Frequently Asked Questions

The following Frequently Asked Questions, answered by the authors of this book, are designed to both measure your understanding of the concepts presented in this chapter and to assist you with real-life implementation of these concepts. To have your questions about this chapter answered by the author, browse to **www.syngress.com/solutions** and click on the **"Ask the Author"** form.

Q: What's a good way to begin getting involved with my child's online activities?

A: Ask your child to teach you about his computer. He'll feel important that you are interested enough to learn about it. As he shows you what the computer can do, ask questions about how he uses certain features, and what he feels is good or bad about the Internet.

Q: If Web services and e-mail programs can use digital certificates to encrypt messages between the two ends of a conversation, do chat programs provide this as well?

A: Instant messaging is playing catch-up, but it's getting there. imici Messenger (www.imici.com) is an instant messenger program that supports 128-bit SSL encryption to send messages, and it works with users of AIM, ICQ, MSN, and Yahoo! chat software. Also, SuidNet (http://suidnet.org) is an IRC network supporting 128-bit SSL encryption with several kinds of client software that you can download from their Web site.

Q: Do Web sites have ratings, like movies?

A: Yes. SafeSurf (www.safesurf.com) is an award-winning rating service that you can configure Internet Explorer to use. You tell IE about the basic classes of sites you don't want to be available, and SafeSurf does the rest.

Q: If I can't block Gnutella-type P2P applications using a firewall, how can I block them?

A: RiFilter is a product from InnoVal Systems Solutions (www.innoval.com) that claims to block Gnutella by supporting the Internet Content Rating Association's (ICRA) standards for rating content on the Internet. Unfortunately, Web sites that don't embed the ICRA standards labels in their Web pages won't get properly filtered, but it's a start.

Chapter 7

If You Become a Victim

Solutions in this chapter:

- Taking Immediate Action

- Managing the Fallout

- Locating Government Resources

- Other Suggested Resources

☑ Summary

☑ Solutions Fast Track

☑ Frequently Asked Questions

Introduction

You thought you were being careful. You thought it couldn't happen to you. After all, you're just an ordinary person—why would anyone target you? But, it happened. Someone opened a charge account in your name and made several thousand dollars worth of charges. Someone obtained a second mortgage on your home and spent your equity money. You're a victim of identity theft. What do you do now?

First of all, realize that you are not alone. Having your identity stolen might be scary, but it can happen to anyone. Remember, as Chapter 1 notes, the FTC takes over 3,000 calls about identity theft each week! Each one of those calls is from someone who is trying to figure out what to do about his or her particular situation.

By the time you suspect that you've become a victim of identity theft, you will have discovered something is amiss with your financial situation. Perhaps you received a call from a collection agency about a loan you didn't know existed. Perhaps you received a credit card bill or bank statement in the mail for an account you never opened. You realize that you are being asked to pay for something you didn't buy or repair bad credit you didn't cause. All the while, you began piecing together a trail of financial damage the boundaries of which you might not fully know for quite some time.

We wish we could tell you about a single company or government program that could repair all the financial and emotional damage for you, but we can't. There's no one company or service "out there" that will do it all. But there *are* services that can help you learn the extent of the financial damage and help you manage the fallout. Law enforcement authorities can help you figure out exactly what happened and, hopefully, catch and prosecute the person responsible. Local law enforcement agencies also have Victims Services Units that can suggest community resources to help you deal with personal or emotional problems you might experience as a result of becoming a crime victim. In this chapter, we examine some of the resources that can help you through the recovery process if you're a victim of identity theft.

Taking Immediate Action

Once you become aware that someone else is using your name or other personally identifying information to obtain services or goods in your name, you should get help putting a stop to the thief's actions as soon as possible. The sooner you report the crime to authorities, the sooner they can apprehend the culprit. The sooner you report stolen credit cards, bank accounts, ATM cards, and so forth, the sooner your money (and credit standing) can be made inaccessible to the thief.

But how do you know that you've been a victim? First, by always being on guard. The last thing you want to do is discover the crime by accident. This means looking for signs of identity theft in your credit report, actively and often.

For this reason, the FTC recommends that the first step you take after you suspect you've become a victim of identity theft is to order a credit report to find any falsified accounts and close them. This needs to happen more or less concurrently with filing a police report, so the full extent of falsified loans, credit cards, and bank accounts can be included in the report. Only then can you begin making repairs to your financial and emotional well-being. This section presents a three-step plan for reporting the crime and closing any accounts that are involved, to make sure all the bases are covered.

Step 1: Filing Police Reports

If you believe or suspect that an identity theft crime has been committed, the first report you should file should be with your local law enforcement. If the crime occurred elsewhere, such as use of your credit card number by an imposter in another state, you'll want to report the crime in the remote state, too. Be sure to inform the local officer in charge of your case about any reports you file in other locations. The officer can determine if Federal or other enforcement agencies need to become involved, and she can help you sort out any cross-jurisdictional issues that might arise. The main tasks you need to complete during this stage are:

- **Notify law enforcement** Police will ask you specific information about the incident, such as how you became aware of it, what documentation you have to support your claim, and so on. The officer will want to examine any evidence you might have. If your computer was involved, for instance, the officer will want to examine it for evidence. He or she will want to examine any falsified account statements you might have received in the mail. If your wallet was stolen, the officer will ask for details about when and where the theft occurred, information about anyone standing nearby at the time, and so on. The office in charge of your case will involve any Federal agencies, such as the FBI or U.S. Secret Service if the situation warrants. The U.S. Secret Service, for instance, might become involved if the theft is part of a larger crime ring, especially if the dollar amounts involved are very high or the crimes involve multiple states jurisdictions.

- **Obtain credit reports** If you are prepared with some credit report information ahead of time, you will be able to expedite the police report filing process. If you learned about the theft of your identity by regularly reading your credit report, good for you! You're a step ahead in the game. As we discuss in Chapter 1, you should frequently examine your credit report to make sure it's accurate. If you haven't yet obtained a copy of your credit report, now would be a good time to order a copy. Details about how to do that, including addresses and phone numbers you'll need, are discussed later in this chapter in the section "Contacting Credit Bureau Services." Be sure and provide a copy of your credit report to the officer in charge of your case, because it might contain valuable information or evidence.

- **Gather relevant information** If you follow our advice in the "Striving for Prevention" section of Chapter 1, this is the point when your list of credit card numbers, bank account numbers, and billing cycle information will come in handy. Police (and you) can more quickly identify falsified accounts appearing on your credit report by comparing it against your list of known, valid accounts. The officer will need a complete list of falsified accounts to include in the report, and he might need to obtain copies of credit applications that were filed by the culprit. The officer might need written permission from you, an affidavit, a warrant, or a subpoena in order to obtain all the necessary documents. You can help speed up the process by requesting these additional documents yourself.

- **Get copies of everything** You will need copies of the police report in subsequent follow-up cycles with credit card companies or banks later on, as you seek their help in closing accounts and obtaining credits for purchases you didn't make. Companies will want to see a copy of the police report, especially if they must take a loss themselves because the account is closed. The report thus needs to list account numbers, loss amounts involved, and dates for each occurrence of loss. If police take billing statements, account statements, or other documents as evidence, ask for copies so you can follow up to close the accounts over the next few days or hours.

Digging Deeper...

Preserving Computer Evidence

If you suspect your computer has been hacked into or that your computer has been used to commit a crime against you or someone else, authorities investigating the action will want to examine the computer for evidence. Make sure that you do not accidentally destroy any evidence before the investigation occurs. If the thief contacts you via e-mail, or you received a threatening e-mail, the message is evidence that might help police track the culprit. It might also be useful in court. Therefore, don't delete any e-mail or other messages involved in the theft.

Note that even shutting down your computer could damage data on your hard disk or purge evidence from memory. If the intruder installed a malicious program, it could even destroy the contents of the hard disk, erasing evidence in the process.

The best way to preserve any potential evidence on your personal computer is to leave it turned on, but disconnected from the Internet or home network. Simply unplug the PC from your home network, cable modem, DSL, or telephone line. Unless the power goes off due to circumstances beyond your control, don't turn off the computer, don't log in or out, and don't run any programs. If the power goes out, just leave the PC turned off. You will effectively be without a computer until authorities have finished their examination, but you will save any further damage to the computer or your personal information that could be caused if you used it while a malicious program is running. When you file your police report, be sure to inquire if it's OK to use the PC again. In a best-case scenario, possibly no intrusion actually occurred and you can go back to using your PC as normal.

If an intrusion has occurred on your PC, you can't be sure of the integrity of any of the files on it. The intruder might have left a backdoor to allow him in again at some point in the future. After the computer has been returned to you and you are free to use it again, you should "wipe" the disk clean (remove all the data on it), restore from the original restore CD-ROM that came with the PC, and then restore any personal files or software from local copies you should have on-hand from performing periodic backups of your PC. Most PC manufacturers have Web sites that provide instructions for reinstalling software along with very helpful technical support to provide assistance in this process.

Step 2: Reporting Fraud and Stolen Accounts

As discussed in Chapter 1, the most common crime associated with identity theft is credit card fraud. In the case of credit card fraud, someone fraudulently opens an account or makes purchases using an existing account in your name. Bank fraud is similar, except money is withdrawn from a bank account using a check, ATM card, electronic fund transfer, or manual withdrawal. Loan fraud involves someone taking out a loan in your name and spending or hiding the proceeds.

All three types of fraud require the thief to impersonate you in order to obtain the financial benefit. After he or she has done this, and you report the account as stolen, you can no longer use the card or account number without the risk of losing more money. You might be able to recover some or all of your loss, but it is not guaranteed.

The losses you incur as the result of identity theft are not limited to the three preceding examples. You'll need to close any and all commercial and private accounts used by the imposter. This includes accounts that don't have an immediate financial impact (such as shopping cards) to prevent them from being used to obtain access to accounts that do. This is where our advice in Chapter 1 to keep a record of your wallet's contents comes in. If your wallet is stolen, you need to know what was in it before you can contact each of the merchants to close the accounts.

In most cases, you can avert having to pay for fraudulent charges made by an imposter, but you'll need to complete an affidavit and provide copies of the police report separately to each merchant involved. This can be a time-consuming process, and it can cost money in the form of notary fees, postage, and copying expenses. As we discuss in a later section, you'll need to keep track of these expenses, so you can recover them later if a judgment is awarded.

Closing Credit Card Accounts

If your credit card information has been stolen, you will need to contact your bank, credit card company, or lender sponsoring the card as soon as possible. If someone uses an existing credit card account number to make purchases over the phone, U.S. mail, or the Internet, it's the same as if your credit card was physically stolen. You'll need to cut up the plastic card for that account and discard it or return it to the issuer (if you still have it) and then immediately notify the card issuer that the theft has occurred. If a new account has been created in your name, it must be closed immediately. As you're examining your records to determine which credit card accounts were fraudulently used, don't forget about lesser-used accounts, like gasoline credit cards and privately issued department store credit cards in addition to bank-issued credit cards, such as MasterCard, Visa, and American Express. A couple key points to keep in mind when closing credit card accounts include:

- **Report the theft immediately** By immediately notifying credit card companies that your card or card number is stolen (within three days of its first fraudulent use), you can limit the dollar amount of unauthorized charges you have to pay to a small amount, usually $50 per credit card. As with filing police reports, your list of credit card and bank account numbers will come in handy at this point and enable you to quickly identify which accounts need to be closed. Usually, a contact phone number is supplied on your credit card statement or bank statement for use in reporting stolen accounts.

- **Request loss recovery** If more than three days have elapsed since the theft, you can notify the bank issuing the credit card within 60 days, in writing, and request to charge the dollar amount back to the original merchant as a billing error. Your billing error claim is based on the fact that the merchant failed to ensure that the purchaser was authentic. If more than 60 days have elapsed between the time a charge was fraudulently made and the date you discovered the card or account number was stolen, you might still be able to recover some of your loss for up to one year under the issuing bank's loss and recovery provisions, but not as a billing error. After one year, you will not be able to recover your loss through the credit card issuer, and you will need to pursue legal channels to recover your loss. In each case, the credit card issuer will ask you to complete a form and provide copies of police reports before they will be able to take any action on your behalf.

Closing Bank and Loan Accounts

If money from your checking, savings, or other bank account was stolen, you won't have the ability to limit your loss automatically, unless perhaps you purchased separate insurance that covers you in cases of theft or personal loss. This is a good reason why using a credit card number instead of your bank's checking account routing numbers when making online purchases is always a good idea, despite recent trends toward online purchasing networks designed to take your personal bank account information instead of requiring credit card numbers. Some points to keep in mind when closing bank and loan accounts include:

- **Report the theft** As with a credit card account, notify your bank if your ATM card is stolen or lost, if money is withdrawn fraudulently using it and/or your ATM PIN, if a book of checks is stolen or lost, if a check is forged in your name, if a loan is taken out in your name, and so forth. You will need to close any existing accounts you have with each bank involved in the theft and open new ones. This is because the thief might have recorded all existing account numbers you held with the bank, and he might attempt to use them again before he is apprehended. Don't forget your IRA accounts, Christmas club, or other specialty savings accounts when examining which ones have had money removed. It's easy to overlook these during the "excitement."

- **Notify check verification agencies** If the thief has forged your name on a check and cashed it, the merchant that cashed the check likely used a check-verification service before cashing it. This type of service checks your name against a list of persons that have a bad habit of cashing bad checks. If your name isn't on the list, the service sends the merchant an authorization number, which is recorded on the cashed check. You can obtain a copy of the cashed check to determine which agency was used. You should then notify the check-verification agency that your account is on a theft hold. By doing this, any further attempts made by the thief to pass one of your checks will be refused a check authorization.

- **Stop payment on stolen checks** You'll also need to stop payment on any checks that might be outstanding and close the account as soon as possible. Stopping payment usually costs a small fee—about $10 per check—so keep track of the fees so you can try to recover them later. Choosing a bank that supports use of a secret password in order to withdraw money from your checking or savings account can help protect against account theft ahead of time, but it won't help now if someone has already helped herself to your ATM card. If your ATM, debit card, or PIN has been stolen, request a new account, PIN, and password, destroy the old card, and close the old account.

- **Notify insurance companies** Theft of information from your home—including records taken from your filing cabinet, home computer, or possibly even the trash—should be covered under a home-owners or rental insurance policy if the items were removed from property covered by those policies. You'll need to establish the value of the stolen information, however, which might be hard to do if it was discarded in the trash prior to being stolen. This is why we recommend in Chapter 1 to always shred unused and cancelled checks, ATM cards, and bank statements prior to discarding them.

- **Place traveler assistance claims** If you were traveling at the time your wallet (or other private data, such as that stored on a laptop) was stolen, your loss might be covered by traveler assistance programs, like AAA, or personal insurance provided as part of a travel package through your travel agent. Homeowner's insurance sometimes covers losses while traveling as well. You should discuss the matter with your agent and place a claim, if this is the case. If your loss isn't covered, now might be a good time to invest in a policy that covers the situation. It happened once, and it might happen again.

Reporting and Closing Other Commercial Accounts

Don't forget, there's a whole list of other ways to commit fraud using your identity besides using your credit card, bank account, or a loan taken out in your name. You'll also need to close the following other types of accounts if the cards or account numbers have been used in an identity theft:

- **Club Memberships** Many people carry membership cards for a local gym or health club, recreation center, golf course, bingo club, swimming pool, dinner club, auto club, or any number of other social clubs that provide access or prepaid services to those who possess a membership card.

- **Grocery or department store shopping cards** Shopping cards are associated with an account for which you provide your name, address, and telephone information when you sign up. Possessing these cards can provide access to this information and might be used to make purchases that otherwise would not be possible.

- **Video rental memberships** Video rental membership cards are an often overlooked piece of identification. When you open an account with a video rental store, you are usually requested to provide a credit card number that the store can use in the event you fail to return the rented media.

Dealing with Compromised Online Accounts

If you become a victim of identity theft, you should change all your passwords immediately. Because there is no guarantee regarding how much information the thief has obtained about you, he or she might have one, some, or all of your usernames and passwords. By changing your passwords, you cut off avenues to further damage your name, credit, and personal safety.

Because identity theft often starts by impersonating a person and then branches into other types of crime, someone with your passwords could potentially commit numerous acts of fraud, send threatening messages to others posing as you, or conduct a variety of other crimes. Online services generally have firewalls that keep logs of who accesses their site, which might be useful in determining who is responsible for stealing your identity.

When someone visits a Web site, the firewall might record the IP address of the computer. An IP address is a number that's assigned to your computer when you log onto the Internet that allows your computer to communicate over the network. IP addresses are unique to each computer on a network, in much the same way street addresses in a city are unique to each house. Just as street addresses ensure that letters go to the proper houses, IP addresses ensure that messages between computers reach the correct destinations. When accessing Web sites, the time, date, and IP address of a computer visiting the site might be recorded in a log. This information can be provided to police in an investigation to determine who accessed the site with your password. After police have this, they can contact the Internet Service Provider who issued the IP address and get the name and address of the person who accessed a site with your password.

Some actions you should take when you're dealing with compromised online accounts include the following:

- **Notify service providers** You should contact any online services you deal with (such as banking institutions, your Internet Service Provider, auction sites, and so forth), so they can take the necessary steps to protect you. This might include changing your password, deleting your current account so you can set up a new account, and preparing for any investigations that might result. Don't use your home computer to do this, because it might also be compromised. Be sure to let police investigators know if you use monitoring software, as discussed in Chapter 6, because this could provide valuable clues about what happened. Use a local Internet café or a friend's computer until the police investigation is finished and you are free to once again use your computer.

■ **Close compromised Web accounts** If a theft involves a Web site account or password, you should delete the account as soon as possible. Don't use the old account anymore to make online purchases, even with a new password. Why? Because the imposter might now know enough about you to guess or crack any new passwords you might choose. If the account is associated with a Web site that doesn't allow you to delete the account online, change the password and then contact the site maintainers in writing to ask for the account to be deleted. This actually won't be easy, because most Web site developers are concerned more with helping people *create* an online account than with *deleting* one. Most Web sites post their contact information as a link off the main page, including phone numbers and addresses, which should help.

■ **Do some investigative work** Contact the Web site's administrator and find out if the Web site keeps network logs for its transactions that include the originating computer's network address. If so, then the imposter's computer address should be recorded in the logs about the time the bogus online purchase was made. If you can demonstrate that the address is different from yours, you might have sufficient evidence that you didn't make the purchase. Your ISP should be able to help you make that determination. Be aware that these kinds of logs are typically huge, so they aren't kept for very long. You should act quickly if you hope to find what you're looking for. Be sure to pass any information you learn to the officer in charge of your case. When all else fails, ask the credit card company for a charge back. If they can't produce a charge slip showing that you signed for the goods or service, then the credit card company should be able to credit your charge account and collect the money from the merchant that failed to properly identify the person making the charge.

Step 3: Notifying the Federal Trade Commission (FTC)

The last reporting step you need to take is to call the Identity Theft Toll-Free Hotline at 1-877-IDTHEFT (1-877-438-4338). The FTC is the central point of contact within the Federal government for reporting incidents of identity theft. Information about identity theft is gathered and distributed to a variety of law enforcement agencies from this centralized service, so ensure that your crime is reported to the FTC if it involves someone impersonating you for financial gain. For more information about the FTC, see the section "Federal Trade Commission" later in this chapter.

Managing Other Fraud Situations

The previous three steps address ways to counter what many people consider to be typical identity theft scenarios instigated for the purpose of fraud. Keep in mind that other types of compromising situations exist, which require a special set of directions to adequately deal with the crime. These are described in the next few sections.

Reporting Stolen IDs

One of the most common types of fraud involves falsified identification, such as a driver's license or Social Security card. When your identification information has been falsified, you should take the following actions:

- **Report stolen driver's license** Your local Department of Motor Vehicles (DMV) can add a fraud alert to your driver's license information. This adds a statement to your DMV report that indicates that you have been a victim of identity theft, but it doesn't cancel the existing license. This protects you in cases in which your license wasn't stolen but other forms of identification were. You should try to obtain a new license number if your license number was stolen, especially if your Social Security Number is the same as your driver's license number.

- **Report Social Security fraud** You can determine if someone has been misusing your Social Security Number by ordering a free copy of your Social Security Statement using a request form (Form 7004). You can find a copy of the request form online at www.ssa.gov/online/ssa-7004.pdf, by phone at (800) 772-1213, or in person at any Social Security Office. If you notice that the report doesn't include earnings for years in which you worked or includes earnings when you did not work, then someone else might be using your Social Security Number. If you believe someone is misusing your Social Security Number, call the Social Security Administration Fraud Hotline at (800) 269-0271. Don't forget that a military ID displays your Social Security Number, so be sure to report any lost or stolen military badges immediately.

Dealing with Telephone Fraud

One of the more profitable phone scams occurring these days is associated with telephone "900" numbers. You might receive a message on your pager or cell phone indicating a phone number you're supposed to call back. The phone number appears to be a local call, but, when you dial the number, it actually routes your call outside the country to a "bill-per-minute" service designed to maximize the amount of time the caller spends on the phone before hanging up. If you discover that you've been the victim of a 900-number scam, follow these procedures to rectify the situation as much as possible:

- **Recognize phone fraud** You typically won't realize you've been scammed until your phone bill arrives. Phone fraud takes other forms, too. Sometimes, you'll receive a notice in the mail, usually with an urgent request for you to place a call to claim a contest prize. Sometimes, the call might not be to an area code you recognize as a toll-call area code. For instance, the number might have a toll-free area code, like 800. Or, someone might take over your cell phone's serial number to make their own calls get charged to your cell phone account, as discussed in Chapter 1.

- **Notify the authorities** In a telephone fraud case, there is no account to close, just long distance charges on your phone bill. Reporting this type of experience to agencies that can deal with the problem universally, such as the Federal Trade Commission, is the best course of action. If the request came through the mail, then mail fraud is also involved. If this is the case, you should notify the U.S. Postal Service.

- **Notify the telephone company** Because there was no way for you to know that you were going to be billed, telephone companies will often remove the charges from your bill.

- **Get a new cell phone** If you discover that your cellular telephone is being billed for calls you didn't make, you should get a new cell phone. If someone has discovered the unique code being used to identify your cell phone to the wireless service provider, your code can be programmed into another cell phone—a process called *cloning*. Cloning is discussed in detail in Chapter 1. Calls made from a cloned phone are billed to the same account as your phone, so always review your charges to make sure you haven't been billed for calls you didn't make.

Dealing with Stolen Wireless Service

Wireless services aren't limited to your telephone any more. The same identity theft problems that apply to cell phones also apply to any wireless handheld devices, such as Palm Pilots and other personal digital assistants, or even a laptop with wireless networking. A stolen PDA can be used to send mail or make calls to people contained in your stored phone book. An identity thief might be very interested in your PDA for the account numbers, passwords, or business information you might have stored there. The thief might surf the Web on your dime until you close the account with your wireless service provider. A couple actions you can take if someone has stolen your wireless service are:

- **Notify wireless service providers** You can very easily set down your Palm Pilot and forget where you put it. If you discover that your palm pilot is missing and might have been stolen, you should notify your wireless provider so you won't be expected to pay for any per-minute access fees that accrue after the date you discovered you PDA was missing. You should always keep a backup of the information contained on your PDA, so now is a good time to review the data to understand what information about you has the potential for abuse after the theft.

- **Review backup data** Most handheld personal assistants come with software or other means of backing up the data stored on them. Usually, you transfer the data over a serial cable or the Internet to another computer. This is always advisable, so you don't lose the information if the PDA is stolen or lost. If you have performed backups of your PDA, now would be a good time to review the information from the last backup, to see the extent of the information stored on it. If you have recorded any passwords, bank account information, or other personally identifiable information that can be changed, you should take steps to change the information immediately, as a precaution. We talk more about changing passwords later in this chapter. Further, you should also refer to Chapter 2 for details about choosing strong passwords.

Managing the Fallout

Even after you've reported the crime and taken the steps described so far in this chapter, the damage is still not done. In addition to losing whatever was taken from you, additional fallout you'll suffer from a theft includes chasing down

reparations, defending your credit history, and carrying the emotional burden—
and you can't even know if or when it'll all be over. If you keep your records
organized and stay vigilant and informed, you will come through intact.

Unfortunately, there won't be a magical ending to your predicament. There's
no finish line; nothing to indicate that the imposter will no longer use any of
your private information. Even if the imposter has been apprehended and con-
victed, you can't be certain that your credit card number or e-mail address wasn't
sold on the Internet or given to a friend. If so, your information could be circulating for years. Only through diligence in monitoring how your information is
used will you be able to determine if an imposter is still active or has ceased
using your identity.

Dealing with all this can take an emotional toll on you as well as a financial
toll. Don't hesitate to seek local victim advocacy groups in your area for help.
Start by asking the law officer in charge of your case for contact information.
Some of the privacy groups listed later in this chapter also offer resources for
helping you deal with this aspect of an identity theft. Other people who have had
similar experiences might be able to offer insight into solving a particular
problem you're having. They might be able to suggest local resources that we
don't know about or other helpful information not suggested in this book.

The next step in managing the fallout is to make repairs to your financial
health. You'll need to contact credit bureaus and creditors to request repairs to
your credit report. This process could take a lot longer than reporting the
crime—a year or more, depending on the damage that was done. You might
decide to pursue legal recourse, which in turn might depend on the outcome of
a criminal prosecution. The upcoming sections offer some resource information
that you can use to make all that easier, beginning with how to contact credit
bureaus and understand your credit report.

Contacting Credit Bureau Services

Credit bureaus collect information about your financial health and store this
information in a database. Whenever you apply for a loan, a credit card, or other
banking service, the prospective lender makes an *inquiry* into your credit history
by viewing your credit report. Credit bureaus make money by charging a fee for
this service to lenders, employers, landlords, and individuals with valid business
reasons for needing this information. All inquiries are recorded on your report, so
other lenders can later determine how many times you have applied for a loan in
recent days.

You might think you already know what's on your credit report, because you opened all the accounts in the first place. But you might be surprised to learn exactly who has been performing inquiries about you. You have the right to view the information and examine your financial situation from the perspective of an outsider. Doing this once or twice a year at a minimum is advisable, in case adverse information is being incorrectly reported.

Table 7.1 lists the major credit bureaus. Most have started offering services to monitor your credit report on your behalf, for a monthly fee. Experian (www.experian.com) offers a service tracking important changes to your credit report for a $79 annual fee.

By checking your credit report often and notifying you of changes when they occur, this credit monitoring service keeps you informed when your financial information is accessed, thereby saving you from having to manually obtain and pay for a new report every day or every week. This type of service could provide your earliest tip-off that someone else is obtaining credit in your name. You might want to consider signing up for one of these services in the event you have been a victim of identity theft, because it won't be possible to tell in advance how often or for how long your identity information might be misused.

If you often receive offers in the mail for preapproved credit cards, those offers might just be how your financial information was stolen, as we examined in Chapter 1. The more credit card offers you toss in the trash, the greater your exposure to dumpster divers. To reduce the number of offers, you need to tell the credit bureaus that you don't want your information shared with the companies sending the offers in the first place. You might remove your name from the mailing list used to generate those offers by calling a toll-free number and requesting removal. This number covers all the credit reporting agencies listed in Table 7.1 for a period of two years: 1-888-5-OPTOUT (1-888-567-8688)

The automated phone system will ask you for your 10-digit phone number, attempt to verify the numeric portion of your home address, and then ask you to say and spell your full name. You will be removed from the list for all four reporting agencies after about five days. You need to remember to remove yourself again in two years, so it would be a good idea to make yourself a calendar note when you place your call.

Obtaining a Report

A really good hacker will have the ability to view your full credit report either through social engineering (such as impersonating your landlord) or breaking into the database. The credit bureaus do everything possible to protect your information, of course, but perfect security is impossible.

Even if you don't believe you are a victim of identity theft, you should be prepared ahead of time by knowing what information about you is available and by understanding the ramifications of someone abusing this information. The best way to do this is to obtain a copy of your credit report from the three major credit-reporting agencies listed in Table 7.1. The Privacy Rights Clearinghouse (www.privacyrights.org) recommends ordering a credit report twice a year, because identity theft is on the rise.

Table 7.1 Credit Bureau Contact Information

Bureau	Equifax	Experian	TransUnion
Order by Mail	Equifax Information Services, LLC P.O. Box 740241 Atlanta, GA 30374	National Consumer Assistance Center P.O. Box 2104 Allen, TX 75013	TransUnion LLC Consumer Disclosure Center P.O. Box 1000 Chester, PA 19022
Order by Phone	(800) 685-1111	(888) 524-3666	(800) 888-4213
Report Fraud	(800) 525-6285	(888) 397-3742	(800) 680-7289
Web Address	www.equifax.com	www.experian.com	www.transunion.com
Fee	$9.00	$9.00	$9.00

Be aware that anyone with a legitimate business need, including landlords and employers, can view your credit report. Your written consent is required only for a current or prospective employer, not for landlords, preapproved credit offers, or other credit inquiries. Thus, an identity thief can impersonate a legitimate person or organization in many ways in order to obtain your credit report, even if he isn't technically sophisticated enough to break into a computer or software application. An identity thief only needs sufficient identifying information so that the credit bureau believes the imposter is a legitimate lender using the credit bureau service.

When you get your own report, take care to investigate and thoroughly understand every line, and satisfy yourself that each entry is correct. If not, you have the right to dispute incorrect information. You should contact each of the credit bureaus in Table 7.1 to determine which agencies are reporting the incorrect information, and obtain instructions for making corrections. Next, let's take a look at a sample credit report and the information it contains.

Digging Deeper...

Obtaining a Free Report

If you have been a victim of identity theft, you are entitled to receive a free copy of your credit report from any of the various credit reporting agencies, so you can determine the extent of the damage. Residents of most states will be expected to pay a small fee that shouldn't exceed the fee listed in Table 7.1. If you're fortunate enough to live in Colorado, Georgia, Maryland, Massachusetts, New Jersey, or Vermont, you can obtain a free report at any time. According to the Fair Credit Reporting Act, you are also entitled to a free copy of your credit report if any of the following are true:

- You are unemployed and intent to apply for employment within 60 days.
- You are receiving public welfare assistance.
- You believe your consumer file contains inaccurate information due to fraud.
- You suffered adverse action, such as denial of credit or insurance, within the past 60 days.

Understanding Your Credit Report: A Case Study

A personal credit report contains information about your financial history and other personally identifying information about you. The Federal Trade Commission has ruled that certain information might *not appear* in your credit report without your consent, such as medical information, bankruptcy information more than 10 years old, debt information more than seven years old, or age and marital status if the inquiry is for a potential employer. This type of information might be collected, but it might not be reported to companies that don't first obtain written consent from you in advance.

Different reporting agencies format the content of their reports differently, so the appearance of your report will vary based on which agency is doing the reporting. Figure 7.1 is a fabricated example of the information a credit report might contain for Mr. Joe User after he has been a victim of identity theft.

Figure 7.1 Sample Credit Report

Generic Credit Bureau Services, Inc.

Personal Information Since 11/1/86 FAD 5/22/01

Name	JOSEPH USER 2222-2222	Reported
Employer	SPAMO SPROCKETS, YOURTOWN SC, VERIFIED 12/94	
Address	555 NOWHERE DR, YOURTOWN, SC, 29999	6/1/98
Address	100 MAIN ST, FUNCITY, CA 90210	1/1/95
AKA	JOE USER	
Phone	554-1212	

Credit Summary From 11/1/86 To 5/22/01

Public Records	3	Collections	3	Negative Trades	1	Inquiries	3
Hist Neg Trades	0	# Trades	1	Revolving	0	Open Trades	1
Hist Neg Occurr	0	Installment	0	Mortgage	0		

Type	High	Limit	Balance	Past Due	Payment	%Avail
Closed	$0	$0	$202	$202	$0	-
Totals	$0	$0	$202	$202	$0	-

Public Records

Reported/ Amount	ECOA/ Subscriber	Assets	Type/ Plaintiff/Attorney	Docket/ Paid	Court/ City, State
06/95 984	C Z 0111111		Civil judgement Pltff: CHEAPO MOTOR CO	95CVM11X	Superior Court
01/98	I Z 0111111		Chapter 7 bnkrptcy discharged Attn: THOMAS SOMEBODY	9802222 03/99	Federal District
05/98 1903	I Z 0111111		Civil judgement Pltff: WIDGETS R US	21FFF	Common Pleas

Collection Accounts

Firm/ID Code	Paid/ ECOA	Placed/ CLSD	VRFD/ CS(MOP)	$PLCD/ BAL	Acc#	Creditor Name	Remarks
ATTN L.L.C. Y 222221	I	04/99	05/00A O9B	83 83	8233	ANYMED CENTER	Placed for collection
CREDBURSYS Y 000000001	I	08/98	03/00A O9B	216 216	2217171717	FIXME HOSPITAL	Placed for collection
CAP RCV SVC Y 91111111	I	05/95	07/96A O9B	57 57	299999	THE FOOT DOCTOR	Placed for collection

Open Accounts

Acct Name/Address	Rptd/ ECOA	Opened Clsd/PD	High/ Limit	Pmt/ Term	Bal	Past Due	Current Status Mths 30 60 90	Hist Status	Rating
O'DAY WIRELESS 3300305 Subscriber code:U 029222 Loan Type:Open Remarks:Closed by consumer	05/01A I	02/01 05/01F	202		202	202	1		O2
Open Account Totals					$0	$202			

Inquiries

Date	Name/Address	Code	MKT	Type Inq/Loan	Amount
03/22/01	FAB AUDIO PRODUCTS	Y288399	FLA	I	
03/19/01	WESTERN UNION	FM2993818	SCT	I	300
02/06/01	WESTERN UNION	FX1036653	CNM	I	50

Page 1

In our fictional example, Joe happens to get a letter from a credit bureau telling him that negative information has been reported about him and advising him to get a copy of his credit report. He orders and receives the report in April and notices that O'Day Wireless has reported a $202 account balance as being 30 days past due. This is alarming to Joe because he doesn't have a cell phone, or so he believes. He also doesn't recall having done any business with Western Union in the previous two months, so why did Western Union inquire into his credit history? He contacts O'Day Wireless, and they confirm that cellular service was indeed set up in February under his name. Joe immediately informs the company that he does not own a cellular phone and requests that the account be closed, which is reported to the credit bureau the following month.

Joe then contacts Western Union and discovers that his bank account has been used to wire funds to someone in February and in March. Fab Audio Products also informs him there is a credit account application from him on file, which was recently approved for a $1,000 credit line, although it hasn't been used to charge anything yet. Joe immediately closes the account with Fab Audio and contacts the authorities to report an identity theft. The sample credit report in Table 7.2 is what Joe now has to either clean up or live with. Fortunately for him, Joe caught the problem early, before anything had been charged to the new account with Fab Audio.

Preparing Your Victim's Statement

Credit bureaus will ask you to prepare a victim's statement before they will make any changes or corrections to your credit report. After this is done, they will add a comment to your report that brings attention to the fact that your identity has been stolen. This is also known as a *fraud alert*, and it will serve as a warning to lenders or merchants who view your credit report in the future.

Somewhere in your victim's statement, you should ask the credit bureaus to include a statement on your report requesting that under no circumstances should merchants or lenders open any credit accounts or offer any loans without speaking to you in person, at a phone number you list in the request. This will also serve to let you know if someone is continuing to use your identity.

Figure 7.2 shows a model letter taken from USLaw.com (www.uslaw.com) that you can use to write your own victim's statement. Adding the fraud alert to your credit report won't stop the imposter entirely, but it can greatly increase your chances by alerting future lenders that a fraud has occurred and that credit should not be extended without first contacting you in person. Inquire how long the fraud alert will remain active and how it can be extended, because these services might differ for each reporting agency.

Figure 7.2 Sample Victim's Statement

Dear Sir/Madam:

This letter is to serve as written follow-up to my phone call to your office on [*Date*]. As I stated in my call to your representative [*Name*], I am the victim of identity fraud. I became aware of the theft of my identity on [*Date*] and in the following manner: [*Brief Description of Crime*]. Thus, I request certain items and assistance from your office. Specifically, please:

Continued

Figure 7.2 Continued

- Provide me with the name of an individual in your office to whom I should address all future correspondence about my credit file and the theft of my identity.
- Place a fraud alert on my credit file, noting that I am the victim of identity theft and that no credit is to be issued without my permission.
- Send a complete copy of my credit report to my home address, which is listed below. I understand that because I am a fraud victim, there is no charge for this report.
- Remove my name from any client list you might provide to other credit grantors or direct marketers.
- Notify all credit grantors or other agencies that have received my credit report within the last year that there has been a fraud committed against me. Please send me a copy of all such correspondence.
- Send me a list of all credit grantors (with phone numbers and addresses) to whom you are sending this information. Notify all companies that have inquired in the last 12 months about my credit that a fraud has occurred against me.
- Send me any booklets or handouts as to my legal rights and obligations, along with any additional information your agency might have to help me deal with this identity theft.
- Do not release my credit report without my permission. Do not change my address without my approval. Place this letter in my credit file. I am attaching a copy of my last utility payment and driver's license to verify my identity.

I have filed a complaint with the [*Name of Police Department*] concerning this crime. The police report number is [*Report Number*]. You might contact [*Name of Investigator or Case Agent*] at [*Phone Number*] to verify that this crime was reported.

Thank you very much for your immediate attention to this matter. I look forward to receiving the information I have requested, along with a copy of my credit report.

Should you need me to supply with any additional information, please notify me as soon as possible. My address is [*Home Address*], and I can be reached during the day at [*Phone Number*] and during the evening at [*Phone Number*].

Sincerely,
[*Signature*]
[*Name*]
[*Address*]
[*City, State and ZIP code*]

Knowing When to Seek Legal Help

As mentioned earlier in this chapter, you should not have to pay for credit card bills or other charges resulting from identity theft (other than the minimum $50 charge for a stolen credit card), nor should the fraud reflect badly on your credit history. The fact that someone impersonated you to cause you damage is not your fault. If creditors pursue you for actions taken by an imposter, you might need to obtain legal help for reversing civil actions or fighting a false arrest.

You might have trouble convincing a creditor or credit bureau to remove fraudulent information from your credit report. This can happen when companies are inexperienced with this problem or are trying to avoid absorbing the cost of a charge back. You might be tempted to pay for bogus credit card or telephone bills just to make the problem go away. Don't do it! You have up to a year to request a creditor to correct a credit card charge if you meet certain requirements, but *not if you've paid the bill*. In this case, the dollar amount must be over $50, you must try in good faith to get the original merchant to refund the money, and the merchant must be within certain distance limits from your home to qualify. If nothing you do is successful, get legal help, especially if the charges are referred to a collections agency or the imposter has engaged in illegal activities in your name.

Keeping Records

Keep records of any notary or postal fees incurred. You can recover the costs later if a judgment is issued. Be sure to keep a log of all phone calls, including dates, names, and other pertinent information when attempting to report the fraud to credit bureaus, law enforcement agencies, credit card companies, and so on. Keep track of the amount of time you spend on each call, and note any long distance charges. Make a note of copying fees, notary fees, and postage expenses you incur. This information will help you establish a basis for restitution later, if you are awarded a judgment. If not, you might be eligible for a tax reduction related to your loss. Consult your tax professional for more information.

Locating Government Resources

Identity theft became a federal crime in 1998 with the passing of The Identity Theft and Assumption Deterrence Act of 1998. Since that time, many states have passed their own laws or have laws pending regarding identity theft, privacy issues, credit reporting, and establishing jurisdiction. This section is devoted to providing a few resources where you can learn more about the laws pertaining to the state in which you live.

Statutes in Your State

FindLaw (www.findlaw.com) is a wonderful Web site where you can search for an attorney based on specialty, statutes based on state or subject area, legal reference materials, and other tools you might need to defend yourself after you have become a victim of identity theft. Figure 7.3 shows documents available about such topics as cyberspace law, electronic signature legislation, and Web forums dealing with legal topics pertaining to the Internet.

Figure 7.3 The FindLaw Web Site Page for Massachusetts Laws

Federal Trade Commission

The FTC is an agency that enforces laws protecting consumers in the marketplace. According to their mission statement, the FTC works "to enhance the smooth operation of the marketplace by eliminating acts or practices that are unfair or deceptive." The FTC maintains the complaint clearinghouse for victims of identity theft (as discussed earlier in this chapter). You'll want to notify the Identity Theft Clearinghouse if you've become a victim of this crime. They can also send you a booklet with more information about coping with identity theft after it has occurred. To obtain a booklet, contact the Identity Theft Clearinghouse at the following address:

> Identity Theft Clearinghouse
> Federal Trade Commission
> 600 Pennsylvania Avenue NW
> Washington, DC 20580

You can also call the toll-free Identity Theft Hotline at (877) IDTHEFT or file a complaint using the online form at www.consumer.gov/idtheft. The FTC also maintains a Web site at www.ftc.gov containing lots of information about protecting yourself online and understanding your rights under the Fair Credit Reporting Act.

Understanding the Fair Credit Reporting Act

During the process of cleaning up your credit report you might need to follow up with companies where purchases were made illegally. Understanding your rights under the Fair Credit Reporting Act (FCRA) will help you understand what actions credit or collection agencies can and cannot take against you. Your full rights under the Act can be found at www.ftc.gov/os/statutes/fcra.htm, but we include a summary of your rights here:

- You must be told if you have been denied credit as a result of information contained in your credit report.

- The information in your report can't be withheld from you. Free copies must be supplied to you under certain circumstances, such as if you have been denied credit.

- You are entitled to dispute information contained in your credit report. The credit reporting agency must investigate your dispute, usually within 30 days, and give you a report of its findings. A summary of your dispute must appear in future credit reports.

- Information that is outdated might not be reported. Generally, the cutoff is 7 years for credit information and 10 years for bankruptcy information.

- Reports cannot be provided to employers without your consent. Reports cannot contain medical information without your consent.

- You are allowed to exclude your name from lists used for unsolicited offers of insurance or credit.

- If any of your rights under the FCRA are violated, you can seek damages.

Other Suggested Resources

Victims of identity theft might find their name or Social Security Number has been added to mailing lists, magazine subscriptions, bank accounts, unwanted credit cards, or other loan services. Unfortunately for the victim, tracking down the service providers and getting removed from lists or having services stopped is a manual process. Chapter 1 presents several opt-out programs for telemarketing lists that a victim can follow after the theft has occurred. Twenty of the states also have individual telemarketing opt-out programs, which you can learn about at the FindLaw Web site (www.findlaw.com).

> **NOTE**
>
> If you find yourself receiving unwanted sexually oriented advertising or other unwanted mail from a particular company, you can request that the U. S. Postal Service stop sending it to you. Simply stop by your local post office and request Form 1500 or Form 2150 to stop mail from a particular company.

Other sites on the Internet offer a wealth of advice and guidance about preventing identity theft and taking action after it has occurred. This section presents a few that you will find invaluable if you have become a victim. Don't hesitate to follow advice you find on the sites mentioned in this book.

Privacy Rights Advocates

You might wonder what privacy rights have to do with identity theft, but the two topics are tightly interwoven. As corporations or other entities collect information about you, the result is a series of databases scattered about with your private information stored in them. Information in one database can be sold and correlated with information in another database to successfully identify you.

This correlating of data isn't merely useful for marketers; this isn't just about getting rid of junk mail anymore. Companies often make big money selling their customer information databases to other companies that can use the information to produce their own service or product. The laws you expect to protect you from rampant misuse of this kind of profiling information are only now being conceived and written.

As this book shows throughout, outsiders can use many means to collect private data about you. Some ways you probably already knew about; others ways, you probably didn't. Looking toward the future, you, as a victim of identity theft, might want to become more involved with privacy groups that stay abreast of the latest information about identity theft, privacy, and laws that protect online data. This section is intended to inform you about the existence of some helpful resources.

The Electronic Frontier Foundation

The Electronic Frontier Foundation (EFF) (www.eff.net) is a 10-year-old donor-supported nonprofit organization dedicated to protecting *your* civil liberties online. EFF supports online privacy by educating the public about technologies being used to violate privacy and by offering suggestions for avoiding or working around those technologies. The EFF Web site offers the latest news about pending legislation and technology that might impact your rights online.

The Privacy Rights Clearinghouse

The Privacy Rights Clearinghouse (www.privacyrights.org) is a comprehensive not-for-profit Web site where you can find lots more information about taking control of your personal information both online and offline. Their Web site offers several fact sheets about identity theft but, more interestingly, provides some victim's stories taken from real cases that might provide valuable insight into your own experience.

The Identity Theft Resource Center

The Identity Theft Resource Center (www.idtheftcenter.org) is a program affiliated with the Privacy Rights Clearinghouse that offers resources in English and Spanish, dedicated to victims of identity theft and people wanting to learn how to prevent it. The Web site offers a self-help section with information about coping with the court experience, organizing your case, and dealing with the emotional impact of identity theft.

Privacy International

If it weren't for the seriousness of the subject matter, the Big Brother awards section of the Privacy International (www.privacyinternational.org) Web site would be funny. The awards are at once laughable and pathetic, shining a spotlight on the people, agencies, and companies making the biggest contributions to loss of privacy. Aside from that, the site covers important privacy news topics around the world; it doesn't limit its coverage to the United States.

The Electronic Privacy Information Center

The Electronic Privacy Information Center (EPIC) (www.epic.org) is a public interest research center in Washington, DC. Established in 1994, the EPIC was created to increase awareness of emerging civil liberties issues, protect privacy both online and offline, protect the First Amendment, and defend our constitutional values. You can learn more about pending privacy legislation, legal actions, free speech online, and freedom of information as well as privacy in the archives section of this comprehensive Web site.

The Privacy Coalition

The Privacy Coalition (www.privacypledge.org) is an organization dedicated to supporting legislation protecting personal privacy. Their Web site contains privacy news and information, including letters to government officials proposing reform. The Privacy Coalition also participates in FTC complaints denouncing monopolistic or predatory business practices affecting your personal privacy.

The Global Internet Liberty Campaign

The Global Internet Liberty Campaign (GILC) (www.gilc.org) takes a global approach to supporting online encryption, promoting the rights of free speech, and fighting discrimination. This site is particularly useful to people who are interested in privacy issues centered in Europe.

Summary

To most people, the computer and the Internet are marvelous inventions that expand the world of communication and entertainment to lengths never before reached. There's no doubt about that. But, your freedom to enjoy knowledge contained on the Internet, to have cheap and private conversations with your friends online, to purchase goods from your home office, and to reach out to other people like you online has an unfortunate side effect. By participating in these activities, you disclose information about yourself that can be used to impersonate you. Throughout this book, we demonstrate precautions you can take, both online and offline, to protect your private data. But sometimes, precautions aren't enough, and you become a crime victim anyway.

This chapter is dedicated to helping you understand what you should do when someone has succeeded in using your identity to commit an associated crime of fraud. You need to begin by understanding what has happened and reporting the crime to police. You'll need to help collect the documents police will need to investigate the theft, such as bank records, credit card statements, and credit bureau reports. If you can obtain these documents yourself, you can speed up the investigation by eliminating the need to complete permission affidavits.

After you have notified police, the next step is to notify the merchants, lenders, banks, and other service providers with whom your identity was fraudulently used to obtain goods or services. In each case, you need to let the appropriate entities know that you have been a victim of fraud, and you need to request that the account be closed. The last organization you should notify is the Identity Theft Center, a central clearing house for identity theft data that is affiliated with the Federal Trade Commission.

Obtaining a credit report might be a new experience for you. A credit bureau report contains information about your financial health. You aren't usually forced to look at your credit report unless you've been denied credit. Because this happens frequently in cases of identity theft, denial of credit might be the first evidence you see that an identity theft has occurred.

You should obtain copies of credit reports from the major credit reporting agencies frequently. Verify the accuracy of the information the reports contain, and vigorously pursue corrections wherever false information exists. You'll need to prepare a victim's statement and provide this, along with a copy of the police report, to credit bureaus in order for them to correct information related to the crime. A fraud alert can be added to your report to warn potential creditors that you have been a victim of fraud and to request that new accounts can only be opened after speaking to you personally. You might need to seek legal help if you have difficulty getting credit bureaus to remove erroneous information from your report.

As you manage the fallout identity theft can cause, you'll benefit from a variety of resources available to help you get through it. The Federal Trade Commission provides a comprehensive Web site devoted to identity theft. Also, many privacy rights groups provide guides, fact sheets, and case studies from other people, just like you, who've been through it all and can offer tips to help you through your own identity theft experience.

Solutions Fast Track

Taking Immediate Action

☑ Catching identity theft early is your most important tool in combating it. Delaying action provides time for continued abuse of credit cards and your bank account.

☑ You should report crimes to authorities where you live and in the state where your information is being used. Report fraud attempts to credit bureaus and creditors, and close accounts that are being used by an imposter. Refuse to pay for charges brought on to you by an imposter. Obtain legal help if necessary.

☑ Call the ID theft hotline to report identity fraud. Your situation might be part of a larger criminal investigation, so it's important to notify federal authorities.

Managing the Fallout

☑ Contact the three major credit bureaus to obtain a copy of your credit report. You have the right to dispute items in the report that are incorrect. Obtain legal help if a credit-reporting bureau is failing to help you remove something that should be removed. Add a victim's statement to your report so additional creditors will reject applications from imposters.

☑ You can stop receiving preapproved credit card offers generated by credit bureau mailing lists if you call the opt-out hotline at (888) 5-OPT-OUT.

☑ Credit bureaus are a good source of information for detecting identity theft. You can order your own reports frequently and examine them for suspicious activity. Alternatively, you can pay a monthly fee for a service that examines your report periodically and notifies you of suspicious activity.

☑ Keep good records about time and money spent cleaning up after an identity theft, so you can claim actual losses in the future.

Locating Government Resources

☑ Laws protecting you from identity theft differ from one state to another. Your rights in one state might not be protected in another state. FindLaw can help you determine your legal protections in your state.

☑ Report Social Security fraud to the SSA hotline at (800) 269-0271. Examine your Social Security statement periodically for evidence of inappropriate use of your Social Security Number.

☑ The Federal Trade Commission is a good source of information about protecting yourself online, and maintains the Identity Theft Clearinghouse, a central agency for reporting identity theft.

Other Suggested Resources

☑ A wealth of information resides on the Internet that can help identity theft victims. Privacy rights groups—such as The Electronic Frontier Foundation, Privacy Rights Clearinghouse, and Privacy International—offer news articles, tips for prevention, guides for managing legal issues, and advice from people who've already been victims.

☑ Stop unwanted mail by filling out Form 1500 with the U.S. Postal Service.

Frequently Asked Questions

The following Frequently Asked Questions, answered by the authors of this book, are designed to both measure your understanding of the concepts presented in this chapter and to assist you with real-life implementation of these concepts. To have your questions about this chapter answered by the author, browse to **www.syngress.com/solutions** and click on the **"Ask the Author"** form.

Q: Would it help if I stored sensitive documents, like copies of my online tax returns, on a CD-ROM instead of my computer's hard drive?

A: Yes, but only if you take the disk out of the computer's CD-ROM drive after each use, and keep it out of the hands of people who might have physical access to it. The idea is to prevent users on the Internet from accessing your information. If information isn't stored on your computer's hard drive, then you don't have to be as concerned about what happens while your computer is connected to the Internet. Don't forget, though, that when you use applications like e-mail and Web browsers, cookies or other types of hidden files might be created on your computer that contain private data you might not know about. Don't assume your computer is free of private data just because you store the documents you *do* know about on a CD-ROM.

Q: I don't use credit cards, and I never buy anything online, so I don't need to worry about identity theft, right?

A: Wrong! No matter how careful you are, you are never 100 percent protected. In terms of your computer use, if you use your computer to file your taxes, send e-mail, post to newsgroups, chat online, or even just surf the Web, the potential remains for your personal information to be stolen and used in undesirable ways.

Q: I just learned that someone else sent derogatory e-mail to my boss using my e-mail address, so my boss thinks the message came from me. What do I do now?

A: Possibly, someone has discovered your e-mail password. You should change your password as a precaution. Just as possible, though, someone might have figured out how to impersonate you in an e-mail without actually knowing your e-mail password. A computer system administrator or other person familiar with reading e-mail *headers* (or *envelopes*) can tell you if this is the case. To determine this, you'll need the original e-mail that your boss received, with the headers intact and displayed. Your boss's e-mail software should have the ability to view the header information, which can be printed or forwarded to you directly. Enlist the assistance of a computer professional from there.

Q: I keep getting these embarrassing pop-up ads on my computer for things like viagra and pornographic sites, but I've never visited anything like that on the Web! Does this mean someone else is using my computer?

A: No. What it means is that you've visited some fairly innocuous Web site that has set a cookie or installed some spyware on your computer that is displaying those ads. If that's the case, you should follow the instructions in Chapter 4 for deleting cookies and temporary files from your computer, and blocking ad-ware. You might have installed some software that contains spyware within it. It's easy to do if you download software from the Internet frequently. If this is the case, the pop-up ads won't go away until you remove the spyware from your computer. Try uninstalling any software that you might have installed about the time the ads started showing up. If that doesn't solve the problem entirely, consider restoring your computer's software from the restore CD-ROM that came with it originally. This will restore your computer to the way it was when you first bought it, so be sure to save any documents or data before doing this. Follow your computer manufacturer's instructions for performing a factory restore, because some computers might not come with a restore CD-ROM.

Q: How can I tell if someone has accessed my computer's hard drive over the Internet?

A: A possible sign of someone accessing your computer is if software that normally works fine suddenly stops working, even though you've made no changes and haven't installed anything new, opened any e-mail attachments, or accessed any files on the disk yourself. The only real way to be certain is to perform regular backups of all the files on your computer's hard drive, so you can compare what's there today with what was there yesterday, the day before, and so on. If files go missing and you didn't delete them, that's suspicious but not concrete proof. You will need the help of monitoring software, as discussed in Chapter 6, to prove for certain whether someone else is accessing your hard drive. You should probably enlist the help of a computer professional if you suspect this is happening.

Q: How can I be certain that nobody has sat down in front of my computer and used it as me while I was away?

A: The monitoring software discussed in Chapter 6 can help. If someone is logging on as you, you can find out who it is by installing a camera on the PC and using monitoring software that records an image from the camera when the mouse moves or at specific time intervals. Your PC then becomes an inexpensive security system. Several kinds of software applications are available that will do this for you; check the Web sites suggested in Chapter 6 for one that suits your needs.

Q: It seems like everyday there's something new about the Internet's lack of security. Should I even be using it at all?

A: Like many opportunities in life, you don't enjoy a reward unless you take a risk. The problem isn't that the Internet isn't safe, because nothing in life is safe. The problem is that few regulations are in place to protect your safety as you go about using it. Automobiles are no less likely to be involved in a crash today than they were in 1950 when seatbelts weren't yet being used; still, the probability of you dying in a car crash is greatly reduced by regulations requiring seatbelts today. Just as, in today's world, it's impossible to create an automobile that can't crash, it's impossible to create an Internet that can't be used maliciously. As the Internet matures, some of the dangers will shake out. Until then, all you can do is understand how you can be affected by it, use it only when necessary, and protect yourself from the worst risks any way you can.

Chapter 8

Configuring Your Browser and Firewall

Solutions in this chapter:

- **Managing Your Web Browser's Security Features**

- **Configuring Your Home Firewall**

- **Applications Port List**

Introduction

Now that you understand the ways that securing your computer and transactions on the Internet helps protect you from identity theft, you're ready to install a firewall and make security improvements to your Web browser settings. Each manufacturer of firewall and Web browser software creates their products to look and feel different from others in their class—yet, at the core, the basic functions are similar. As we demonstrate in Chapter 4, all browsers receive cookies and can block them; you just need to know how. Likewise, all firewalls block incoming network connections and can block outbound connections too if you want to enable this feature.

Knowing what you want to do is a good start, but translating what you want to do into configuring specific menu items is another matter. Sometimes, if you can just see one or two examples of software configurations that do what you want, you can figure out how to configure your own software in the same way—even if it's not the same as the software in the example. Toward that end, this chapter provides examples for enabling some of the important security features in the three most popular Web browsers we discussed in Chapter 4. This chapter also provides examples for configuring firewalls, including two of the most popular personal firewall products and an external firewall product for people securing multiple computers in the home. Configuration examples in this chapter are provided for the following applications:

- Internet Explorer
- Netscape
- Opera
- ZoneAlarm Pro
- BlackICE Defender
- Siemens DSL/Cable Router

Managing Your Web Browser's Security Features

Not all browsers provide the same ability to manage your Web privacy in the same way. By understanding how browsers differ, you can make good choices about which browser, and which configuration options, best protect your private information as you traverse the Web. Everyone has a different expectation for security and privacy, so you should adopt the browser with security features that most suit *your* needs. In this chapter, we look at three popular browsers and discuss various features each one provides for keeping your Web browsing experience private.

> ### NOTE
>
> Most browsers have an option that allows you to enter your personal information profile. A form typically asks for the kind of information you'd put on a business card. The browser can then insert the information into Web forms, e-mails, or news postings without having to retype it. This feature makes life easier, certainly, but it also stores private information you might not want to be viewable by everyone. There is a small risk that the information might be shared with the wrong service, your computer could be stolen, or the information could otherwise be obtained without your knowledge. You should evaluate the value of using this feature against the risks it brings. If you don't really need it, don't use it.

Internet Explorer Version 6

Let's begin with Windows Internet Explorer version 6 (IE 6), which uses the concept of *Security Zones* to allow you to classify Web sites by level of trust. Zones enable you to choose one set of security settings that are more permissive for use with Web sites you trust, and another more restrictive level of security to be used with Web sites you don't trust or have never seen before. Microsoft provides four zones for your use, shown in Table 8.1.

Table 8.1 Understanding Security Zones in Internet Explorer

Zone	Use This Zone For	Default Security Level
Internet	Everything not yet classified	Medium
Local Intranet	Sites on a local network	Medium-Low
Trusted Sites	Sites you use often and trust	Low
Restricted Sites	Sites you are testing	High

Microsoft's Security Zones allow you to make decisions about which specific security features should be enabled for each zone and what Web sites you want to be allowed to use each zone's settings. To make life easier for IE newcomers, Microsoft has provided a reasonable default security level for each zone. To empower users wanting to take more control over their security, Microsoft provides the ability to change the entire zone's default security level or change individual security features separately for each zone. Your own settings should be at least the default settings or higher. If IE 6 is your browser of choice, you should review your settings to make sure they are at least at the levels shown in the table.

Figure 8.1 shows the four zones in the **Security** tab displayed when you click the **Tools | Internet Options** menu along with their relative security levels. For security, all Web sites are considered to be in the more restrictive *Internet* zone until you manually place them the more permissive *Trusted Sites* zone or the more restrictive *Local Intranet* or *Restricted* zones. To add a Web site to a particular zone:

1. Highlight the zone you want to change.

2. Click the **Sites** button.

3. Type in the site's URL.

4. Click **OK**.

Figure 8.1 Using Security Zones in Internet Explorer 6

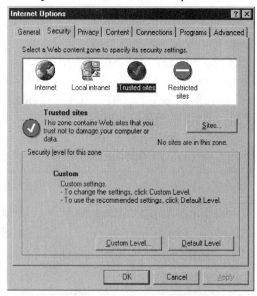

Each zone has its own set of configuration options, which you can view or edit by clicking **Custom Level**. The security configuration for the more permissive Trusted Sites differs significantly from the security configuration for the Internet zone, which is shown in Figure 8.2. After you choose a security level from the scroll box at the bottom of this screen and click **Reset**, each security feature inside the upper scroll box changes to a setting that's an appropriate default value for the level that was chosen.

Setting the Internet zone to **High**, for instance, disables most of the browser features. This is the safest setting for the Internet zone, but the disabled features are commonly used to view flashy animated or music-enabled Web sites. As a result, certain sites might not display properly under the **High** setting. Avoiding sites that use these features is a better approach, but you might not always be able to. Only you can decide if using lower zone security so you can view a site is worth the risk of potentially downloading a malicious ActiveX control, Java applet, Java script, and so on.

Figure 8.2 Setting a Zone's Security Level in Internet Explorer 6

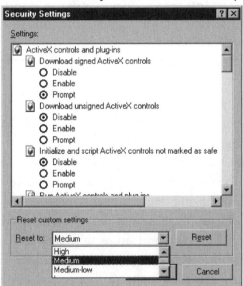

Alternatively, you can change the setting for each security feature individually. Table 8.2 lists the meanings of the setting options for any given security feature. A feature that is set to **Prompt** will be enabled or disabled based on your response in a pop-up window that will display each time the feature is required by a Web site you visit. The **Prompt** setting is considered safer than **Enable** but not as safe as **Disable**, because this setting allows you the possibility of making a poor choice. Disable is always the safest way to go. We examine a few modifications to the default settings later in this chapter when we discuss beefing up your browser settings.

Table 8.2 Understanding Internet Explorer Security Options

Option	Feature Defaults To	User is Prompted for Action
Enable	On	No
Disable	Off	No
Prompt	N/A	Yes

NOTE

A complete discussion of all the various settings for the more than 20 IE6 security features is well beyond the scope of this book. If you'd like to learn more about Internet Security Zones, a good place to start is the Microsoft TechNet article at www.microsoft.com/TechNet/prodtechnol/ie/ reskit/ie5/part1/ch07zone.asp.

IE 6 also provides a nice feature for managing cookies, shown in Figure 8.3. In Chapter 4 we show how to delete cookies in IE 6, but perhaps, instead, you want to allow cookies in some situations and block them in others. You can do this using the security slider bar that is available from the **Tools** menu, under the **Internet Options | Privacy** tab. Choosing a privacy level with this slider causes cookies to be blocked to varying degrees in the Internet zone. The recommended setting for this slider is **High**. You can also define certain Web sites to be treated differently, by clicking **Edit** at the bottom of this same screen and typing in their address. You might use this feature if, say, you want cookies to be off by default (slider bar is set to **High**) but there's one or two sites that you use frequently that require cookies to be turned on in order for you to interact with them correctly. The slider bar setting would then apply to all other Web sites by default.

Table 8.3 shows the variety of settings that Internet Explorer uses to determine how cookies will be handled. To configure how cookies are handled in Internet Explorer 6 through the Privacy Settings section of Internet Options, follow these steps:

1. Click the Windows **Start** menu, select **Settings**, and then click the item labeled **Control Panel**.

2. When the **Control Panel** appears, double-click **Internet Options**.

3. Select the **Privacy** tab, and then move the slider bar to determine how you want cookies to be handled.

Figure 8.3 Setting Privacy Levels in Internet Explorer 6

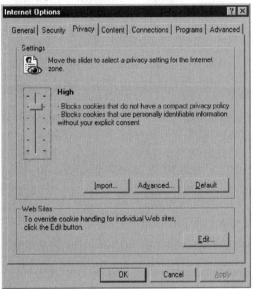

Table 8.3 Privacy Settings for Internet Explorer 6

Setting	How Cookies Are Handled
Accept All Cookies	Cookies from Web sites are not blocked, and Web sites will be able to read existing ones on your machine.
Low	Cookies from third-party sites that don't include a privacy statement that can be read by the computer are blocked. Those from third parties that attempt to use personally identifiable information without your implicit consent are deleted when Internet Explorer is closed.
Medium	Cookies from third-party sites that don't include a privacy statement that can be read by the computer are blocked as well as those from third parties that attempt to use personally identifiable information without your implicit consent. Also, cookies from first-party sites that attempt to use personally identifiable information

Continued

Table 8.3 Continued

Setting	How Cookies Are Handled
	without your implicit consent are deleted when Internet Explorer is closed.
Medium High	Cookies from third-party sites that don't include a privacy statement that can be read by the computer are blocked as well as those from third-party sites that attempt to use personally identifiable information without your explicit consent. Cookies from first-party sites that use personally identifiable information without implicit consent are also blocked.
High	Cookies that don't include a privacy statement that can be read by the computer and those that attempt to use personally identifiable information without your explicit consent are blocked. This applies to all Web sites.
Block All Cookies	Cookies from Web sites are blocked, and Web sites won't be able to read existing ones on your machine.

One of the downsides to Internet Explorer is that, because it is the default browser included with every Windows computer, it is the most common browser in use and therefore the most targeted for hacking. If a criminal has reason to expect that you'll be using Internet Explorer, he might be more inclined to use a known exploit for an older version in order to gather information from your computer, for instance. However, Microsoft makes frequent security patches available to deal with new exploits, so this might be less of a concern if you always install security patches as soon as they are available. We talk more about obtaining and installing security patches at little later in this chapter.

NOTE

Some sites might directly instruct you to enable specific browser features, such as Java or ActiveX controls, if you want to view the site the way it was intended. You should have a healthy mistrust for following those instructions. In the vast majority of cases, making the change will cause no immediate harm. However, a remote chance exists that the requested change might be overkill, might be abused by other sites you'll visit in the future, or might enable a Web server to do something malicious using a software bug in your browser.

Netscape 6.2

At the time of this writing, Netscape version 6.2 is the latest available. Instead of grouping Web sites with similar security requirements together in a zone with a name, Netscape approaches the security of each Web site individually. This allows you to manage your own security requirements for each site separately.

From the **Edit| Preferences | Privacy and Security** menu, several security options are available for managing cookies, passwords, and other personal information (see Figure 8.4). Selecting **Cookies** from this menu allows you to set default values for how cookies should be handled. Details of these options can be seen in Table 8.4. You should check the box labeled **Warn me before storing a cookie** so Netscape will alert you when a Web site attempts to store the cookie on your system. You then have the option of allowing or disallowing that particular site's cookie.

Figure 8.4 Managing Security Settings in Netscape 6.2

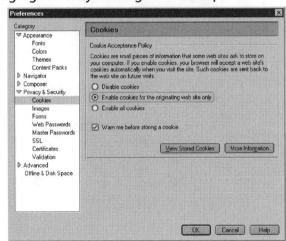

Table 8.4 Settings for Cookies in Netscape:

Setting	How Cookies are Handled
Disable cookies	Cookies from Web sites are blocked.
Enable cookies for the originating Web site only	Cookies from third parties or those received through e-mail (in which the message contains a Web page) are blocked.
Enable all cookies	Cookies are accepted from all Web sites.

One of the more interesting features of Netscape 6.2 is its easy-to-access option to **View Stored Cookies** from within the **Preferences** dialog box, which brings up the **Cookie Manager**. From the Cookie Manager, you can view and remove one or all cookies stored by Netscape. Figure 8.5 demonstrates some cookies that have been set for Joe User. One cookie in particular shows that information stored inside the cookie file includes Joe's full name and home address (555 Nowhere Way). This utility can give you information about a site's cookie, before you decide whether to disable future cookies from the site. Being able to easily view the contents is very useful. The more private information contained in a cookie, the more likely it should be removed. Cookies should be disabled by default. If you run across a Web site that requires cookies and you can't live without using its services, turn on cookies for just the one site.

Figure 8.5 Viewing Cookies Using Netscape 6.2

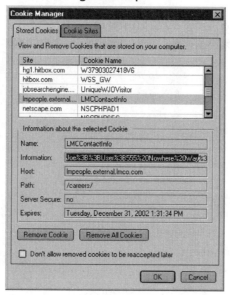

> **NOTE**
>
> The cookie shown in Figure 8.5 also demonstrates the need to protect all files on your computer, no matter how obscure or hidden, because they might contain important information you don't want made available for viewing. If you were to accidentally share your entire hard drive or even just the directory where the cookie file is stored, you could be giving away the ability to steal private information about you. See Chapter 5 to learn how to disable or set correct permissions for file shares.

Next on the agenda for securing your browsing experience using Netscape 6.2 is to turn off automatic storing of information in forms. Netscape provides this feature so you can automatically save private information, such as name, address, and credit card number, which you type into forms on the Web. Netscape will replay the information for you at a later time. This feature makes life simpler but stores sensitive data unnecessarily on your hard drive. Unless you really need this feature, you should turn it off. From the **Preferences** menu, click **Forms**, and uncheck the box as shown in Figure 8.6 before clicking **OK**.

Figure 8.6 Securing Form Data Using Netscape 6.2

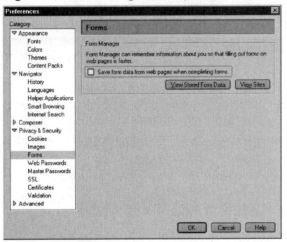

Netscape provides a password manager that can store your passwords each time you type them into a Web page. By storing your passwords in Netscape, you don't need to write them down in a less secure way, such as in a notebook or plain file on your computer. Should you use this feature? If you do, you rely on Netscape to provide security for those passwords, to properly encrypt them while they are stored on your hard drive. No doubt Netscape does due diligence in this regard, but accidents are also possible. Using this feature is certainly better than writing passwords on a sticky note on the front of your monitor. However, an even better approach would be to use the tricks presented in Chapter 2 and Chapter 4 for remembering passwords associated with each individual Web site, so you don't need to store them anywhere except your memory. The Web Password Manager is turned on by default. If you don't absolutely need this feature, you should turn it off by clearing the box in the **Web Passwords** menu, as shown in Figure 8.7.

Figure 8.7 Managing Passwords Using Netscape 6.2

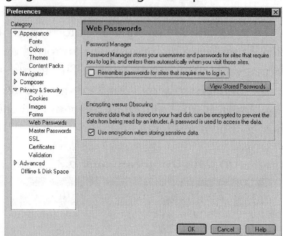

Finally, Netscape allows you to disable Java and Java Scripting, but not for individual Web sites. Java is either on or off for all sites. If it's off (the most secure setting for a Web surfing computer), some sites you visit might not display correctly. However, Netscape is somewhat less targeted for attack than Internet Explorer, because fewer people use it. The recommended setting is off, although this means that Web sites requiring Java might not display properly. If you can live without the features described here and don't care to view any sites requiring Java, Java scripting, or cookies, then Netscape with these features disabled is a good choice for safe Web surfing.

Opera 6

If you're like most people, you've heard a lot about Internet Explorer, at least a little about Netscape, and have never heard of Opera (www.opera.com). That's because Opera is the newcomer on the block. You can download a free trial version of Opera that displays an ad banner, or you can pay a small fee and receive a licensed version without any advertising. Opera provides some very useful security features that don't exist in other browsers, so we want to spend a few minutes telling you about how they can help protect you against theft of your private information as you surf the Web.

At first glance, Opera looks like any other browser, until you click **File | Preferences** and view the flexibility that's built into it. For instance, in the **Network** menu, you'll find a scroll bar that lets Opera identify itself to Web servers as Opera, Internet Explorer, or Netscape. Why is that useful? If a Web site were programmed to exploit a bug in Opera, it would check to see what type of browser you're using before launching the attack. By masquerading as Netscape or IE, you might be able to avoid being bitten by certain exploits aimed directly at Opera.

Opera's **Privacy** menu provides a comprehensive set of options for managing cookies that covers all the bases, shown in Figure 8.8. You can turn off cookies, adding individual exceptions later, if necessary, using the **Edit Server Filters** feature. It's a good idea to also turn off automatic redirection, which helps ensure that you don't get tricked into thinking you're viewing one site when you're actually viewing another. Opera's Privacy options include the following:

- **Enable referrer logging** Allows sites to note pages you came from and refer to one another. By disabling this feature, some sites might not function properly.

- **Enable automatic redirection** Allows a site you visit to redirect you to a different site.

- **Use cookies to trace password protected pages** Causes pages within a site you authenticated using a password to be deleted from your hard disk when you exit Opera.

Figure 8.8 Managing Cookies in Opera 6

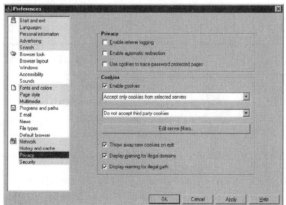

In addition to these settings, the Cookies section contains a checkbox that allows you to control whether cookies are enabled or disabled. If disabled, the only items you'll be able to change are **Enable referrer logging** and **Enable automatic redirection**. This is because everything else on this dialog box deals specifically with cookies and thereby needs them to be enabled if the settings are to apply.

Below the **Enable Cookies** checkbox are two drop-down lists that specify how cookies are handled. The settings in the first drop-down list are selected first; these settings are detailed in Table 8.5.

Table 8.5 Settings for upper drop-down list in Opera Privacy Preferences

Setting	How Cookies are Handled
Automatically accept all cookies	Cookies from Web sites are not blocked.
Accept only cookies from selected servers	If selected, you must specify which servers you'll accept cookies from by clicking the **Edit Server Filters** button on the dialog.
Display received cookies	You are prompted as to whether you want to accept or reject cookies as they are received.
Do not accept cookies	Cookies from Web sites will not be accepted.

The settings you then choose in the lower drop-down list apply to any setting in the first, except **Do not accept cookies**. If this is selected, it doesn't matter how cookies are handled. The settings for the second drop-down menu are detailed in Table 8.6.

Table 8.6 Settings for Lower Drop-down List in Opera Privacy Preferences

Setting	How cookies are handled
Only accept cookies for the server	Accepts cookies set by the active server (that is, the server you're receiving the current page from) and all pages within that server's domain.
Don't accept third-party cookies	Cookies sent by third parties are not accepted.
Display third-party cookies	You are prompted as to whether you want to accept or reject cookies as they are received.
Accept from any servers	Cookies from any server are accepted.

One of the more interesting features of Opera 6 is that it gives you simple control over pop-up advertising, as shown in Figure 8.9. Selecting **Refuse pop-up windows** effectively disables those annoying ads that pop up when you visit certain Web sites. Although, the option won't disable advertising from within the Opera browser.

Figure 8.9 Refusing Ad Pop-Ups in Opera 6

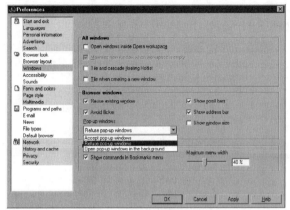

Configuring Your Home Firewall

We chose the products in this section based on their popularity and/or price. The personal software products are available for free trial on the Internet, so you can download and try them out before buying. The Siemens DSL/cable router was chosen mostly for its price—it's the least expensive external NAT (network address translation) firewall we found at the local large computer store. Knowing that price is an important factor, we felt it was important to demonstrate that you can use inexpensive products to improve your home network's security. However, we wouldn't classify the Siemens DSL/cable modem as the most secure external firewall you can buy, by any means. For this reason, our discussion will include comments, where appropriate, to help you understand the products' limitations as well as benefits. Hopefully, all this will help you decide if a product is right for you and give you some foundation for making a decision about what you're looking for in an external firewall.

BlackICE Defender for Windows

BlackICE version 3.0.53 for Windows is firewall software produced by Network Ice, which was subsequently bought by Internet Security Systems. You can buy or download a copy for evaluation at www.iss.net/products_services/ hsoffice_protection/buy.php.

When you install BlackICE for the first time, an icon for the BlackICE service will appear in the system tray. To edit the BlackICE settings or view the log files it makes, right-click the icon. You will then see the configuration screen shown in Figure 8.10.

Figure 8.10 BlackICE Firewall Tab

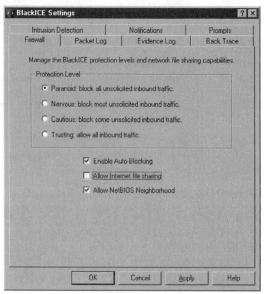

The **BlackICE Settings** dialog box contains seven tabs that allow you to configure various types of settings. The **Firewall** tab allows you to select a protection level without having to know very much about how firewalls operate. We recommend the **Paranoid** setting, which blocks any computer on the Internet from *originating* a conversation with your computer. If you interact with Web-based applications that won't work without session cookies, you might find that the **Paranoid** setting causes those applications not to work correctly. You might also have trouble viewing streaming media (such as listening to music or watching video) or using applications that need to open multiple connections back to your computer from the server (such as NetMeeting or other video teleconferencing programs). You might need to experiment to find the highest acceptable setting that is right for you.

If you check the box to **Enable Auto-Blocking**, intruders who attempt to connect inappropriately to your computer will be prevented from doing so.

Clearing this check box will cause BlackICE to record information about the attempt (such as the IP address of the remote computer) in the log files but won't attempt to stop the connection from occurring.

If you need to share files or printers with other computers in the home, you'll need to clear the check box to **Allow Internet file sharing**. You'll also need to make sure the box to **Allow NetBIOS Neighborhood** is checked (on). If you only have one computer in the home and don't need to share files or printers from it to another computer at work or elsewhere on the Internet, you should turn off this feature by leaving both boxes unchecked. If you have several computers in the home or use the computer to connect to an employer's network by dial-up or other means, you'll need to make sure the box to **Allow NetBIOS Neighborhood** is checked (on).

If you want finer control over blocking incoming connections with BlackICE, you can manually configure connections using the **Advanced Firewall Settings** feature shown in Figure 8.11. To get to this screen, click the BlackICE icon in the system tray to bring up the BlackICE Defender monitoring window. From the monitoring window, select the **Tools** menu, click **Advanced Firewall Settings**, and then click the **Add** button to see the screen in Figure 8.11.

Figure 8.11 BlackICE Add Firewall Entry Dialog Box

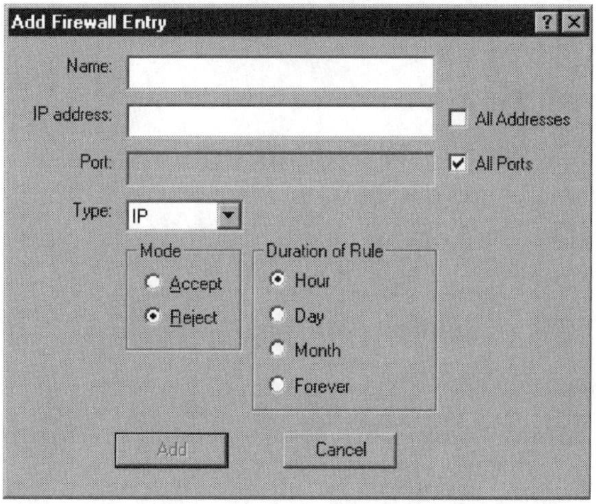

This screen lets you take one of several actions. First, let's say you need to make your computer completely available (visible) to a selected few computers. For example, a teacher might want to provide multiple services—such as Web content, shared files stored on disk, and e-mail services—to other computers in an Internet-enabled classroom but not to other computers on the Internet. To do this, you can enter the allowed computer's IP address and leave the **All Ports** check box checked. This will enable the allowed IP address access to all services on the firewalled computer. If the **Accept** button is checked, all incoming connections from the single IP address will be allowed (accepted). The teacher would repeat the process for each of his student's computers.

Or, let's say the teacher wants the same scenario but one of the student's computers should not have access to the teacher's computer. If the **Reject** button is checked, all incoming connections from this single IP address will be blocked (rejected).

This is a powerful feature, enabling you to punch a rather large hole through your firewall by simply forgetting to uncheck the **Accept** button. Be careful when using this screen to make sure it shows exactly what you intend. If you don't have a specific need to make your computer be seen by others on the Internet, (that is, you're not running any Web server or e-mail server that you want people on the Internet to be able to see), you won't need to configure anything at all using this screen.

Alternatively, let's say the teacher wants to provide only Web service to his students and all other services will not be made available to them. He can select a single IP address and specify only certain incoming services to be allowed or blocked. The steps he would take to configure this are:

1. Enter the remote computer's IP address.

2. Clear the **All Ports** box.

3. Type the number **80** into the **Port** field. (Port 80 is the common port for Web service, but not all Web services use this port. See the TCP/IP ports list at the end of this chapter for a list of common services and the ports they use.)

4. Choose **TCP** as the protocol **Type**.

5. Select **Accept Mode**.

6. Choose a length of time this service should be allowed.

Again, unless you specifically need to allow computers on the Internet to access services you provide on your computer, you shouldn't configure anything using this screen.

Packet Log Menu

Use the BlackICE **Packet Log** tab to configure the size and naming convention for BlackICE log files, as shown in Figure 8.12. Make sure that logging is enabled (ensure that the check box is checked), because it's not enabled by default.

Figure 8.12 BlackICE Packet Log Tab

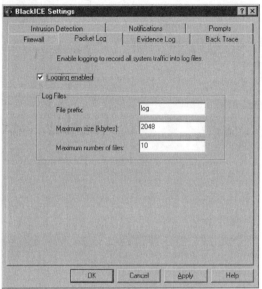

Evidence Log Menu

When BlackICE detects an incoming connection that looks suspicious or matches one of its patterns as a known intrusion attempt, it can save information about the connection as evidence. This is a nice feature to enable, as shown in Figure 8.13, because it offers details that could be used for locating or prosecuting an intruder.

Back Trace Menu

BlackICE allows you to configure how you want to gather information about intruders at the time they make a connection, shown in Figure 8.14. We recommend that you enable both indirect trace and direct trace. Be aware that the DNS lookup indirect trace might cause delays in processing, so you might need to turn this off if your connections are too slow.

Figure 8.13 BlackICE Evidence Log Tab

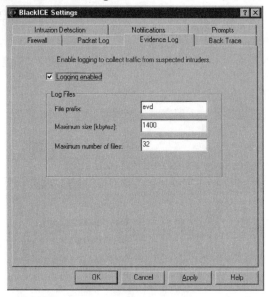

Figure 8.14 Back Trace Tab

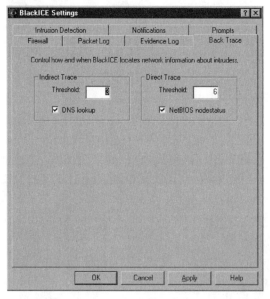

Intrusion Detection Menu

BlackICE isn't just a firewall; it's also an intrusion detection system. As such, it will record all connection attempts other computers make, if those connection attempts are recognized as potentially threatening. Sometimes, connections that appear threatening to an intrusion detection system are actually innocent, because you might trust some computers and not others. If you have several computers on a home network that you trust, you might not want to fill up log files with useless event information about them. Figure 8.15 shows an intrusion detection configuration that trusts the computer with IP address 192.168.0.1. This is the IP address of another computer sharing the same home network as the computer on which BlackICE is running.

Figure 8.15 BlackICE Intrusion Detection Tab

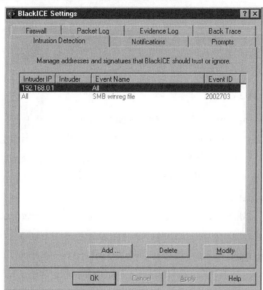

To add a trusted computer to the BlackICE **Intrusion Detection** screen, click the **Add** button, and enter the IP address of the trusted system, as shown in Figure 8.16. You'll need to get the IP address from the trusted computer by running the command **ipconfig** (in Windows NT/2000/XP) or **winipcfg** (in Win 9x/Me) on the trusted computer. To run either command, take these steps:

1. Click the **Start** menu on the Windows desktop.

2. Click the **Run** menu option.

3. Type the command into the **Open** text box.

Figure 8.16 BlackICE Addresses to Trust

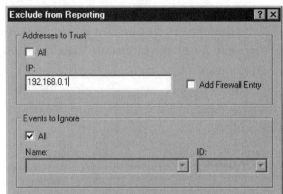

Notifications Menu

By default, BlackICE provides **Visible Indicators** (alerts) of suspicious events in the **Event Notifications** screen shown in Figure 8.17. Clicking the first option button (exclamation mark only) tells BlackICE that you want to see only critical alerts. Clicking the second button tells BlackICE that you want to see critical or serious alerts, which are considered somewhat less severe. The third setting (all three indicators) tells BlackICE that you want to see all events, regardless of their severity. You can also configure similar settings for **Audible Indicators**. Be sure to check the **Enable** box for **Update Notification**, so you'll know when BlackICE checks for upgrades and patches to its software.

Prompts Menu

Finally, Figure 8.18 displays the BlackICE **Prompt**s screen that tells BlackICE how you want to interact with its help functions. You can receive **Beginner** tips, which provide more information; **Intermediate** tips, which provide less; or you can choose to receive **None** at all.

After you have configured BlackICE, it will record intrusion attempts, which you can view by clicking the BlackICE icon in the system tray to view the screen shown in Figure 8.19. This screen sorts alert information based on individual events (on the **Events** tab), the source of those events (on the **Intruders** tab), or a view over time (on the **History** tab). If someone attempts to break into your computer, attempts to scan your computer to see what services are running, or to infect it with a malicious program, this is where BlackICE **Defender** will tell you about it. Clicking the **advICE** button takes you to a Web site that explains the attack and what you can do about it. You'll need to refer to this **Events** tab often to stay on top of what is happening to your computer. Finding a port scan alert appear in the **Events** tab within a few minutes of connecting your (otherwise unprotected) computer to the Internet is not uncommon.

Figure 8.17 BlackICE Event Notifications

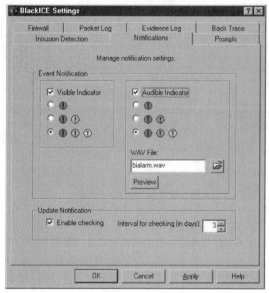

Figure 8.18 BlackICE Prompts

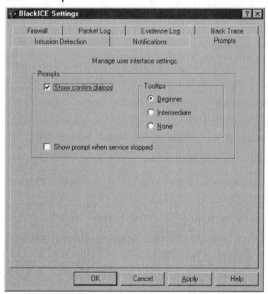

Figure 8.19 BlackICE Defender Event Alerts

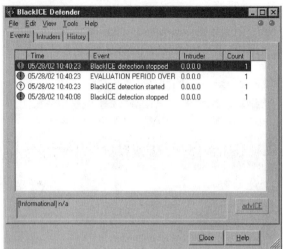

Zone Alarm Pro for Windows

This section is devoted to showing you the configuration options for ZoneAlarm Pro version 3, manufactured by Zone Labs Inc. (www.zonelabs.com). ZoneAlarm Pro is firewall software that runs on the same PC that is being protected. By default, an icon is installed in the system tray, on which you can click to get to the main configuration screen. Figure 8.20 shows the main configuration screen. From here, you can tell the firewall just about everything it needs in order to protect your computer. Alternatively, ZoneAlarm will automatically prompt you by default whenever it needs to know how you want to handle a particular event involving the Internet.

The first action you need to perform after installing ZoneAlarm Pro is to change the password that is used to make configuration changes to the firewall. Click **Set Password** to make the change.

The **Check for Updates** section tells ZoneAlarm whether it should check the manufacturer to see if there are any manufacturer-recommended upgrades or patches. You can set this to manual if you are in the habit of checking for these upgrades yourself periodically. Otherwise, set it to automatic, to help you remember to perform upgrades regularly.

In the **General** section, you tell ZoneAlarm how you want it to start up. Because ZoneAlarm can't help you if it's not running, make sure the **Load ZoneAlarm Pro at startup** check box is checked (it should be, by default). ZoneAlarm can also hide information about you when you contact the manufacturer for updates or other information. To enable this check the check boxes under **Contact with Zone Labs**, as shown in Figure 8.20.

Figure 8.20 also shows a red stop sign near the top. Use this **Stop** button as an emergency panic lock to stop Internet activity in progress. Generally, use of this button shouldn't be required, but it's nice to know you can halt a conversation in progress, if needed.

Figure 8.20 ZoneAlarm Main Configuration Screen

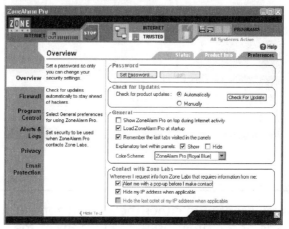

Firewall Menu

Figure 8.21 shows the **Firewall** configuration screen for the Trusted zone, viewing the **Zones** tab. For ZoneAlarm Pro software, *Trusted* zone means your home network, where your home computer resides. The *Internet* zone means everything else "out there." The **Firewall** screen shows that the network, on which a home computer resides, 192.168.0.0, is the network being protected by ZoneAlarm Pro. At the time the software is installed, it detects the network address information for the computer and displays it here. Prior to installing ZoneAlarm Pro, the computer used in this example was already configured for Internet access, and its IP address had already been assigned by a broadband modem. The IP address could just as easily have been manually entered onto the computer or assigned to the computer automatically when we connected to a dial-up ISP. In any case, ZoneAlarm Pro would detect it at installation.

If we were to later create a new network that this computer would protect, in addition to this particular computer with the 192.168.0.0 address, we could manually enter the new network information here, in this screen. That's more of an issue for a small business than a home computer user, so we won't go into detail about how that's done. Just remember this screen and consult the ZoneAlarm Pro manual if you need this feature.

Figure 8.21 ZoneAlarm Pro Firewall Configuration Zones Tab

> **NOTE**
>
> You can manually configure either the Trusted zone or the Internet zone by choosing one or the other using the buttons at the top-center of this screen. All other configuration screens apply to the Trusted zone only.

The **Main** tab of the **Firewall** configuration screen, shown in Figure 8.22, demonstrates the settings we recommend for connecting to the Internet safely. ZoneAlarm lets you configure settings using one of two methods. The first is a slider bar, as shown in the figure. Choosing a setting with a slider bar lets you choose among several sets of configuration settings that are appropriate for each level of the slider bar. The second configuration method is to manually configure each setting individually, which you might do by clicking the **Advanced** button in the lower-right corner of the screen. We describe the features enabled in each of the slider bar settings throughout this discussion, but we don't go into the advanced configuration features. If you are interested in manually configuring ZoneAlarm Pro, consult the software manual for more information about these settings.

With **Internet Zone Security** set to **High**, all attempts by outsiders to connect to your PC will be blocked by ZoneAlarm Pro, as if your PC were invisible. File and printer sharing are disabled using the **High** setting, preventing you from sharing any files or printers with any other computers, including those that might reside in your home, sharing the same home network. Your computer can still connect to servers residing on the Internet. However, servers residing on the Internet won't be able to *initiate* conversations with your PC.

If you want to share files and printers with computers in the home but not with computers on the Internet, choose the **Medium** security setting for the Internet zone. This setting takes your computer out of stealth mode, however. The **Low** setting allows all incoming traffic and is not recommended.

Figure 8.22 ZoneAlarm Pro Firewall Configuration Main Tab

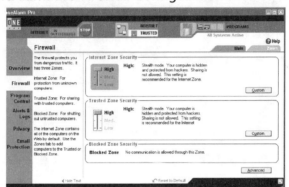

Program Control Menu

In the next screen, called **Program Control**, you can tell ZoneAlarm how you want it to behave when it needs to do outbound filtering, that is when you run an application on your computer. Note that there is an **Advanced** button which is not covered in this discussion. Consult the software manual for ZoneAlarm Pro for more information about manually configuring advanced features. Although you will be primarily choosing among only three settings in the slider bar (**High, Medium**, or **Low**), each one has an important bearing on how you will interact with ZoneAlarm Pro after you choose it. ZoneAlarm Pro provides a comprehensive set of instructions in its help facility, to guide you in making wise choices when ZoneAlarm prompts you for action, regardless of the setting you choose. Figure 8.23 is an example of the detailed level that the help facility goes to in explaining the choices you can make when action is required.

Figure 8.24 shows the **Program Control** screen set to the **High** setting. In this mode, ZoneAlarm will watch not only the applications you run on your computer but also any component of those applications, such as add-on libraries, modules, or configuration components that might change as the result of a software upgrade or alteration to the software's configuration. With this setting,

ZoneAlarm Pro will detect if you run software that attempts to load a component that has changed since the last time you ran the software. ZoneAlarm will then prompt you with an *alert* to decide if that software should still be allowed Internet access, given the changed component.

Figure 8.23 ZoneAlarm Pro Help Screen

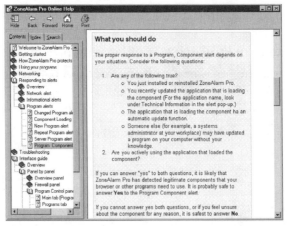

Figure 8.24 ZoneAlarm Pro Program Control High Setting

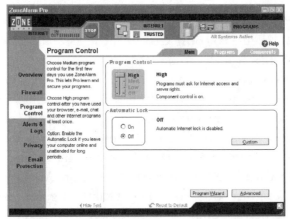

An *alert* is a small window, such as the one shown in Figure 8.25. It will pop up to ask permission for the software to access the Internet, along with a brief explanation of what application or component is requesting the access. If you agree, click **YES**. If you click **NO**, the software will not be allowed to send data to an Internet server now or the next time you run it. If you want to see what programs have been granted access to the Internet so far, you could click the

Programs tab to see a list of programs and their current status. The **Components** tab will display a list of components within those applications and their respective status as well. If you check the box labeled **Remember this answer the next time I use this program**, ZoneAlarm Pro will not ask you this same question again. In this way, ZoneAlarm learns your firewall preferences as you actually use your computer's software.

There's no way to determine, within ZoneAlarm Pro itself, what kind of data is being sent to the Internet server, other than what you are told in the alerts. The data being sent might contain a password or other private data, or it might just contain information the software needs in order to do what it's designed to do. It will help if you are familiar with the software you run, in order to decide the risk of clicking **OK** when prompted. The help screen for ZoneAlarm will also walk you through a decision-making process, to help in that regard. Further, familiarizing yourself with common services—such as DNS, SMTP (e-mail server at your ISP), POP or POP3 (e-mail client on your computer), and so on—might also help. A list of TCP/IP port numbers (doors into your computer) used by these services is provided at the end of this chapter.

In Figure 8.25, Microsoft Works is trying to locate its update server. It wants to send the name of its update server to DNS name service, to get the IP address for the update server. After it has this information, MS Works will ask its update server if a software update is available for MS Works. In this case, choosing **Yes** is OK, because you would want MS Works to know if an update is available that you should install.

Figure 8.26 shows the **Program Control** slider set to **Medium**. With this setting, ZoneAlarm still checks each application you run and still prompts you for action with an *alert* each time you run an application that requests to send data to a server on the Internet. It doesn't monitor each individual component, as with the **High** setting, however. **Medium** is the default and recommended setting by ZoneAlarm, at least for the first few days you run the firewall. You will receive fewer alerts, so interacting with ZoneAlarm will seem less confusing with this setting. As you become more familiar with its operation, you can then move to the higher security setting.

Figure 8.27 shows this same **Program Control** slider with the **Low** setting enabled. With this setting, you will not receive an alert each time you run an application that needs to send data to the Internet. Instead, ZoneAlarm will attempt to inventory the software installed on your computer and thereby "learn" what applications will request Internet access. It will automatically grant access to the Internet to any and all applications you run. This is the lowest security setting and is not recommended.

Figure 8.25 ZoneAlarm Pro Pop-up Action Screen

Figure 8.26 ZoneAlarm Pro Program Control Medium Setting

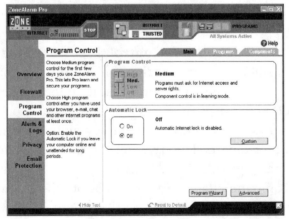

Note that so far, we haven't checked the button for **Automatic Lock**. This button can turn off Internet access for all applications after a period of inactivity or when your computer's screen saver activates. If you choose **On**, you can provide more information by clicking the **Custom** button to see the screen shown in Figure 8.28. In this screen, you can set the inactivity timer or you can rely on the one used by your screen saver. You can choose whether you want programs to be allowed or disallowed access to the Internet when the computer is inactive. We recommend that **Automatic Locking** be turned **On** and set to block all access to the Internet during periods of inactivity.

Figure 8.27 ZoneAlarm Pro Program Control Low Setting

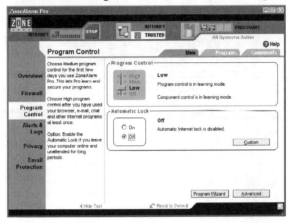

Figure 8.28 ZoneAlarm Pro Screen Lock

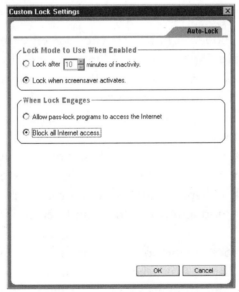

Alerts and Logs Menu

Figure 8.29 shows the **Alerts & Logs** screen for ZoneAlarm Pro, along with the settings we recommend. These settings will log all events the firewall sees, displaying only the most important ones to you. By default, all types of events are enabled, so clicking the **Custom** button is unnecessary unless you want to disable certain software events from being logged, which is not recommended. Note that you can choose the **Log Viewer** tab to view the log entries that ZoneAlarm has recorded.

Figure 8.29 ZoneAlarm Pro Alerts & Logs Screen

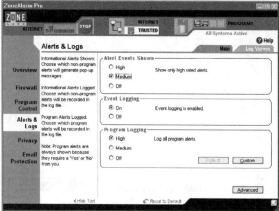

Privacy Menu

Figure 8.30 shows the ZoneAlarm Pro **Privacy** screen with recommended settings. The **High Cookie Control** setting allows you to block all cookies that Web sites attempt to set on your computer. By default, all Web sites are controlled by this setting. If you want to change the behavior of this setting based on the address of various Web sites, you might do so by clicking the **Sites** tab and entering information for those locations.

By default, blocked cookies don't include session cookies, even on the highest setting, unless you choose them explicitly by clicking **Custom**. Session cookies are cookies that Web-based applications need in order to identify your interaction with the application, as distinguished from a third person's interaction with the Web server.

If you choose to block session cookies, it will not be possible to do work using Web-based applications that need session cookies in order to operate. If you never use this type of application, it's safe to turn them off. Just be aware they are not turned off by default, so choosing the **High** setting won't interfere with your favorite Web-based applications that require session cookies.

Figure 8.30 ZoneAlarm Pro Privacy Screen

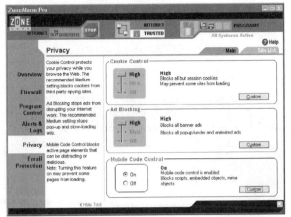

Ad Blocking allows you to disable pop-up ads and banner ads while browsing the Web. You can select certain types of ads you want to block or allow, but we block them all as a matter of course.

Mobile Code Control refers to the Active-X and Java capabilities of your Web browser, discussed in Chapter 4 of this book. Instead of configuring multiple browsers on your computer to allow or disallow these features, you can enable or disable them all at once here. We recommend them to be disabled unless you absolutely must have them enabled. If this is the case, you'll need to choose **Off** in this screen and then configure each of your browsers separately to either allow or block these features.

Email Protection Menu

Figure 8.31 demonstrates the ZoneAlarm Pro **Email Protection** screen. With this feature turned on, your computer will be protected with additional safe-guards to any e-mail scanning software you might be running. This feature scans attachments and quarantines e-mail that might contain malicious attachments, viruses, and so forth. We recommend this setting to be on, even if you run additional e-mail scanning software from Trend Micro, McAfee, and so forth. It's always better to have two sets of eyes watching than one.

Siemens Speedstream SS2602 DSL/Cable Router

The Siemens Speedstream Model SS2602 is a *port filtering* NAT router for home or small office use. We discuss port filtering and NAT in Chapter 5, if you need to refer back for details about this type of firewall. Use this router with broadband modems that don't provide any NAT or other firewall capability. Even if your broadband modem provides NAT, it probably doesn't provide any outbound port filtering or ability to set time of day restrictions on services that are allowed through it—a deficiency this product can help resolve.

Figure 8.31 ZoneAlarm Pro Email Protection Screen

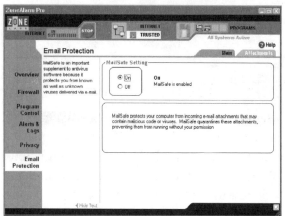

The Siemens router is installed as the network-based firewall shown in Figure 8.32. You might recall this same diagram from the discussion of network-based firewalls in Chapter 5. You can think of the Siemens router as having two doors—one that you will connect to the Internet (WAN) and one that you will connect to your home computer(s) (LAN).

Connect the Siemens router (network-based firewall, in the diagram) to your broadband DSL/cable modem using the 8-pin RJ45 Ethernet cable that comes with it. The Siemens router also has two 8-pin RJ-45 LAN ports for connecting two computers, two hubs, or one of each to the firewall. Other types of external firewalls might only have one LAN port or might have several more.

NOTE

Even though the product is labeled DSL/cable router, you can also connect it to an ISDN router, such as the Cisco 760. Any broadband modem that provides an Ethernet connection for the LAN (that is, where the home computers are connected), will work just fine with this product.

Figure 8.32 Installing the Siemens External DSL/Cable Router

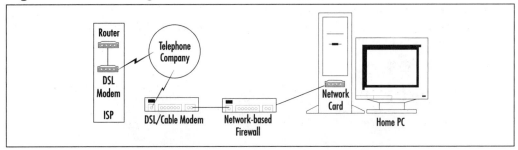

Pros and Cons of Using the Siemens Router

Because the filtering is based only on ports, a service is either on or it's off. You don't have the ability to say "this internal IP address can go to service Y on external address A but not external address B." There are also only a few outbound filtering settings you can configure at once, so the vast majority of outbound traffic will be allowed. This makes the product ideal for a household with several computers sharing a single Internet connection, such as one in which a parent wants to restrict the times a child's PC is allowed to access the Internet while placing no restrictions on the parent's computer. But if you have a small business network where you need to restrict certain computers in different ways than other computers, you probably should buy a different product that allows an unlimited number of filtering rules.

Configuring the Router on the Network

Siemens provides detailed and simple instructions for cabling and initial setup in the documentation that comes with the product. It walks you through the installation of the hardware, and then sets up your PC's browser so that it can connect to the Siemens router in preparation for configuring it. You will configure the router using your PC's browser, by connecting to the Web server running on the Siemens. Before attempting to configure the router, you'll need to make sure you can get to the Siemens configuration screen that looks like Figure 8.33. If you have trouble with this or any of the steps discussed in this section, contact the Siemens technical support staff for additional assistance.

The first item on the agenda is to change the password. The initial password is admin. Type **admin** and click the Login button to get to the Siemens **Status** screen and configuration menu, shown in Figure 8.34. To change the password, follow these steps (be sure to choose a strong password using the methods presented in Chapter 2):

1. Click Simple **Setup**.

2. Click **Change Password**.

3. Enter the new password.

4. Click **Save**.

Figure 8.33 The Siemens Configuration Login Screen

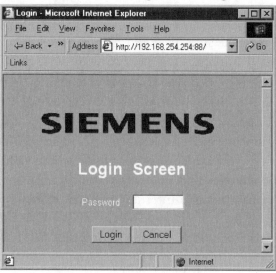

Figure 8.34 Siemens Configuration Menu

Figure 8.34 also shows the initial network settings for the Siemens router. Note that these settings configure themselves *automatically* as defaults when you install the router, provided that your broadband DSL/cable modem is capable of

assigning IP addresses (they usually are—if not, you will need to set the WAN IP address manually using the **Simple Setup** menu). If so, you don't need to make any changes to the Siemens configuration to get to this step. The DSL/cable modem assigns an address to the WAN port of the Siemens router as soon as the router is powered on.

The Siemens router in turn assigns IP addresses to the PCs on your home or small office network. It should use a different range of IP addresses than the DSL/cable modem, so there won't be any conflicts in the addresses that get assigned. You'll need to make sure that the LAN PCs are configured to accept automatically assigned IP addresses for them to work with the Siemens router— instructions for this two-step process are included in the Siemens installation guide. Follow the steps for each computer that will be protected by the firewall.

The end result is that you will have two networks, each with its own unique addresses—one between your broadband DSL/cable modem and the Siemens firewall (known as WAN/ Internet), and one between the Siemens firewall and your PCs (known LAN, and labeled as Speedstream Router in Figure 8.34. We refer to this network as the LAN throughout the rest of this section).

In the example figure, this screen shows that:

- The Siemens firewall is running (Enabled).

- Network Address Translation (NAT) is enabled.

- The Siemens is serving automatic IP addresses (DHCP) to computers on the LAN.

- The IP address on the LAN-side of the Siemens (Speedstream Router) is 192.168.254.254 (this address is a default factory setting in the Siemens router.)

- The IP address on the WAN-side of the Siemens (Internet) is 10.0.0.4 (this address is assigned to the Siemens router by the broadband DSL/cable modem).

- The Siemens will send all its traffic to the DSL/cable modem (Gateway IP) located at IP address 10.0.0.1 (which was preassigned to the DSL/cable modem prior to installation of the Siemens router).

Note that the router is fully configured at this point to protect your home or small office computers. You can change the date and time or any of the preceding setup information under the **Simple Setup** menu, but it really isn't necessary due to the automatic configuration features when you power on the Siemens router. However, you might want to enable additional features of the Siemens router, such as outbound filtering or setting date/time restrictions for services, which are presented next.

Configuring Advanced Settings

The **Advanced Setup** menu (notice the **Advanced Setup** link shown in Figure 8.34) allows you to configure some of the more advanced features of the Siemens router. Click **Advanced Setup** to see the menu items shown in Table 8.7. The automatic setup process makes changes to the first two menu items (**LAN** and **Firewall**) unnecessary. We begin with a discussion of the **Virtual Server** menu.

Table 8.7 Advanced Setup Menu

LAN	Configures TCP/IP network settings for the LAN-side of the Siemens router. Example: change the LAN IP address.
Firewall	Turns the firewall on and off. Example: if you need to temporarily disable the firewall and reenable it later.
Virtual Server	Settings for making LAN computers visible to the Internet. Example: allowing an inbound connection to a service that is normally blocked by default.
Special Applications	Settings for allowing inbound services that need multiple ports to operate. Example: video conferencing or certain kinds of gaming software.
Client Filtering	Settings for blocking outbound connections. Example: disabling LAN access to the Internet at certain times of the day.
Misc	Setting for administrator time-out and so on.

Virtual Server *Menu*

The **Virtual Server** menu lets computers on the Internet find services running on your home PC. That is to say, if one of the computers on your home network is running a service that you want for computers on the Internet to use, such as a Web server or video conferencing service. As we discuss in Chapter 5, this is often called "poking a hole" in the firewall, because normally, all incoming connection attempts are blocked (disallowed) by default.

As an example of using this feature, let's say you have a Web server on your home PC and you want it to be viewable from the Internet. Let's also say that the Siemens has assigned an IP address of 192.168.254.170 to your home PC and that you have set up your Web server with a default listening port number 80. (Fully configuring Web servers is beyond the scope of this book but, for now, just understand that all Web servers will use this port by default, unless you change it in the Web server's configuration somewhere.)

Someone sitting on the Internet is not going to find your Web server at IP address 192.168.254.170, because you have placed your new Siemens Firewall between them and your server, and the firewall, which is enabled, will block all incoming connections to that server from any computer on the Internet. The **Virtual Server** menu tells the Siemens firewall what to do with the traffic. By default, unless a rule is configured, all inbound traffic will be dropped. This doesn't affect outbound traffic, which is allowed by default. In other words, if you type a URL into your home PC browser, seeking to view a Web site on the Internet, that's outbound traffic (which is allowed, by default). If computers on the Internet type your Web server's URL into their browser, that's inbound traffic and is disallowed by default. You'll need to use the **Virtual Server** menu to make your server visible. To do this, you must tell the Siemens firewall that any incoming connections for port 80 are to be redirected (forwarded) to Web server software running on port 80 of your Web server's IP address.

This configuration has already been made in Figure 8.35. The first line tells the Siemens, in effect, "If a new connection comes in from the Internet looking for services running on port 80, send that traffic to the LAN PC with IP address 192.168.254.170, which runs the requested service on port 80." Essentially, this opens up a hole in your firewall to allow Web traffic inside. A port is just a door number into your computer; different services can be found at their respective port (door) numbers. All inbound connections for port 80 will be redirected, or *forwarded*, to a specific computer on a specific port. For this reason, this type of setting is also known as *port forwarding*.

Unless you run a server on one of your PCs, you don't need to do any port forwarding. If you do, you'll need to configure the Siemens to use the appropriate port for the particular service you provide, such as e-mail server, X-Windows server, and so on. For your convenience, we've included a list of TCP/IP ports, along with some services that (if installed) commonly use those ports, later in this chapter. In all likelihood, you won't be running any of these services and won't need to make any changes to the **Virtual Server** menu.

Figure 8.35 Configuring a Virtual Server

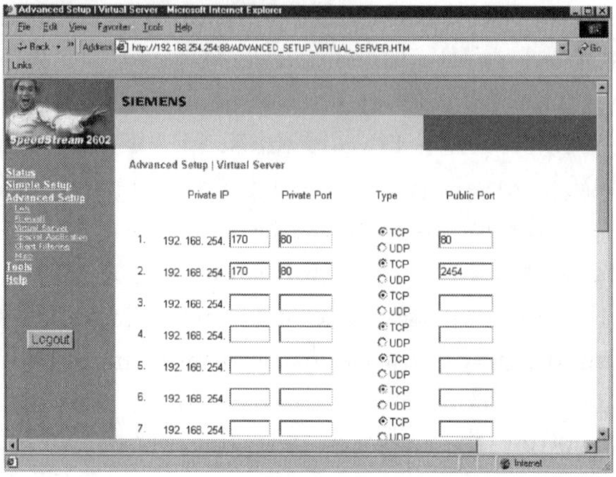

Note the second line of Figure 8.35, which has a different public port than private port number. This setting tells the Siemens firewall, in effect, "If a new connection comes in from the Internet looking for a service on port 2454, send that traffic to the PC at 192.168.254.170, and find the service on port 80."

Why might you need to do this? Let's say the default port number for the service you want to provide is 80 (a Web server, in this particular case). Computers on the Internet will look for your Web server on port 80 by default. Someone who's trying to find a Web server to break into might perform a scan of all computers that are running a service on port 80, because this is the default port number for the service the intruder is interested in. If you use port 80 as the public port, the scan will be able to see this, and the intruder will know you have a Web server running. But with this virtual server configuration, the intruder won't see anything running on port 80. She'll only see your Web server if she scans for port 2454, which is much less likely, because nothing of particular interest to intruders commonly runs on that port number. By using port forwarding to a different port number, you reduce the likelihood that your Web server will be discovered and compromised, because focusing on a Web server she finds in her scan for port 80 is easier than taking the time to check every single port number (remember, there are over 65,000) on every single IP address she's interested in.

Your Web server is still available to anyone who knows to look for it on port 2454 instead of port 80. Your friends, who know this, simply append **:2454** (or whatever number you're using) to the end of the address they type into their browser to access your Web server. The Web service is *not* actually hidden, but it does ensure that external users won't find the service in its normal spot. There are many more advanced reasons for using this feature that are beyond the scope of a typical home user, which are not discussed here.

Special Applications *Menu*

Some kinds of applications, like Microsoft's NetMeeting videoconferencing application, don't run on a single port; they require multiple ports. This is because they are made up of several components, each of which uses different ports to process different actions. The **Special Applications** menu does exactly the same thing as the **Virtual Server** menu, only it opens up wider ranges of ports to accommodate these *special applications*. Leave this menu blank if possible, because you shouldn't allow inbound connections unnecessarily. You need to keep the number of incoming connections allowed into your network to a bare minimum. Consult the manual for your particular application to determine the port ranges it requires and enter them into the **Special Applications** menu, if you find you do need this feature.

Client Filtering *Menu*

The **Client Filtering** menu option is the only one that limits outbound connections, such as those originating from your home PC(s). This option restricts what the PCs on your home network can see on the Internet and at what times. It has no bearing on the visibility of your PC to the Internet, only the visibility of the Internet to your PC.

Let's say you want to allow a family member to use your computer but not after midnight and not before 6 A.M. during the week. Let's say your PC has been assigned IP address 192.168.254.122 (run **ipconfig** or **winipcfg**, as discussed earlier in this chapter, on the PC to find out the actual IP address in your case) by the Siemens router. Using the **Client Filtering** menu, you can tell the Siemens firewall to block all traffic from IP address 192.168.254.122 to any service (port) on the Internet on weekdays between the hours of midnight and 6 A.M. as shown on the first line of Figure 8.36.

Let's also say you don't want him ever to download files from the Internet using FTP, and you don't want him using Telnet or ssh to bypass your time rules by opening a shell on someone else's computer. The second line in Figure 8.36 shows that the ports for FTP (20 and 21), Secure Shell (22), and Telnet (23) are blocked at all times. Line 3 blocks 192.168.254.122 from using Gnutella at all times, and line 4 blocks it from using IRC at all times.

Figure 8.36 Client Filtering

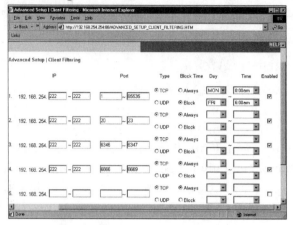

Applications Port List

In the advanced settings of the firewall discussed in the preceding sections, you need to know the correct port number for a given service you want to allow or disallow through the firewall. As we mention in Chapter 5 and earlier in this chapter, a port is similar to a door into your computer. Your home address is similar, then, to your computer's IP address.

You can think of the services on your computer as people standing at each of the doors of your home. If a visitor knocks at your front door, the front door person answers, and the two can then talk. If the visitor knocks at your back door, the back door person answers, and those two can then talk. Each door provides access to talk to a different person. After awhile, the visitor will learn that to talk to Person A, he needs to knock on the front door, but to talk to Person B, he needs to knock on the back door. If he knocks on the back door and nobody is standing there, he can't get inside. To make it easy to remember next time he visits, he makes a list of all the doors, numbers them, and then records the names of the people he'll find behind each one.

Services work in much the same way, except there are over 65,000 virtual doors into your computer. They are called *ports* in the TCP/IP network protocol specification. Each type of software that listens for incoming connections—such as Web server software, Internet game server software, videoconferencing software, e-mail server software, and so on—can usually be found on a specific *well-known* port unique to that type of software. A port is described as well-known for a particular service when it is normal and common to find that particular software running at that particular port number. For instance, Web servers run on port 80 by default, and FTP file transfers use ports 20 and 21. Your computer likely sends e-mail to your ISP's SMTP server running on port 25. It might download your incoming e-mail from your ISP's POP server using port 110.

Thus, there is a common mapping between different types of software and the ports they commonly listen on. Whatever port number your software is using is the port number you must use when poking a hole in a firewall, as discussed earlier. In order to determine what port number to use, you need to know what port number the given software is using. To make that determination easier, you can refer to a list of the common services that run on Windows computers along with their respective well-known ports.

Table 8.8 is just such a list. It is a tool you can use to map TCP/IP port numbers to the name of the service that commonly uses that port. You can think of a port as a door into your computer. This list describes the services your computer might be running, along with the port number (door) where each service can typically be found. There are over 65,000 of them in all. Your computer could be running one, several, or none of these services. Each port number is typically associated with one certain service, although some programs are known to share ports with other programs.

Note that in Table 8.8, we've included some of the more common Windows services you might see, along with some common games and some of the more common Trojans that might infect your computer. You shouldn't consider this list to be a complete representation of everything that might possibly be running on your PC.

Also, if you've never heard of some or most of the services in Table 8.8, don't worry about it. Just refer to this list for more information when prompted for action by your firewall software or viewing firewall log files. Sometimes, firewall software records port numbers only in log files but not service names. ZoneAlarm might pop up an alert using a port number that is unfamiliar to you, with no service name attached. It helps to have this list as a reference in these cases, so you can decipher what those messages mean and make better informed decisions about what to do next.

If you're looking for a particular port number and don't find it on this list, a good place to search for it online is at the Snort Intrusion Detection Open Source page (http://snort.sourcefire.com/ports.html). You'll notice that even Trojans, which we discuss in Chapter 2, have well-known port numbers. Unfortunately, for nearly every possible port number, someone has written a virus or Trojan that could be running there. For a bigger list of Trojans listed by the port they use, check out the Blackcode Web site at www.blackcode.com/trojans/ports.php.

Table 8.8 Common Services Port List

Port Number	Name of Service	Comment
1	tcpmux	Port Service Multiplexer
5	rje	Remote Job Entry
7	echo	Echoes a character or line
9	discard	Discard
11	systat	Shows the active users
13	daytime	Displays the current time
15	netstat	Displays network status
17	qotd	Displays a quote
18	send/rwp	Message Send Protocol
19	chargen	Character Generator
20	ftp-data	Transfers files across the Internet
21	ftp	Transfers files across the Internet
22	ssh	Run commands on a remote computer
23	Telnet	Run commands on a remote compute
25	SMTP	Simple Mail Transfer Protocol, which is the primary Internet e-mail protocol
31	msg-auth	Trojan
33	dsp	Display Support Protocol
37	time	Time
38	RAP	Route Access Protocol
39	rlp	Resource Location Protocol
42	nameserv, WINS	Windows name service
43	whois	Displays users of Unix systems
49	Login, TACACS	Log into the system
50	RMCP	Remote Mail Checking Protocol, plus DRAT Trojan
53	DNS	Domain Name Service for the Internet
57	MTP	Private Terminal Access
59	NFILE	Trojan
63	whois++	VIA Systems FTP and whois++
66	sql*net	Databases talk to each other using this

Continued

Table 8.8 Continued

Port Number	Name of Service	Comment
67	bootps	Used to boot one computer using another
68	bootpd/dhcp	One computer assigns an IP address to another
69	TFTP	Trivial File Transfer Protocol
70	Gopher	Look for files to download
79	finger	Find out who's logged on
80	www-http	The mail port used by Web services
88	Kerberos, http	Alternate Web server port
98	linuxconf	Configure computers running the Linux operating system
101	HOSTNAME	Reports the name of the computer
105	Csnet-ns	Mailbox Name Server
106	poppassd	Eudora-compatible password changer
109	POP2	Older protocol for downloading mail from your ISP's mail server
110	POP3	Better protocol-download mail from your ISP's mail server
111	Sun RPC Portmapper	One of the biggest targets for scanning
113	identd/auth	Advertises who you are and who is logged in
115	sftp	Secure FTP
117	uucp	Old protocol used for transferring files
119	NNTP	Network News Transfer Protocol
123	NTP	Network Time Protocol
129	PWDGEN	Password Generator Protocol
133	statsrv	Trojan, Statistics service
135	loc-srv/epmap	Location Service
137	netbios-ns	Windows networking name service
138	netbios-dgm	Windows networking
139	Netbios	Windows networking
143	IMAP	E-mail protocol mostly used internally, not over the Internet
144	NewS	Network Extensible Window System

Continued

Table 8.8 Continued

Port Number	Name of Service	Comment
152	BFTP	Background File Transfer Protocol
161	SNMP	Reports statistics about network usage, can be used to administer systems remotely
177	XDMCP	X-Windows Display Manager Control Protocol
218	MPP	Netix Message Posting Protocol
220	IMAP3	Protocol used for e-mail
259	ESRO	Efficient Short Remote Operations, Checkpoint FW-1 admin
366	ODMR	On-Demand Mail Relay
387	AURP	AppleTalk Update-Based Routing Protocol
389	LDAP	Directory service
407	Timbuktu	Remote administration tool plus file sharing
434	Mobile IP	Mobile IP Agent
443	SSL	Secure Sockets Layer, for secure Web browsing
444	snpp	Simple Network Paging Protocol
445	SMB	Protocol used to connect to a Windows shared drive
458	QuickTime TV/ Conferencing	(Obsolete)
468	Photuris	Photuris Key Management
500	ISAKMP	Used for authentication
512	biff	Common Unix tools
513	who	Common Unix tools
514	syslog	Common Unix tools
515	lpr	Printing
520	RIP	Routing Information Protocol
521	RIPng	RIP Next Generation
531	IRC	Trojan, chat
543	Klogin	AppleShare over IP
545	QuickTime, Kerberos	Apple QuickTime Server, Kerberos Encrypted Remote Shell

Continued

Table 8.8 Continued

Port Number	Name of Service	Comment
554	RTSP	Real-Time Streaming Protocol
555	phAse Zero	Trojan
563	NNTP over SSL	Secure protocol for use with downloading news
593	MS-RPC	Microsoft Remote Procedure Call over HTTP
608	SIFT/UFT	Sender-Initiated Unsolicited File Transfer
631	IPP	Internet Printing Protocol
635	mountd	Connect to Unix file shares
636	sldap	Secure directory service
642	EMSD	Efficient Mail Submission and Delivery
648	RRP	NSI Registry Registrar Protocol
660	Apple MacOS Server Admin	AppleShare IP Remote Manager
666	Doom	Game
687	Asip-reg	AppleShare IP Registry
700	buddyphone	Internet telephone
705	AgentX for SNMP	Simple Network Management Protocol
777	AIM spy application	Trojan
901	swat	Samba software
993	s-imap	Secure IMAP client for downloading e-mail
995	s-pop	Secure POP3 client for downloading e-mail
1024-5000	mIRC	Chat program uses this *wide* range of ports
1027	ICQ	Chat program
1029	ICQ	Chat program
1032	ICQ	Chat program
1062	Veracity	Veracity Enterprise Monitor
1080	SOCKS	Internet proxy server
1085	WebObjects	Apple software for creating Web sites
1117-5190	Audiogalaxy	Uses this Wide range of ports

Continued

Table 8.8 Continued

Port Number	Name of Service	Comment
1227	DNS2Go	Dynamic DNS, AIM Video Chat
1243	SubSeven	Trojan
1338	Millennium Worm	Trojan
1352	Lotus Notes server	Database and e-mail
1381	Apple-licman	Apple Network License Manager
1417	Timbuktu-control	Remote administration tool
1418	Timbuktu-observe	Remote administration tool
1419	Timbuktu-send files	Remote administration tool
1433	Microsoft SQL Server	Database
1434	Microsoft SQL Monitor	Database
1494	Citrix ICA Protocol	Remote display terminal software for Windows
1503	T.120	Microsoft NetMeeting
1521	Oracle SQL	Production database
1525	Pdap-np	Prospero
1526	Pdap-np	Prospero
1527	tlisrv	Oracle database software
1604	Citrix ICA	Browser
1645	RADIUS Authentication	Password server often used by employer networks
1646	RADIUS Accounting	Accounting server often used by employer networks
1680	Carbon Copy	Remote control software from Microsoft
1717	Convoy	Microsoft Clustering services
1720	H.323/Q.931	Telephony over data networks
1723	PPTP control port	Virtual private network
1755	Ms-streaming	Microsoft Streaming
1818	ETFTP	Enhanced Trivial File Transfer Protocol
1863	MSN Messenger	Chat program
1973	DLSw DCAP/DRAP	Backdoor worm
1985	HSRP	Network protocol

Continued

Table 8.8 Continued

Port Number	Name of Service	Comment
1999	Cisco AUTH	Trojan
2001	Glimpse	Search engine
2049	NFS	Network File System
2064	Distributed.net	Encryption-cracking tool
2106	ekshell	Kerberos encrypted remote shell
2140	DeepThroat	Trojan
2301	Cpq-wbem	Compaq Insight Management Web Agents
2427	stgcp	Simple Telephony Gateway Control Protocol
2504	WLBS	Windows Load-Balancing Service
2535	MADCAP	Multicast Address Dynamic Client Allocation Protocol
2543	SIP	Session Initiation Protocol for teleconferencing
2592	netrek	Game
2727	MGCP call agent	Media Gateway Control Protocol
2628	DICT	Dictionary
2998	ISS Real Secure Console Service Port	Intrusion Detection Software
3000	Firstclass	Remote control software, Remote Shut Trojan
3031	Apple AgentVU	Trojan
3100	Delta Force	Game
3128	squid	Web proxy server
3130	ICP	Communication between Squid proxy servers
3150	DeepThroat	Trojan
3264	ccmail	Lotus mail
3288	COPS	Common Open Policy Service
3305	Odette-ftp	Odette FTP
3306	mySQL	Personal database
3389	RDP Protocol	Terminal Server
3521	netrek	Game

Continued

Table 8.8 Continued

Port Number	Name of Service	Comment
3568	Delta Force	Game
3569	Delta Force	Game
3999	Delta Force	Game
4000	ICQ, Blizzard Battlenet, Command and Conquer	Chat program, game, game
4321	rwhois	Remotely checks to see who owns a DNS domain
4333	mSQL	Personal database
4590	ICQ Trojan	ICQ Trojan
4827	HTCP	Hypertext Caching Protocol
5000-5001	Yahoo! Messenger	Voice chat
5004	RTP	Windows XP Remote Desktop Protocol
5005	RTP	Windows XP Remote Desktop Protocol
5010	Yahoo! Messenger	Chat program
5050	Yahoo! Messenger	Chat program
5100	Yahoo! Webcams	Chat program
5190	AIM	AOL Instant Messenger Chat Program
5423	Apple VirtualUser	Remote administration tool
5631	PCAnywhere data	Remote administration tool
5632	PCAnywhere	Remote administration tool
5800	VNC	Virtual network computer display
5801	VNC	Virtual network computer display
5900	VNC	Virtual network computer display
5901	VNC	Virtual network computer display
6000	X Windows	Alternate Windows server for Unix
6112-6119	Blizzard BattleNet	Online gaming
6346	Gnutella default port	File sharing
6502	Cserver pages	Build Web applications using this software
6667	IRC	Internet Relay Chat Trojan

Continued

Table 8.8 Continued

Port Number	Name of Service	Comment
6670	VocalTec Internet Phone	Virus
6699	napster	File sharing
6712	Sub Seven	Trojan
6713	Sub Seven	Trojan
6776	Sub7	Very common Windows Trojan
6891-6901	MSN Messenger	Chat program uses this *wide* range of ports
6970	RTP	Apple QT4 Real-time Transport Protocol
7070	RealServer/QuickTime	Streaming audio and video
7778	Unreal	Online game
7648	CU-SeeMe	Video conferencing
7649	CU-SeeMe	Video conferencing
8010	WinGate 2.1	Web/anonymous proxy server
8080	HTTP	Alternate Web server port
8181	HTTP	Alternate Web server port
8383	IMail WWW	Web mail
8875	napster	File sharing
8888	napster	File sharing
10008	cheese worm	Virus
11371	PGP 5 Keyserver	Serves encryption keys for Pretty Good Privacy software
12345	Netbus	Trojan
12346	Netbus	Trojan
12456	Netbus	Trojan
13223	PowWow	Tribal Voice Messaging software
13224	PowWow	Tribal Voice Messaging software
14237	Palm	Hotsyncs your palm to a PC across the Internet
14238	Palm	Hotsyncs your palm to a PC across the Internet
18888	LiquidAudio	Music streaming

Continued

Table 8.8 Continued

Port Number	Name of Service	Comment
21157	Activision	Activision Gaming Protocol
22555	Internet Phone	Vocaltec Web Conference/Internet Phone
23213	PowWow	Tribal Voice Messaging software
23214	PowWow	Tribal Voice Messaging software
23456	EvilFTP	Trojan
26000	Quake	Online game
26214	Dark Reign	Game
27001	QuakeWorld	Online game
27010	Half-Life	Online game
27015	Half-Life	Online game
27960	QuakeIII	Online game
28800-29000	MSN Gaming Zone	Online games
30029	AOL Admin	Trojan
31337	Back Orifice	Trojan
32777	rpc.walld	Send messages to remote computer users
39213	Sygate Manager	Remote control for Sygate software
41000-50000	Audiogalaxy uses this wide range of ports	Music file transfer
54320	Back Orifice 2000 default port	Trojan
65000	Stachelradt	Denial of Service Trojan

Index

SYNGRESS SOLUTIONS...

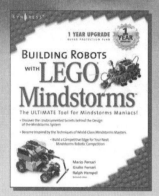

AVAILABLE NOW!
ORDER at
www.syngress.com

Building Robots with LEGO MINDSTORMS

The LEGO MINDSTORMS Robotics Invention System (RIS) has been called "the most creative play system ever developed." This book unleashes the full power and potential of the tools, bricks, and components that make up LEGO MINDSTORMS. Some of the world's leading LEGO MINDSTORMS inventors share their knowledge and development secrets. You will discover an incredible range of ideas to inspire your next invention. This is the ultimate insider's look at LEGO MINDSTORMS and is the perfect book whether you build world-class competitive robots or just like to mess around for the fun of it.

ISBN: 1-928994-67-9

Price: $29.95 US, $46.95 CAN

AVAILABLE NOW!
ORDER at
www.syngress.com

Journey to the Center of the Internet

Not your typical computer book, *Journey to the Center of the Internet* brings readers a brilliant techno-tale in the spirit of the classic science fiction novel and includes over 40 narrated animations taking you inside the "stuff" that makes the Internet run.

ISBN: 1-928994-75-X

Price: $29.95 US, $46.95 CAN

AVAILABLE AUGUST 2002!
ORDER at
www.syngress.com

Scene of the Cybercrime: Computer Forensics Handbook

FIGHT BACK. Track Down Cybercriminals and Bring Them to Justice! Terrorism. Theft. Child pornography. Vandalism. Many of the offline world's most troubling crimes now thrive online—and in a world of global Internet connectivity all of us are vulnerable. This pioneering book will unite these two key groups in common cause, showing them step by step how to fuse their expertise to trace and capture today's increasingly dangerous cyberfugitives.

ISBN: 1-931836-65-5

Price: $59.95 US, $92.95 CAN

solutions@syngress.com

SYNGRESS®